20
BATTLES

I0165702

EVERT KLEYNHANS & DAVID BROCK KATZ

20
BATTLES

Searching for a South African Way of War

1913–2013

DELTA BOOKS

JOHANNESBURG • CAPE TOWN

All rights reserved.
No part of this publication may be reproduced or transmitted,
in any form or by any means, without prior permission
from the publisher or copyright holder.

© Text: Evert Kleynhans & David Katz (2023)
© Cover images: Front cover – John Liebenberg /Africa Media Online (tank);
   South African National Defence Force Documentation Centre (helicopter);
   Back cover – Ditsong National Museum of Military History,
   Masondo Reference Library, Various Photo Collections.
© Images: Department of Defence Archives (p. 193, p. 207, p. 235, p. 249);
   Ditsong National Museum of Military History, Masondo Reference Library,
   Various Photo Collections (p. 21, p. 37, p. 51, p. 67, p. 81, p. 109, p. 127, p. 137,
   p. 153, p. 167, p. 181); L Olivier Private Photo Collection (p. 262).
© Maps: Jonathan Ball Publishers (2023)
© Published edition: Jonathan Ball Publishers (2023)

Published in South Africa in 2023 by
DELTA BOOKS
A division of Jonathan Ball Publishers
A division of Media24 (Pty) Ltd
PO Box 33977
Jeppestown
2043

ISBN 9978-1-92824-822-4
ebook ISBN 978-1-92824-823-1

*Every effort has been made to trace the copyright holders and to obtain their
permission for the use of copyright material. The publishers apologise for any
errors or omissions and would be grateful to be notified of any corrections that
should be incorporated in future editions of this book.*

jonathanball.co.za
twitter.com/JonathanBallPub
facebook.com/JonathanBallPublishers

Cover by mrdesign
Design and typesetting by Martine Barker
Maps by Jan Booysens
Set in Aktiv Grotesk and Adobe Caslon Pro

CONTENTS

LIST OF MAPS

LIST OF ABBREVIATIONS

Abbreviations are defined in brackets where they first occur in the text. The most frequently used abbreviations are listed here:

ACF	Active Citizen Force
Armd Bde	Armoured Brigade
Armd Div	Armoured Division
CAR	Central African Republic
CGF	Coast Garrison Force
DRA	Defence Rifle Associations
FACA	Forces Armées Centrafricaines
FAPLA	Forças Armadas Populares de Libertação de Angola
FNLA	Frente Nacional de Libertação de Angola
FOMAC	Central African Multinational Force
GEA	German East Africa
GOC	General Officer Commanding
GSWA	German South West Africa
Mot Bde	Motorised Brigade
MPLA	Movimento Popular de Libertação de Angola
OC	Officer Commanding
PLAN	People's Liberation Army of Namibia
RLDF	Royal Lesotho Defence Force
RPG	Rocket Propelled Grenade
SAAF	South African Air Force
SADF	South African Defence Force
SA Div	South African Division
SAEC	South African Engineer Corps
SAI	South African Infantry Regiment
SA Inf Bde	South African Infantry Brigade
SAMR	South African Mounted Rifles
SANDF	South African National Defence Force
SAP	South African Police
SAPF	South African Permanent Force
SSB	Special Service Battalion
SWA	South West Africa
SWAPO	South West Africa People's Organisation
UDF	Union Defence Force
UNITA	União Nacional para a Independência Total de Angola

PREFACE

The concept for this book was born in the lecture rooms of the Army, War and Defence colleges of the South African National Defence Force (SANDF). The authors have enjoyed a profitable decade-long association through their academic endeavours in the Department of Military History at the Faculty of Military Science of Stellenbosch University.

Dr Evert Kleynhans is a senior lecturer in the Department of Military History, while Dr David Brock Katz is a research fellow in the same department. During our lectures at the various defence force colleges, it emerged that there was a lack of instructional material concerning examples of South African warfare through the ages. Students expressed frustration at the lack of African content and demonstrated their hunger for South African-oriented material – no matter its supposed political sensitivity. They appealed for military history directly relevant to the defence force's various historical deployments on the African content and further afield.

Our journey revealed not only the glaring lacuna in South African military historiography but also the existence of a distinct, and yet largely uncodified, South African way of war. South African military doctrine evolved from centuries of internecine conflict among the peoples of southern Africa, including the all-encompassing South African War (1899–1902). In addition, South African forces, after the formation of the Union of South Africa in 1910, took part in the suppression of internal unrest, both world wars, the Korean War and the decades-long Border War, bringing them into conflict, at one time or another, with the Axis powers (Italy and Germany), the Soviet Union indirectly, the liberation movements, Cuba and its proxies and the armed forces of Angola.

South Africa's unique doctrine and way of war evolved with every historical engagement and, in the process, it was constantly modified and built up. Upon closer inspection it becomes evident that the SANDF and its predecessors, the Union Defence Force (UDF) and the South African Defence Force (SADF), indeed developed a distinctive method of manoeuvre warfare and directive command style. Unfortunately, to the present day the doctrine remains an enigma and largely uncodified.

True to the nature of warfare, South Africans have learned and re-learned the lessons of earlier conflicts. Numerous false starts, misdirected efforts and spurious or irrelevant mentors have hindered various attempts to record South Africa's tactical and operational doctrine. Jan Smuts followed the common trend of one on the losing side and, following his experience in the South African War, tried to emulate the British victors. He was determined that, upon the establishment of the UDF in 1912, its discipline, uniforms and doctrine would be modelled on those of the British Army. Fate dealt his 'modernisation' endeavours a cruel blow when he was forced to use reservists from the moribund Defence Rifle Associations (DRAs) to put down the strikes of the Witwatersrand mineworkers in 1913–1914 and then later the 1914 Afrikaner Rebellion. Incidentally, the bulk of Smuts's reservists were veterans of the erstwhile Boer republican commandos.

During the First World War, circumstances again obliged him to reverse his anglicisation policy in the latter stages of the campaign in German South West Africa in 1915, when the UDF adopted a distinctive Boer republican doctrine based on the deployment of a large mounted infantry component. The same mounted infantry and their doctrine would accompany Smuts to German East Africa in 1916, where they were central to his operations in that theatre. However, on the Western Front, the nature and conduct of the war were entirely different, which largely removed the South Africans' freedom of movement and prevented them from taking the operational initiative. The deployment of South African infantrymen in static positions characterised by trench warfare, massive artillery barrages and near-suicidal assaults, came at a considerable cost in manpower – especially at the Battle of Delville Wood in 1916.

During the interwar period, demobilisation, rationalisation and stringent budget and manpower cuts placed the defence force in a precarious position. Yet, on several occasions the UDF had to support the South African Police (SAP) to suppress the mounting internal uprisings that challenged the authority and legitimacy of the state both within the Union and within its mandated territory of South West Africa (now Namibia). The most prominent deployments took place during the 1922 Rand Revolt and the Bondelswarts Rebellion of the same year.

The Second World War saw the UDF transform the Boer mounted infantry model into motorised infantry brigades, supported by token armoured forces. By trading horses for vehicles, the UDF utilised much of the same light infantry doctrine of their mounted forebears in the Boer republican forces. These forces, using manoeuvre and combined arms and logistical self-sufficiency, quickly overran the Italian defenders in southern Abyssinia (Ethiopia) and Italian Somaliland (now part of Somalia) in January 1941. However, after the occupation of Addis Ababa in April, the proverbial open flanks so conducive to manoeuvre warfare disappeared and the South Africans were forced to contend with more resolute Italian defenders who occupied key high-altitude terrain. The new operational environment severely challenged the hitherto successful South African way of war, especially during the battles of Combolcia and Amba Alagi.

The South Africans emerged from their East African campaign flushed with victory, their manoeuvre doctrine vindicated. They had run circles around the Italians, though at the cost of annoying the British, who looked askance at the UDF's reluctance to engage in frontal attacks. The UDF's next destination was the wide-open expanses of the North African desert. Here they would meet two challenges, one from the Axis forces and the other from the British command style, which was anathema to the more flexible South African approach of directive command. The British lacked ideas on how to combine the South African motorised infantry with their armoured brigades. The South Africans, denied the flexibility that their doctrine demanded, found themselves in static positions at Sidi Rezegh (1941) and then later Tobruk (1942), two disasters that cost them dearly in casualties they could ill afford.

Plenty of evidence also exists of the otherness of South African doctrine when compared to that of the British. The South African way of war was an enigma to the British officers under Smuts's command in German East Africa in 1916. His style of leading from the front, penchant for battles of encirclement, over-sensitivity to battle casualties and preference for Boer-style directive command, which allows initiative down to the lower levels of command, left the British bewildered, unimpressed and more often frustrated.

The British preference for frontal assaults and battles of annihilation held no sway in South African ranks. This misunderstanding of South Africa's unique manoeuvre doctrine and its attendant directive command style led to open conflict between British and South African generals during the Second World War and particularly in the East African and Western Desert campaigns. Frequently, orders issued by the hard-pressed British were half-heartedly followed or completely ignored by South African commanders who had no desire to expend lives pointlessly.

In 1943, the decision was taken to form a South African armoured division for service in the European theatre of operations. The 6th South African Armoured Division was duly constituted and after a period of intensive training in the Western Desert, the division deployed to the Italian theatre in April 1944. There the South Africans would be tested in a new operational environment distinct from the previous African theatres, and not at all conducive to armoured and manoeuvre warfare. In fact, the Battle of Celleno, fought in June 1944, would be the only instance in the campaign during which the division's entire armoured complement deployed in unison. In fact, the Allied operational command left little room for South Africa to practise its home-grown manoeuvre doctrine in the Italian theatre. For the remainder of the campaign, the South African armour was relegated to support roles, while the infantrymen bore the brunt of the fighting across the challenging, built-up and mountainous terrain against extremely resolute German defenders – the engagement at Chiusi in June 1944 serving as a prime example.

The period after the Second World War and up to the Battle of Ongulumbashe in August 1966 – the start of the Border War – witnessed many changes in the South African defence establishment beyond the mere name change from the UDF to the SADF. South Africa's experience in the Italian campaign as a fully fledged armoured division left the SADF with a conventional structure and organisation more aligned to American and British doctrine. However, the Border War proved to be an exercise in unravelling and reversing some of the conventional lessons learned and the structure and organisation acquired by the UDF in the Italian theatre. The SADF proceeded to build a more flexible and manoeuvrable defence force suited to the growing challenges of a highly mobile cross-border war in the trying bush terrain of northern South West Africa (SWA) and southern Angola.

During the Border War, the SADF conducted several large-scale cross-border operations into Angola. These ranged from brief forays to more lengthy operations during which it intermittently occupied large tracts of the operational environment to interdict and offset the People's Liberation Army of Namibia (PLAN) and the Forças Armadas Populares de Libertação de Angola (FAPLA) and their Cuban and Russian allies. For the purposes of this book, the principal operations were Savannah (1975–1976), Cassinga (1978) and Protea (1982), as well as Moduler (1987), Hooper (1987–1988) and Packer (1988). These operations in turn tested the organisation, doctrine and force design of the SADF and would in the long run leave an indelible imprint on the nascent SANDF, established in 1994.

The SANDF was constituted from the SADF, the armed wings of the African National Congress and the Pan Africanist Congress and the Self-Protection Units of the Inkatha Freedom Party, as well as the armed forces of the former Bantustans (Ciskei, Transkei, Venda and Bophuthatswana). It was an exercise in compromise, integration and rationalisation, but for the most part the semi-conventional nature of the SADF, especially in terms of organisation, force design and doctrine, remained in place. From 1994 the SANDF was increasingly called upon to intervene in regional peacekeeping, peace support and other operations. In the democratic era, the deployments of the SANDF during Operation Boleas in Lesotho, in 1998, and the so-called Battle of Bangui in the Central African Republic, in 2013, are the prime instances with which to investigate the further evolution of a South African way of war.

The quest to rediscover a South African way of war was marked by many well-intentioned but ultimately misinformed initiatives. Historically, South African generals resorted to the teachings of JFC Fuller and were attracted to the strategy of the indirect approach, as espoused by

BH Liddell Hart. The ideas of these theorists formed the basis for the disastrous British tank-heavy brigades that the Germans consumed piecemeal in the Western Desert. British military philosophers saw the tank as a war-winning weapon and neglected the fundamental role of a combined-arms team. The advice and mentorship of Friedrich von Mellenthin, a staff officer in Rommel's Afrika Korps, was sought in the 1970s, despite the dissimilarity of the German way of war to South Africa's brand of manoeuvre warfare. South African officers also attended Israeli staff courses and imbibed the lessons delivered by visiting Israeli officers on their brand of warfare.

Lessons learned at a high cost during the South African War and the two world wars seemed casually forgotten and clearly neglected as South African military leaders sought out foreign doctrine in the four corners of the world. Finally, a South African manoeuvre doctrine using a combined-force approach emerged from the fog of foreign consultants. Military literature began to hark back to the days of the Boer commandos, but, inexplicably, reference to the UDF in the two world wars remained absent. A relic of the confusing journey towards rediscovering the South African way of war can be found in the *South African Staff Officers' Operational Manual*, which refers to 'Blitzkrieg', 'The Indirect Approach', and 'Mission Command', among other foreign doctrines, paying homage to Fuller and Liddell Hart, but making no references whatsoever to the fathers of South Africa's defence force, Louis Botha and Jan Smuts, nor to the many key battles that South Africans fought across Africa and in Europe. The SANDF has also not progressed its operational doctrine since the advent of a democratic dispensation in 1994. Instead, it has subsumed many of the traditions and structures of the SADF and has unfortunately inherited its amnesia in seeking the roots of, and building on, its doctrine.

In *20 Battles: In Search of a South African Way of War, 1913–2013*, the authors seek to address a glaring lacuna in the historiography of South Africa's unique manoeuvre doctrine. Some of the more important battles that shaped – or should have shaped – our operational military philosophy can be found in these pages. The examples chosen place a lens on instances where South African manoeuvre doctrine progressed, remained static or even regressed during the course of the battle. However, this ever-evolving doctrine runs like a golden thread through these pivotal engagements, giving a clue as to where our military ideas come from, where they are now and how they will develop in the future. History is an indispensable tool for soldiers and soldiering, giving insight into the mistakes committed in the past in the hope of ensuring that they can be avoided in the future. More importantly, history gives an insight into what is possible under adverse conditions. These battles represent the foundation stones on which our military doctrine can be built, and we hoped that their reintroduction will again reveal South Africa's unique way of war.

The title of the book may be misleading to the casual observer, for *20 Battles* in fact goes far beyond mere battlefield analysis. The book uses a select mixture of battles and operations from contemporary South African military history to analyse organisational and doctrinal changes in the defence force over the span of a century. In doing so, it moves between the tactical and the operational levels while critically evaluating the evolution of the South African way of war.

1

INDUSTRIAL STRIKES, 1913–1914

The formation of the Union of South Africa in 1910 signalled the dawn of a new age of reconciliation between Afrikaners and English speakers after the calamitous South African War. Louis Botha, a Boer war hero, became South Africa's first premier, with his loyal lieutenant, Jan Smuts, at his side. These two great men were determined to heal the wounds of a bitter war that tore asunder white South African society. Both men harboured long-cherished dreams of the Union as a vehicle not only for reconciliation and unity but also for the foundation of a future Greater South Africa that would encompass most of the territory stretching up to the equator. However, the enterprise would soon tear apart the uneasy truce between the two white 'races' of South Africa.

The dismissal of the anti-imperialist and nationalist James Barry Munnik (JBM) Hertzog from Botha's cabinet in 1912 scuppered Botha and Smuts's reconciliation efforts. Afrikaner nationalists yearned for the restoration of the old Boer republics and many English speakers remained fiercely loyal to the British crown. Apart from divisions along language and cultural lines, politics and economics played a strong role in dividing whites. Anti-capitalist labour unions seeking job reservation and protection from cheap black and Asian labour proved alarmingly militant.

The discontent of the black majority had grown since the signing of the peace treaty at Vereeniging in 1902. The coming of Union meant that black political aspirations had again been sidelined in favour of white unity. The British and liberal whites had promised blacks at least an extension of the Cape franchise system throughout the Union. However, the notion of extending black representation beyond the Cape was stillborn. South Africa was a country divided against itself in multiple instances and on many fronts.

Smuts and the founding of the Union Defence Force

Faced with a fragile political situation, Smuts set his sights on creating a homegrown South African defence force. He hoped that its formation would contribute to nation-building and, more importantly, that it would be available to counter the ever-present threat of internal strife. It could even be used in the unlikely event of a threat beyond South Africa's borders. The need to deal with the divisive political landscape, meet any internal threat and cater to external threat perceptions presented Smuts with several challenges. Political conciliation at the strategic and operational level would necessarily shape the structure of any future defence force.

Contributing to the less-than-ideal structure of the future Union Defence Force (UDF) was the overriding requirement of pandering to political expediency rather than military necessity. Many UDF appointments and structures were more the result of compromise and concessions than pure ability and expertise. Before Union in 1910, a short-term solution to defence was the formation of volunteer units within the four colonies to replace the ever-dwindling British military presence. Afrikaners and Englishmen joined these British-style volunteer regiments, spurred on by the constant threat of a black uprising. Proof of black political dissatisfaction had manifested itself in 1906 with a Zulu uprising known as the Bhambatha Rebellion. The rebellion was put down by colonial troops under the command of Col Duncan McKenzie. Machine guns and artillery were deployed against Zulu fighters armed with spears and cowhide shields. Although the rebellion was easily subdued, the campaign highlighted deficiencies in the colonial militias and the defence organisations and policies in the colonies. Military necessity led to closer military cooperation between the colonies, which resulted in the creation of a regional military force, a precursor to the UDF.

In May 1910, Smuts was appointed the Union's first minister of defence, and also became the minister of the interior and the minister of mines. Roland Bourne, a veteran of the South African War, was appointed under-secretary for defence to assist Smuts. With the creation of the UDF in July 1912, Smuts faced Afrikaner resentment and a deep mistrust of anything to do with the British military. At the opposite end of the political spectrum, the Unionists demanded a defence force that went beyond the mere ability to deal with internal matters. They sought a South African military that could be deployed anywhere in Africa in support of British forces.

Smuts had the unenviable task of accommodating the aspirations of both pro- and anti-British factions. Marthinus Steyn, former president of the Orange Free State, and John X Merriman, an elder statesman from the Cape Colony, wanted to avoid ushering in a policy of militarism in the Union and for South Africa to stay clear of the quarrels of Europe.

Smuts's emphasis on designing a defence force to meet internal threats was greeted with the full backing and cheers of the House of Assembly in March 1911. However, Smuts drew the House's attention to South Africa's strategic role in the world and its importance as the custodian of gold and rare minerals that were sought after by the rest of the world. He ably demonstrated the need to expand South Africa's defence policy to protect its newfound status. Furthermore, there were language and cultural differences between the two white 'races', and also differences between rural and urban citizens. These 'lines of cleavage' would have to be tackled to construct an equitable system of defence supported by the entire community.

Smuts was determined at this early stage that any system of defence had to be effective, efficient and economical. He suggested a small permanent force, supplemented by a citizen force in times of need. He foresaw the day that British forces would leave the subcontinent and that South Africa would have to fill the void.

Smuts proposed several small, permanent rapid-reaction forces that would fulfil the dual roles of a police force and a conventional military unit. They would be reinforced with an artillery component when needed in more conventional situations. The former Cape Mounted Rifles, together with its attached artillery corps, was the ideal example. Dual police and military roles could be replicated throughout the country and would hopefully make for the economical and efficient use of resources.

The crux of the matter was the shape and structure of the future citizen force. Here Smuts favoured compulsory military service over a volunteer system, tempered by the realisation that a compulsory system would yield too many soldiers and come at too great an economic and political cost. Therefore, he proposed a system of taking volunteers first so as to harness those who were most keen to offer service. The country would be divided up into military districts, each with a permanent officer who was to register all those eligible for military duty in his area.

Discovering a South African way of war

Smuts was determined to place the UDF on a doctrinal path closer to the British system than to the old Boer republican commandos. Understandably, it is often the loser in war who desires to model their future doctrine along the lines of the victor. Smuts identified the two major weaknesses experienced by the Boer republics during the South African War: the lack of highly trained officers and the poor discipline of the rank and file. These shortcomings in Boer doctrine robbed them of fighting power despite their being the 'best fighting material in the world'. The UDF would have to address these two issues and 'not merely rely on the self-devotion of the people of South Africa'.

By a kind of sleight of hand, the permanent component of the UDF and the citizen force would be modelled on the colonial mounted-rifles system and regular infantry. At the same time, veterans of the Boer republican commandos would be relegated to the rifle clubs and enrolled in a veterans' reserve. The yearly citizen force intake would eventually bolster the UDF numbers, with recruits receiving more disciplined, British-oriented conventional training rather than learning the Boer commando system. The committee to establish the UDF would be heavily influenced by British officers such as Field Marshal Lord Methuen, commander of British military forces in South Africa, and Col Henry Lukin, the Commandant General of the Cape.

Further initiatives towards a more professional army included the construction of a military college, which would provide training for officers and address the problem of an insufficiently qualified officer corps. Smuts emphasised the South Africanisation of the whole process, and he looked forward to a time when the army would be commanded by South African graduates of the military college.

The signs of political expediency peppered the process and structures of the newly formed UDF. The system of drawing citizen force officers from the ranks and from the districts they came from ensured that a certain division along language lines was perpetuated in the UDF. According to Smuts: 'We are not going to have an alien system of officers imposed – English officers on the Dutch-speaking section or Dutch officers on the English-speaking section.' Political barriers had the unfortunate effect of producing two military components streamed along language lines – mounted infantry and regular infantry. The former was mainly Afrikaans/Boer in character and staffed by Afrikaans officers recruited in the mainly Afrikaner rural areas. The latter was English in character, staffed by English-speaking officers and drew Afrikaner and English recruits from the urban areas.

The debates in the House of Assembly highlighted the tensions the future UDF would have to contend with. When the Defence Bill was first submitted to Parliament, both sides of the House vigorously debated the issue of black participation and the internal and external threats the UDF would need to consider. It was quite apparent from the replies of the opposition and the backbenchers that they perceived the main threat to the Union to emanate from the black population.

Colonel Charles Crewe took the opposite view, and saw little threat from the black population, referring to it as a 'danger which he did not believe existed'. He went on to say that it did not exist because 'civilisation and enlightenment and fair play had done a great deal to show the native races that they were not the enemy of the whites in this country'.

John X Merriman was another who disagreed that blacks were the 'natural enemy', and he rather thought that 'They ought to be our natural friend'. His concern was that blacks would become a problem only if they were mismanaged and he called on the government to 'govern the natives properly'. Merriman turned to the external threat posed by Germany and Portugal, whose colonial possessions lay on South Africa's borders. TL Schreiner saw that the destiny of South Africa 'was to be both a white and a black man's country'. He saw an opportunity to raise a military corps among the 'coloured people', who he believed had no better in the world, and if led by a 'proper' European, they would follow him to their death.

Hugh Wyndham also raised some points of concern. The first was that

Smuts had announced the replacement of the volunteer system without putting forward an alternative. His second concern was the formation of an intelligence department.

The notion of armed coloureds or blacks being drawn into the defence force to fight locally or overseas, as proposed by Schreiner, drew antagonism from much of the House. General Tobias Smuts, a distant relative of Jan Smuts, hoped that South African troops would never be used to fight on behalf of the British Empire. Training coloured troops and placing them on the same footing as white troops would be immoral, and they would be a menace. He also represented old-school Boer military thought in cautioning against too much discipline and drill. His emphasis was on good riding and shooting skills.

When the Defence Bill was introduced into Parliament for the second reading, Smuts dealt with the exclusion of coloureds. He explained that although the Bill placed no compulsion on coloureds to undergo military training, it also did not exclude them from volunteering for service. The government would always consider any proposals put forward for volunteer service, he said. The fact was that at the time the Bill was passed, many coloureds were serving in the Cape Mounted Rifles and the Cape Mounted Police. Crewe pointed out that the House had no right to exclude any volunteer, and he referred to the excellent service blacks had provided as scouts in the Basutoland campaign of 1881.

Sir George Farrar identified a problem that would become a reality in the 1914 Afrikaner Rebellion and also in the campaigns in German South West Africa (GSWA) and German East Africa (GEA). He warned against the impression that the rural population, consisting mostly of Afrikaners, would supply the mounted infantry while the urban population, predominantly English-speaking, would provide the regular infantry and technical and signal capabilities.

In December 1914, Hugh Wyndham wrote about the results of a divided command and a complete absence of organisation:

> We have at the present time two entirely different military organizations operating side by side in the field. One is the commando system, which in reality is no system at all, & the other is a somewhat faint copy of the British system. However, we are getting along all right.

Botha interjected to support Smuts and assured the House that racial divisions belonged to the past and that all citizens had a role and a duty to defend South Africa. He looked to the proposed defence force as a powerful tool to remove racial divisions once and for all. Some of Botha's (and therefore the Boer) predilection for tactical thinking was revealed in the debate. He stressed that the priority was to ensure that all soldiers learned how to shoot and judge distances properly. Botha raised the important issue of discipline and the need for good officers, but he stressed the need to find an economical solution. He did not mention a formal officer training college. But he did stress the urgency of forming a defence force to take over the country's defence should Britain withdraw its troops at any time and leave South Africa defenceless. Smuts addressed the question of discipline and was at pains to reassure the House that the UDF would not simply be taking over the British Military Code but that it would be modified to suit South African conditions.

Smuts was determined to create a modern defence force capable of engaging a modern enemy and modelled on European lines; and he chose not to recreate the old Boer forces and their way of war. To achieve this, he called upon a select group of staff officers, many of them former enemies, such as Tim Lukin, Roland Bourne and Jack Collyer. He consulted Field Marshal Lord Methuen and his chief of staff, Brig Gen George Aston, who stayed on in South Africa until 1912 at Smuts's request. Collyer specifically assisted Smuts in preparing a Defence Act for the Union. The preparatory work was completed in mid-1912 and consensus was obtained in the Cabinet on the proposed Defence Act.

Smuts welcomed the recruitment of senior officers and warrant officers from the British Army to train the new UDF. He had the vision to realise that the UDF would become an effective modern fighting force only with the assistance of expert battle-hardened personnel, most of whom would come from the former colonial and British enemy.

The introduction of the South Africa Defence Bill in February 1912 was greeted with much criticism and scepticism in Afrikaner quarters. There was considerable resistance to compulsory training, British military discipline, British-style uniforms and the fact that Smuts considered defence to be an imperial matter. Once passed by Parliament, the Defence Act inextricably bound up the UDF with the system of imperial defence by recognising that South Africa was dependent on the Royal Navy to protect it from a seaward invasion by a foreign power. The Governor General, the Rt Hon Viscount Gladstone, approved the Act on 13 June 1912 and it was officially gazetted the following day.

The UDF, as Smuts's brainchild, was thus established on 1 July 1912. It consisted of the South African Permanent Force (SAPF), the Active Citizen Force (ACF), the Coast Garrison Force (CGF), the Rifle Associations (or resurrected commandos), the Royal Naval Volunteer Reserve (RNVR) and the Cadet Corps. In terms of the Act, the UDF was formed to defend 'South Africa', which, for Smuts, was a geographical expression that extended past the Union's borders and included all territory south of the equator.

The small SAPF, consisting of a headquarters, instructional and administrative staffs and five regiments of the South African Mounted Rifles (SAMR) – each regiment supplied with an artillery battery – would be supplemented in times of conflict by an ACF component. The need for a permanent structure to house the artillery component of the UDF had been discussed by Smuts in the House during the second reading of the Defence Bill. He had alluded to the excellence of the State Artillery units of the former Boer republics and the sterling service they had rendered in the South African War. He doubted that a volunteer artillery unit would ever be able to reach the level of expertise of a permanent force unit.

The SAMR was a military constabulary like the Cape Mounted Rifles, tasked primarily with police work in their respective geographical areas. By May 1913, the total strength of the SAMR had grown to 103 officers, 348 non-commissioned officers and 1 565 riflemen, while the so-called non-European section consisted of nearly 2 000 black and Indian constables. This mounted constabulary with artillery support would form a strike force in times of need. Therefore, Smuts saw in the mounted riflemen an efficient and economical way of internal policing, coupled with a trained permanent artillery component.

Unsatisfactorily, provision was not made for a Chief of the General Staff. An alternative arrangement was made by which the three military executive commanders – the Commandant-General of the Active Citizen Force, the Inspector-General of the Permanent Force and the

Commandant of the Cadet Corps – were placed under the direct control of Smuts as the minister of defence, who was in turn advised by a Defence Board. On the eve of the 1913–1914 labour unrest, the complement of the ACF was approaching 77 000 men, the majority of whom consisted of the 42 000 commandos in the Rifle Associations (see Table 1).

ACTIVE CITIZEN FORCE	
December 1913	Complement
ACF and Coast Guard Garrison	23 462
Cadet Corps	11 318
Rifle Associations	42 000
Total	76 780

TABLE 1: *The numbers behind the Active Citizen Force*

Labour unrest

The year 1914 would be a busy one for the fledgling UDF. Its first operational test came from a violent industrial strike called by the South African Federation of Trades on the Witwatersrand in January 1914. It was essentially a continuation of the general strike of 4 July 1913 in which all the mines and power stations on the Reef had been brought to a standstill.

Smuts, caught unprepared by the magnitude of the unrest, could not deploy sufficient manpower via the newly formed UDF and requested assistance from the imperial troops garrisoned in South Africa. The imperial troops, together with policemen and special constables, and a small contingent of the ACF, were unable to curb acts of vandalism effectively. Heavy-handed policing at an attempted crowd dispersal resulted in the deaths of 20 strikers and five innocent bystanders at the Rand Club in central Johannesburg. The combined imperial and Union government forces lacked the strength to suppress the strike, forcing Smuts and Botha to convince the Chamber of Mines, which represented employers, to reach a humiliating agreement with the strikers. Smuts emerged from the experience determined not to allow the strikers to gain the upper hand again.

The situation remained tense throughout the remainder of 1913 and labour relations worsened again in early 1914, when a possible retrenchment of railway workers was announced. A strike was called by the unions for 8 January 1914, and labour action soon spread nationwide. A spate of violent incidents led Smuts to declare martial law for the first time since the establishment of the Union.

Smuts mobilised the defence force's SAPF and ACF components once it became apparent that the outnumbered police would not be able to contain the rapidly deteriorating situation. The SAPF and ACF had been formed only in July 1913 and could therefore not be expected to quell the riots without the assistance of the Rifle Associations (Citizen Force Class B Reserve). The Rifle Associations had been created to make provision for those who had not been drafted and had not volunteered for citizen force training to receive a modicum of musketry training. Provision was also made for young men not actively trained to enter a Rifle Association.

In reality, the Rifle Associations contained many members of the erstwhile Boer commandos. These commandos were drawn mainly from the rural areas, and many were Boer republican veterans of the South African War. Calling up the commandos was contrary to Smuts's vision of building a modern defence force closely aligned to British military doctrine, uniforms and discipline. The commandos who rode out against the strikers in 1914 wore civilian clothes and did not follow the UDF's rank structures; they would form the dominant component of the UDF's deployment and, in this way, would exert an influence on the proceedings equal to their superior numbers. A total of eight Transvaal, 22 Free State and two Natal commandos were called up and placed under the command of the veteran Boer general, Koos de la Rey.

The system was not a voluntary one, as every citizen was compelled to adhere to their call-up instructions under the Defence Act of 1912. There were those, of course, who did not obey the instruction to report for duty, for political or economic reasons. They were, however, in the minority, and many burghers saw this as an opportunity to experience the commando life of their fathers or brothers who had been old enough to fight in the South African War. Desertion was an offence according to the new law, and anyone found guilty was liable to punishment.

The Defence Act stipulated that every member of the ACF who performed the duties of a mounted infantryman was required to bring his own horse and rifle. The UDF, out of necessity, acquired horses for those burghers who did not own one prior to the call-up. Rifles were also issued to those burghers who reported without one. Suitably equipped, the commandos were transported with their horses via the railway network to their various assembly points.

The modernisation process imposed on the UDF by the Defence Act had hardly taken effect when the Rifle Associations were called up. These burghers had received little modern training and uniforms and knew nothing of the new UDF rank structure. The commandos had retained their old Boer leadership system and rank structure of commandants, field-cornets, assistant field-cornets and ordinary burghers.

The deployment took place in the way of the traditional Boer military commando system, with each man required to report for duty with his horse and rifle. Participation in the quelling of the strike provided a feeling of nostalgia to many Afrikaners and presented an opportunity to fight against the English once again, albeit in the form of urban strikers. According to Deneys Reitz, when addressing the commandos during the strike, the commandant general of the Citizen Force, General Christiaan Beyers, said, 'the English townspeople have forgotten what a Boer commando looks like, and … [it is] time to refresh their memories.'

The strike offered the traditional Boer leadership an opportunity to rebuild the old military and political networks and give many youngsters a taste of commando life. The strikes of 1914 oiled the machine of the rebellion that would follow shortly. This would be the last time that the traditional Boer commando system would be used by the UDF, as each successive deployment would take on more and more of the modernising influences instituted by Smuts through the Defence Act.

Smuts was perhaps misguided in relying so strongly on the old Boer commando structure. Even though the call-up took place in the context of the new UDF, it was not without the obvious risk that it could revitalise certain nationalist elements in the commandos and strengthen the Boer republican leadership networks. Indeed, a few short months later, it would be used to conjure up rebellion.

Fortunately, only a small number of workers went on strike beyond the Witwatersrand and so the greater portion of the UDF's fighting power was deployed there. A general strike called for 13 January was preceded by various acts of sabotage and attempted sabotage. As the strike got under way, Smuts declared martial law in the affected districts and implemented censorship of the media. The crackdown resulted in the arrest of hundreds of strikers and union leaders, and the remaining strike leaders made a last stand by barricading themselves in the Trades Hall at Fordsburg. The government forces cleared the area of civilians and demanded the immediate unconditional surrender of the strikers. The strikers fired upon government forces advancing on the hall and defied the call to surrender. The saga was brought to an end on 15 January 1914 when government forces threatened to use artillery: the strikers immediately surrendered. Apart from a few sporadic incidents, the UDF had effectively broken the back of the strike.

The labour unrest of 1913–1914 became the first test for the fledgling UDF. The defence force was designed primarily to suppress internal uprisings and insurrection rather than to combat an external threat. The UDF also became a vehicle of political reconciliation instead of a formation in which personnel were selected purely on merit. Many of its members and institutions were the products of compromise rather than effectiveness. Despite financial and political constraints, Smuts desired a modern army based on the British model – a far cry from the Boer republican commando system from which he had emerged. His determination in this regard manifested in the former commandos being relegated to the Rifle Associations, where they languished.

It is ironic, then, that the mobilisation of the former Boer republican commandos to quell the industrial strikes of 1913–1914 set in motion a process by which Boer doctrine would gain ascendancy over the more rigid British doctrine. It placed the UDF on a trajectory that favoured a style of warfare based on manoeuvre. A further unintended consequence of using the commandos was the opportunity it afforded Afrikaner nationalist networks to forge old ties anew. During the Afrikaner Rebellion of 1914, the ability of the rebels to mobilise efficiently against Smuts and Botha can be traced back to their participation in the suppression of the industrial unrest of 1913–1914.

Smuts would again be forced to rely on the former Boer republican commandos during the second phase of the GSWA campaign of 1915. The UDF's first action of that campaign, and its first entanglement with a foreign foe, occurred at Sandfontein in 1914. It is a story of betrayal and lost opportunity.

The battle of Sandfontein, 1914

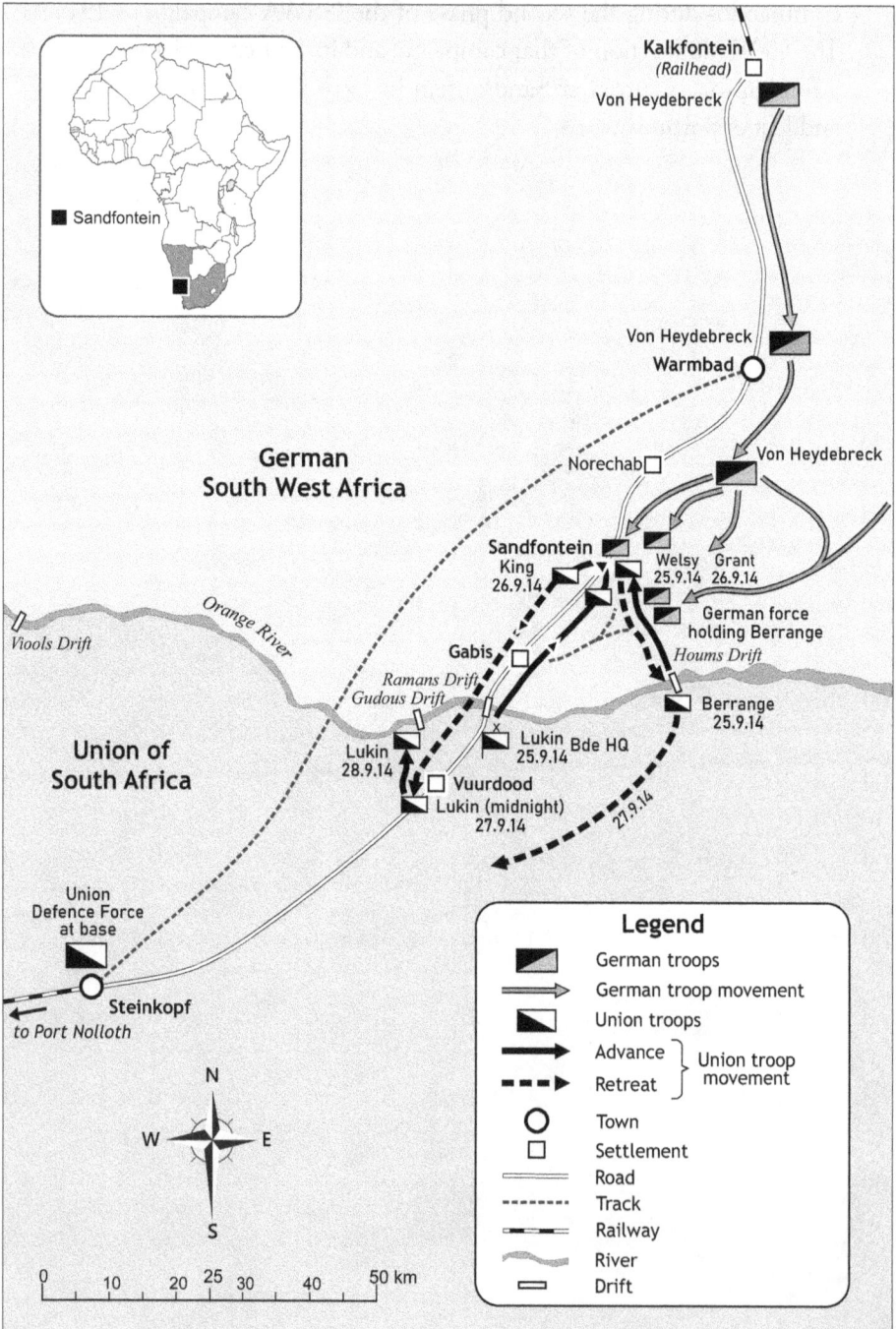

Kalkfontein
(Railhead)
Von Heydebreck

Von Heydebreck
Warmbad

German
South West Africa

Norechab
Von Heydebreck

Sandfontein
King
26.9.14

Welsy
25.9.14

Grant
26.9.14

German force
holding Berrange

Orange River

Viools Drift

Gabis

Ramans Drift
Gudous Drift

Houms Drift

Berrange
25.9.14

Union of
South Africa

Lukin
28.9.14

Lukin
25.9.14 Bde HQ

27.9.14

Vuurdood
Lukin (midnight)
27.9.14

Union
Defence Force
at base

Steinkopf

to Port Nolloth

N
W   E
S

Legend

	German troops
	German troop movement
	Union troops
	Advance } Union troop
	Retreat } movement
O	Town
□	Settlement
	Road
	Track
	Railway
	River
	Drift

0 10 20 25 30 40 50 km

Sandfontein

2

SANDFONTEIN, 1914

In a First World War campaign that is now almost completely forgotten, the Battle of Sandfontein took place on 26 September 1914 in one of the world's most remote locations. The battle marked the fledgling UDF's first foray against a foreign power after its deployment a few months earlier to suppress an internal uprising on the Witwatersrand.

Fortunately, the Battle of Sandfontein has been rediscovered by several South African historians in the past two decades and offers an interesting lens through which to view the evolution of South African military doctrine and the divisive political and military aspects of the Union's early history. It has become a litmus test for gauging the efficacy of the Union's fragile political system and muddled military doctrine.

The battle resulted in the ignominious defeat of the South Africans at the hands of the *Schutztruppe* (protection force), the colonial militia of German South West Africa. Within days of the fiasco, the Afrikaner Rebellion tore South Africa apart politically. The crisis, brought about by defeat and rebellion, abruptly interrupted Smuts's grandiose plan to conquer GSWA rapidly. Sandfontein marked both the low point and the turning point of the UDF's military fortunes. In its wake, Smuts and Louis Botha decisively crushed the rebellion and placed the invasion of GSWA firmly back on the agenda.

With war clouds gathering over Europe in August 1914, South Africa contained all the combustible elements needed for a political inferno. The wounds of the South African War had barely started to heal and the prospect of war in Europe deepened the divide between those who supported imperial Britain and those who did not. As a self-governing dominion of Britain, a politically divided South Africa found itself automatically at war with the Central Powers – Germany, Austria-Hungary, the Ottoman Empire and Bulgaria – and precluded from pursuing neutrality. Britain's confidence in the loyalty of the Union was solid, but there were doubts about whether Botha and Smuts could count on the allegiance of their fellow Afrikaners: on the eve of the war, the two leaders no longer enjoyed the support of the majority of Afrikaners. In future elections, the two would look to English-speaking politicians on the opposition benches to bolster their parliamentary numbers. They seized the opportunity and made an unsolicited offer for the UDF to take over imperial garrison duties in South Africa, thus freeing British troops for service in Europe.

South Africa would defend its territory by using its army exclusively. The departure of British troops fulfilled Smuts's objective of elevating South Africa's status and many South Africans across the political divide welcomed the opportunity to rid the country of 'foreign forces'. Loyal participation at Britain's side when war was declared on 4 August significantly enhanced South Africa's status in the Empire. War could reinvigorate the stalled prospects of territorial expansion in the direction of Portuguese-ruled Mozambique and the High Commission Territories of Bechuanaland, Basutoland and Swaziland. The possibility of adding German colonial territory to the Union was also an attractive prospect.

South Africa enters the First World War

Lewis Harcourt, the British colonial secretary, accepted Botha's offer to relieve the imperial garrison on 7 August, but he went a step further in asking the Union government to 'seize such part of German South West Africa as will give them the command of Lüderitzbucht, Swakopmund and the wireless stations there or in the interior': the German wireless stations posed a considerable risk to Allied shipping around the Cape coastal route. The prospect of denying GSWA ports to German shipping would further enhance British sea power in the South Atlantic and the Indian Ocean.

Smuts and Botha ordered extensive military preparations to launch an attack on GSWA before gaining the approval of Parliament and key opposition figures such as JBM Hertzog and Marthinus Steyn. The alienation of a large sector of the Afrikaner population ensured that any military endeavour beyond South Africa's borders would necessitate the frequent casting of eyes back to the home front. South Africa could ill afford heavy losses or significant defeats in its quest to conquer German territory in a tenuous political environment. Despite having to walk a political tightrope, Smuts proceeded with alacrity to plan for the speedy conquest of GSWA.

Smuts's ambitious project, which involved the conquest of the entire territory of GSWA, went beyond British requests to occupy GSWA ports and neutralise wireless stations there. Smuts's ambition required increased levels of forces beyond those immediately available. Smuts, the prodigious workaholic, even busied himself with the details of assembling the army and dealing with issues of fly infestation, horses and their whereabouts, and the constant stream of officers complaining about each other. He faced many challenges, ranging from a lack of small arms, all types of ammunition and artillery to a dearth of capable junior officers able to command effectively or fill staff functions.

A hopelessly confused command structure aggravated the haphazard proceedings. Even while on campaign, Botha never relinquished his post as prime minister. He decided to take full command of the field force in September 1914, leaving Smuts, the defence minister, with the administrative and organisational work of officer placement, recruitment, force disposition and provisioning. Smuts busied himself with these essential tasks by engaging with the various role-players to build a credible military force for the coming campaign. However, the command structure followed political expediency rather than merit, diminishing the UDF's effectiveness. This was only partially mitigated by the special relationship between Botha and Smuts.

Smuts's plan

Smuts formulated the bold and brilliant plan that included the simultaneous seizure of Lüderitzbucht and Swakopmund and an invasion across the southern border of GSWA. Following a seaborne landing, four separate columns would converge on the capital, Windhoek. The plan called for the 'C' Force under Col PS Beves, with approximately

2 000 men, to land at Lüderitzbucht. With the help of the Royal Navy, its primary task was to destroy critical infrastructure such as the wireless station. The next objective for this group was the advance along the railway line to Aus with the objective of reaching Seeheim/Keetmanshoop.

Further south, Maj Gen (Sir) Henry Timson Lukin commanded 'A' Force, with 2 500 men. He would land at Port Nolloth and advance to Sandfontein, the capture of which would provide him with a gateway into southern GSWA and the first staging post with excellent water resources. A further advance to Kalkfontein would take him to the southern terminus of the German railway system. Lukin's next objectives were to reach Warmbad and then, further along the railway line, to meet Col Beves at Seeheim/Keetmanshoop.

Joining Lukin and protecting his right wing was the 'B' Force under Lt Col Manie Maritz, with 1 000 mounted men. He would invade GSWA from the southeast, with Upington as his base of operations, and protect Lukin's exposed right flank. Even though Maritz was supposed to take part in the campaign, his anti-British sentiments and support for Germany meant he was vehemently opposed to any invasion of GSWA. He would eventually be the first senior commander to come out in open rebellion, in October 1914, and join the Germans with some of his loyal commando, placing Lukin and his force in great jeopardy.

The most significant and crucial formation was the 'D' Force, commanded by Col Duncan McKenzie, with 4 000 men. 'D' Force was to land at Walvis Bay and advance to Swakopmund, with Windhoek as the final objective. The capture of the colonial capital would sever the rail link to Keetmanshoop and render the German defence south of the city untenable. Opposing the 9 500 converging Union troops would be the approximately 5 000 men of the *Schutztruppe*.

The 'D' Force was fundamental to the success of the delicately balanced operation. Failure to land at and seize Swakopmund would allow the Germans to concentrate their forces either against Lukin in the south or against Beves at Lüderitzbucht. For as long as McKenzie held Swakopmund in strength, threatening Windhoek, the Germans would have to glance back over their shoulders should they have any intention of attacking either Beves or Lukin.

The mechanics of Smuts's plan, although ambitious, were based on sound doctrinal foundations. Koos de la Rey had instilled the essence of Boer manoeuvre warfare in Smuts during the latter phases of the South African War. Smuts planned to rely on manoeuvre, coupled with the Clausewitzian concept that recognised the superiority of simultaneous advances when using exterior lines (a concentration in time) over an enemy using interior lines (a concentration in space). The Germans, using their extensive railway network, would be operating on interior lines of communication, but in itself this did not give them a marked advantage. Interior lines afford a force operating from a central position the opportunity to concentrate swiftly at a higher tempo than an enemy operating on exterior lines. In this way, a numerically inferior enemy can achieve superiority at a decisive point. The Germans would try to squeeze every advantage afforded them via their interior lines and well-developed railway system, allowing them to concentrate their forces rapidly against any one of Smuts's advancing groups in turn.

Smuts had no choice but to operate on exterior lines. According to Clausewitz, strategic convergent attacks have the advantage that an attack on any single enemy force affects other enemy forces due to the insecurity brought about by having a victorious army in its rear. The advantage of exterior lines is the threat of envelopment. The requirement for operating on external lines is superiority in numbers or fighting power, good communications between the individual converging wings and speed in executing movements. The arrangement for an effective convergent attack must be that 'the advance [is] made offensively from every point possible, and at the same moment exactly'.

A further advantage of splitting the UDF into four almost equal wings was that the desolate and arid terrain lent itself to supplying smaller formations more easily. Smuts's four wings advancing simultaneously would place the *Schutztruppe* in the horns of a dilemma, as any concentrated attack on one of the wings would leave the defence in front of the attackers heavily outnumbered. Smuts's strategy carried risks but bore the promise of not merely defeating the *Schutztruppe* but cutting them off and eliminating them.

Smuts grounded his manoeuvre warfare plan on successful landings at all three ports either simultaneously or in close sequence. He and Botha persistently implored the British to land the 'D' Force at

Swakopmund well before Lukin's advance to Sandfontein. Ultimately, the UDF's failure to occupy Swakopmund placed Beves and Lukin in a precarious position at the operational level.

The Germans' best chance of delaying the inevitable was in concentrating their forces and attacking each UDF wing in turn, using the operational mobility afforded by the railways and the tactical mobility of their mounted infantry. The *Schutztruppe* would have struggled to achieve numerical superiority against any of Smuts's formations. Doing so would have severely weakened the fighting power of those opposing the simultaneous advance of the other wings.

The *Schutztruppe*, while operating on interior lines, would have to contend with the challenging logistics and exhaustion of rapid movement over vast distances. In the 18th century, Frederick the Great, a successful practitioner of concentration on interior lines, noted another disadvantage of concentration in space applicable to the logistics of his day when he wrote: 'These kinds of wars ruin the armies by fatigue and the marches that one must have his men make.' Botha demonstrated the point when in the last battle of the GSWA campaign, at Otavifontein in June–July 1915, the exhausted Germans had all but expended their capability to manoeuvre.

The UDF as a blunt instrument

At the outbreak of the First World War, the UDF was a blunt military instrument. Structural flaws reduced its fighting power and the command structure lacked a formal general staff component that, in a modern army, could provide vital information in support of command decisions and free up the commander to conduct the actual battle. The general staff would plan, coordinate, administer and organise logistics for operations and campaigns.

Smuts managed with the secretary of defence, Sir Roland Bourne, in place of a chief of staff. But Bourne was a civilian with no military status and advised Smuts to the best of his limited ability. (Brig Gen Jack Collyer, one of the few trained staff officers, fulfilled an essential role in the campaigns in South West Africa and East Africa, and became Chief of the General Staff at the end of the war.) The shortage of staff officers was apparent throughout the UDF, with few having received any

Typical Union Defence Force infantry that fought at the Battle of Sandfontein, 1914

Schutztruppen *on parade in German South West Africa*

formal training. The lack of staff meant that, at the outbreak of war, there were neither mobilisation plans nor operational plans for the upcoming campaign in GSWA. Unwieldy structures such as the Council for Defence and three separate, independent military executive commanders for the SAPF, ACF and Cadets had more to do with representivity and political expediency than with providing an effective military command.

Most of the formations deployed to GSWA in Smuts's initial plan were members of the ACF Class 'A' Reserves, who had received British-type training and were derived from ex-colonial formations led by British officers. The situation was reversed after Sandfontein, when the UDF made extensive use of the ACF Class 'B' Reserves consisting of Rifle Association members who were mainly ex-republican commandos. There were obvious political considerations behind Smuts's initial reliance on the UDF's more English elements for the preliminary deployment to GSWA, including the open and vociferous opposition of Afrikaners to the whole enterprise. Botha and Smuts would fall back on old Boer tactics and force structures after the first phase of the GSWA campaign ground to a halt.

In the light of a precarious political situation and an ill-prepared military, Smuts's ambitious plan for the invasion of GSWA seemed at the outset to be beyond the UDF's grasp. Keen to seize the entire GSWA territory instead of merely fulfilling the British request to occupy the ports and neutralise the wireless stations, Smuts increased his force levels substantially. The increased manpower exacerbated problems with the UDF's already stretched logistical and planning system. The expanded force required naval escorts and resources not envisaged in the original British plan. The location and choice of invasion points were not in dispute, as some historians believe, but the operation's scale and ambition were contentious. The British were anxious that Smuts's grandiose and expanded plans would delay the task force, and they were concerned that the South Africans had not yet executed any part of the invasion plan because of their efforts to assemble the enlarged force.

The invasion of German South West Africa

Lukin's 'A' Force landed at Port Nolloth on 31 August and immediately experienced delays in disembarkation, due partly to the poor state of the port but also to disorganised staff work. According to Lukin, disembarkation was not expected to be completed before 16 or 17 September. Smuts assured the British that the remainder of the expedition would sail on 5 September and that the increased number of troops had not caused any delay. The problem now lay with the British, who could gather enough escorts for the expedition only by 12 September. Chaotic procedures at Port Nolloth (ten days to land the stores, for example) delayed the GSWA expedition a few days beyond 12 September and suggested that disembarkation at the other ports would also entail a lengthy process.

The delays at Port Nolloth meant that the Walvis Bay part of the expedition would take place one week after the landings on 14 September at Lüderitzbucht. Unfortunately, inclement weather forced a decision to land troops at Lüderitzbucht only on 14 September and delayed the Walvis Bay expedition's departure to 26 September. The landing at Walvis Bay would then only be complete by 11 October. Additional delays meant the transport vessels were retained at Port Nolloth and could return to Cape Town only by 17 September. As a result, Beves belatedly occupied Lüderitzbucht on 18 September. The worsening political situation on the home front, including the growing threat of rebellion and the resignation of several senior UDF officers, cast doubt on the campaign plan and the prospects of making a landing at Walvis Bay.

The UDF's failure to secure Walvis Bay/Swakopmund simultaneously with Lüderitzbucht, combined with an offensive by Lukin in the south, placed Beves in a precarious position. Moreover, the resignations of key officers cast further doubt on the Walvis Bay/Swakopmund landings.

Maj Jan Kemp resigned on 13 September, and Gen Christiaan Beyers resigned his position as Commandant-General of the citizen force some days later. Lt Col Manie Maritz had been agitating against the invasion of GSWA ever since he had received news about it on 15 August, most probably through Beyers. It was an open secret that Maritz was opposed to the operation. Smuts suspected Maritz of treachery early on and openly confronted him at the Commandants Conference in August. Maritz's recalcitrant behaviour during September did not go unnoticed by the government. Together with crucial delays in the seaborne operations, a perfect storm was brewing, which placed Beves in considerable jeopardy. Inexplicably, and contrary to Smuts's usual ruthless and decisive nature, he failed to act against Maritz even in the face of mounting evidence of his treachery.

In the absence of a landing at Walvis Bay/Swakopmund, Lukin became critical to the fortunes of Beves's force, which was busy offloading at Lüderitzbucht. Lukin's force, straddling the southern border of GSWA, would have to provide a crucial diversion to protect Beves. Smuts bargained that the threat of Lukin's launching a flank attack towards Warmbad would prevent a German concentration against the port. Crucially, Maritz was to protect Lukin's right flank, and cooperation between their two forces was essential.

The original Smuts plan, based on the occupation of both Walvis Bay and Swakopmund, called for Lukin to strike through Raman's Drift on the Orange River and successively capture the towns of Warmbad and Kalkfontein. Such a thrust by Lukin would also discourage any German move to invade the Union. The after-battle report clearly states that the 'A' Force's operational objective was the capture of Warmbad and then Kalkfontein. It was 'anticipated' that this would lessen the chances of an invasion from GSWA and 'materially assist' the forces landing at Lüderitzbucht. However, Lukin would have to do this without the UDF distracting the bulk of the *Schutztruppe* at Swakopmund, as Smuts had originally intended.

Already compromised by delays in the operation, the simultaneous advance on exterior lines was further thrown out of kilter when it became apparent that Maritz would not cooperate in covering Lukin's flank. Furthermore, there were strong indications that he would go into open rebellion. Instead of Maritz's force bolstering Lukin, it began to menace him. If Maritz switched sides, it would bolster the enemy's numerical strength, which would change the delicate balance of fighting power.

As we have seen, the usually decisive Smuts had taken no immediate action to remove Maritz after the resignations of Beyers and Kemp, despite all the evidence of his lack of support for the campaign. Instead, on 23 September, he ordered Maritz to advance to Schuit Drift from Kakamas and head to Ukamas to assist and cooperate with Lukin's force. Smuts's decision to test Maritz's loyalty rather than replace him is testament to the challenging political climate, where decisiveness gave way to expediency.

Increasingly desperate to divert German attention away from Beves and allow reinforcements to arrive at the scene, Smuts pressed Lukin to advance expeditiously to Sandfontein. Lukin was wary of the German threat gathering to his north and, unsure of Maritz's intentions, expressed his reservations to Defence Headquarters. As the official history records:

'Headquarters had to request high pressure to the verge of self-sacrifice on the part of General Lukin to which he most loyally responded.'

The Battle of Sandfontein

Owing to bungling at Defence Headquarters, Lukin did not receive vital intelligence that the Germans were assembling a force near him. He is quoted as saying that had he received this intelligence timeously, he would have withdrawn promptly. In any event, he should have expected a robust German response to his advance and should have provided a sufficient force forward able to defend itself adequately. He possessed reliable information of the enemy's determination to oppose his advance on Kalkfontein and that the Germans would use the railway to concentrate considerable forces against him.

However, Lukin's report paints a different picture and lays the blame on an intelligence failure. He maintained that scouts should have detected the large force of 1 800 Germans and their ten guns, and that had he known of the impending attack by so large a force, he would have withdrawn from Sandfontein within three to four hours. Lukin did not consider advancing with the 1 200 men at his disposal, using only a fraction of his forces to do so. He committed a cardinal error best encapsulated years later by Gen Heinz Guderian, the great exponent of manoeuvre warfare, who cautioned against attacking in penny packets with the retort '*Klotzen, nicht Kleckern*' (Strike together, not divided).

Sandfontein consisted of a group of three wells located on the route from Steinkopf in the Cape Province to Warmbad in GSWA. The road to Warmbad crosses the border, marked by the Orange River, at Raman's Drift. The distance between Raman's Drift and Warmbad is 72 km, with Sandfontein midway between the two points. The terrain consists of ridges and stone koppies intersected with narrow sandy defiles. Mounted troops were restricted to the roads that followed the defiles.

The landscape breaks into a five-kilometre-long sandy plain in the vicinity of Sandfontein, and the wells are marked by a conspicuous conical koppie 45 m in height. The koppie at Sandfontein is overlooked by groups of ridges to the southeast and north at ranges between 600 m and 1 000 m. The approaches to the wells have several stony outcrops that afford an attacker cover as they advance. The Germans advancing from

Warmbad had numerous approaches to Sandfontein that would allow them to surround the defenders there quickly. With Maritz removed from the picture, the Germans had unfettered access to all the approaches to Sandfontein.

On 25 September Lukin occupied Sandfontein with a combat strength of 120 members of all ranks. Reinforcements dispatched from Raman's Drift comprised two 13-pounder guns of the Transvaal Horse Artillery and two machine guns with four troops of the South African Mounted Rifles, making a combat strength of 122 men. The combined combat force would eventually total 237 members of all ranks. The reinforcements reached Sandfontein at dawn, unaware that the Germans were in the vicinity and had already effectively surrounded the small garrison. Patrols were sent out to reconnoitre the area. Ominous dust clouds were observed to the northwest and the telephone link to Raman's Drift was cut. Sporadic rifle fire broke out to the northeast and soon large numbers of enemy mounted troops emerged onto the plain. The South Africans withdrew their forces and took up defensive positions around the koppie to shorten the defence perimeter.

The fog of war soon descended on the encircled South Africans and events unfolded so quickly that it is impossible to describe their proper sequence. While the defenders' attention was on the attacking Germans in the northeast, they found themselves attacked simultaneously from the southwest by a body of troops emerging from the direction of Raman's Drift. At first, the South Africans thought it was a friendly force, as it came from the same direction as the reinforcements earlier that morning. The South Africans, heavily outnumbered by at least four bodies of the enemy, from four different directions, were pressed from all sides. Any offensive action by the defenders was out of the question. A retreat would have meant abandoning the guns and equipment in addition to the only water source for 30 km.

The Transvaal Horse Artillery soon unlimbered their guns and added their fire to the growing confusion. The first rounds were well short of the intended targets, but, once adjusted, began to fall among the advancing enemy troops. However, the Germans soon laid down effective counterbattery fire from the hills to the northwest, causing immediate casualties among the gunners. The guns were swung around to meet this unexpected threat. They began to lay down a steady stream of fire on the German battery ensconced in the hills. An extended artillery duel ensued, with the South Africans barely holding their own against the superior numbers of German guns.

The South Africans were able to deploy their machine-gun section to good effect in the northeast of the perimeter and their defensive fire was able to hold off determined German attacks from this quarter. The machine-gun pack animals were driven to the relative safety of the south slope of the koppie. Unfortunately, they became a target for the German machine guns and were either killed or scattered en masse. The same machine guns, firing from the east, effectively suppressed the defenders, and the South Africans began to register significant casualties, being unable to move in the open against the withering fire.

A second battery of German guns came into action at 08:30, adding to an already critical situation. One battery firing from the northeast and the other from the northwest were able to envelop the exposed Transvaal Horse Artillery guns with deadly effect. The Germans scored a direct hit on one of the guns at 10:30, temporarily silencing it. The artillerymen, having suffered 50 per cent casualties, were also running short of ammunition and eventually had no option but to abandon the guns for the relative safety of the koppie. The German gunners were now at liberty to direct all their fire at the defenders huddled around the koppie.

The Germans were gradually tightening the noose around the South African positions and by 13:30 they were within 600 m of the defenders. Any hope of relief vanished as the distant sounds of gunfire from the direction of Raman's Drift grew ever fainter. The suffocating heat of the midday sun beat down on the thirsty defenders and added to their misery. The German shelling of the South African positions continued relentlessly, with an estimated 3 000 shells landing among the defenders during the entire action. At 17:00 the action was nearing its end phase, with the Germans having achieved complete firepower superiority with combined artillery, machine-gun and rifle fire. At 18:00 the defenders finally raised the white flag on the summit of the koppie. A brave but fruitless defence ended and marked the UDF's first action against a foreign power, one that would go down in history as an unfortunate defeat. South African casualties amounted to 67, including 16 fatalities. The Germans suffered similarly, with 60 casualties and 14 fatalities.

On 26 September, Lukin's forces advanced on Sandfontein unsupported by Maritz, who was now in open rebellion. The advance of Lukin's force in such small numbers was a tactical error in the face of the uncertainty of Maritz's allegiance. Furthermore, Lukin was responsible for other grave tactical errors, such as the lack of adequate reconnaissance. However, the operational-level failure to occupy Swakopmund, as Smuts had planned, sealed Sandfontein's fate.

Smuts laid the blame for the reversal at Sandfontein squarely on Lukin. He dispatched a telegram to Lukin on 28 September in which he admonished him for taking 'too large a risk in leaving so small a force at Sandfontein and your main force so far away at Steinkopf'. Smuts revealed the operation's overall strategic concern when he pressed Lukin to hold the Orange River and not retire further after the defeat at Sandfontein. Smuts was concerned that Lukin would no longer pose a threat to the German flank, leaving the enemy free to deal with the smaller forces at Lüderitzbucht.

In another communication, he instructed Lukin to move most of his forces from Steinkopf to the Orange River and adopt an aggressive posture to keep the enemy away from the vulnerable Beves. Smuts announced the abandonment of the Walvis Bay/Swakopmund expedition and instead dispatched McKenzie's 'D' Force to Lüderitzbucht on 30 September. Smuts and Governor General Sydney Buxton suggested that HMS *Kinfauns Castle*, an armed merchant cruiser, remain at Walvis Bay for a few more days to make the Germans believe that the UDF was still planning to land a force there. Subterfuge would alleviate some of the risk Beves faced at Lüderitzbucht, considering the Sandfontein fiasco and the cancellation of the Walvis Bay landing.

In August 1914, the UDF – formed a mere two years earlier – was still unprepared for conventional warfare against a first-class European power such as Germany. The fledgling military was more suited to the role of internal policing.

Added to this, the amalgamation of the former Boer republican and colonial forces was nowhere near complete when war broke out.

Hasty preparations, coupled with political expediency, resulted in the UDF effectively fielding two different armies, each with its ingrained doctrine. On the one hand, there was the primarily Afrikaner-led and -manned mounted infantry that languished in the almost moribund Rifle Associations. On the other hand, the bulk of the active UDF consisted of British-style colonial-era regiments who provided mounted and regular infantry very much in line with British training methods and following British doctrine. These units dominated the ACF and the SAPF. Political factors ensured that the invasion of GSWA was undertaken with formations that were modelled on the British colonial way of war.

Had events not overtaken Smuts's vision of a first-class modern army, the British-style regiments would eventually have dominated the UDF. In addition, the yearly intake of recruits would have received British-style training delivered by British instructors in a steady process of modernisation that Smuts favoured.

Smuts's plan for the invasion of GSWA called for a bold simultaneous advance that would place the enemy in a quandary. Yet British commanders such as Beves, McKenzie and Lukin showed a lack of urgency and alarming hesitancy in advancing against the *Schutztruppe*. When Lukin eventually advanced on Sandfontein, he did so with small numbers that left them vulnerable to attack. His doomed expedition was betrayed by Maritz, who deserted him in the hour of need.

However, out of the UDF's darkest hour at Sandfontein came the deployment of the commandos to suppress the Afrikaner Rebellion and subsequently to conquer GSWA. This marked a paradigm shift in doctrine and set the trajectory for the future of South African manoeuvre warfare.

No matter how unprepared the military or fragile the political situation on the home front, Smuts was prepared to risk a war, and even to use the UDF as a blunt instrument, to acquire German South West Africa.

The Battle at Otavifontein, 1915

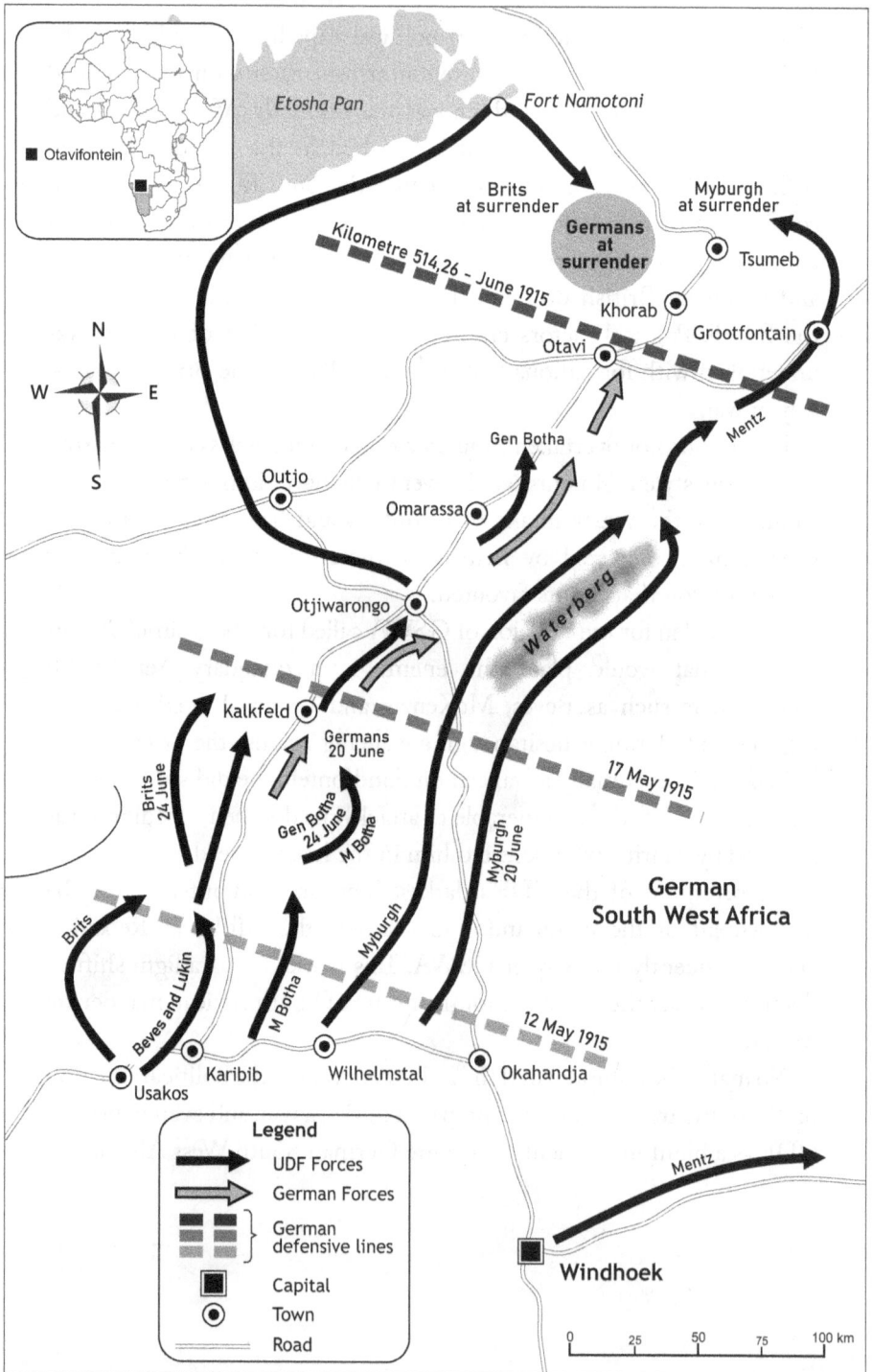

Etosha Pan

Fort Namotoni

Brits
at surrender

Germans
at
surrender

Myburgh
at surrender

Kilometre 514,26 – June 1915

Tsumeb

Khorab

Grootfontain

Otavi

Mentz

Gen Botha

Outjo

Omarassa

Otjiwarongo

Waterberg

Kalkfeld

Germans
20 June

17 May 1915

Brits
24 June

Gen Botha
24 June

M Botha

Myburgh
20 June

German
South West Africa

Brits

Beves and Lukin

M Botha

Myburgh

12 May 1915

Karibib

Wilhelmstal

Okahandja

Usakos

Legend

- UDF Forces
- German Forces
- German defensive lines
- Capital
- Town
- Road

Mentz

Windhoek

0   25   50   75   100 km

3

OTAVIFONTEIN, 1915

Initially, Smuts had planned a campaign of manoeuvre for the conquest of GSWA, and he split the UDF invasion force into four thrusts, separated by many kilometres and converging on the capital, Windhoek. He initiated manoeuvre warfare at the strategic level in the hope of facilitating it at the operational level.

Smuts's original plan fell apart when a combination of poor logistical planning, faulty execution and the outbreak of the Afrikaner Rebellion put paid to the planned landings in Walvis Bay/Swakopmund. In 1913–1914, he had taken a political gamble when he used the almost dormant commandos to suppress the Witwatersrand strikes. This had reinvigorated the old Boer republican networks, which the Afrikaner rebels used to good effect in the Afrikaner Rebellion a few months later. Yet even though the Afrikaner Rebellion was crushed, the belated occupation of Walvis Bay/Swakopmund failed to restore manoeuvre at the operational level of war.

The second iteration of Smuts's plan relied on the thousands of loyal commando members who were used to suppress the rebellion. The UDF's numbers swelled to 40 000 men and Smuts could now make use of a bludgeon instead of a rapier. Prime Minister Louis Botha took overall command of the forces in the field. Limited manoeuvre occurred at the tactical level, but the necessity of conforming to the railway system, due to the larger numbers involved, robbed Botha of operational manoeuvre options. A nimbler force, as Smuts had originally envisaged, would have achieved quicker results at a lower logistical cost.

Poor logistics and unforgiving terrain were not the only factors that

31

dampened the possibilities of manoeuvre. From Col Duncan McKenzie and Lukin to Botha, a strong aversion to risking defeat or a high number of casualties meant that the UDF's advance was sluggish and predictable, thus mitigating its overwhelming numerical superiority. Eventually, though, the strategic advantage gained by advancing along four routes in superior numbers, and then reaching more suitable terrain, unlocked the operational possibilities for manoeuvre.

Manoeuvre warfare restored

Botha finally managed to resolve his logistical issues, and the fall of Gibeon in the south at the end of April 1915 enabled him to launch his attack on Windhoek. His first objective en route to the capital was Karibib, which lay at the railway junction linking southern and northern GSWA. Cutting the railway threatened to trap the remaining German defenders in the south.

After attempting to juggle his meagre transport and water resources between the mounted brigades, with only partial success, Botha, in a letter dated 3 March, pleaded with Smuts for more transport. He complained of the agonisingly slow progress of refurbishing the railway line. On 7 March, he wrote that the engineers had laid only 42 km of track in two months – far less than a kilometre a day. The enormous forces at his disposal could not all be used in the combat zone, but they consumed precious resources and stifled the tempo of the advance.

Smuts responded to the transport crisis by scouring the country for wagons, mules, donkeys and drivers. The capture of Gibeon coincided with the extension of the northern railway line to Trekkoppies, further alleviating Botha's supply problems. The concerted efforts resulted in Botha accumulating five days' worth of supplies by 25 April, allowing him to resume his advance.

Smuts's Southern Force offensive also played a major role in unlocking Botha's path in the north after his offensive had stalled due to logistical constraints. Smuts arrived on the scene to take command of the Southern Force in April 1915 and immediately restored manoeuvre warfare to his sector. His ability to coordinate the three widely dispersed arms of his offensive unhinged the German defences, giving them no option but to beat a hasty retreat towards Windhoek.

During the period between the battle at Riet, on 19 March, and 25 April, Botha's mounted infantry component doubled in size. He now commanded a mounted force of 8 868 men and 16 guns. The 3rd and 5th mounted brigades, commanded by Brig Gen MW Myburgh, joined the 1st and 2nd mounted brigades under Brig Gen CJ Brits. Botha's infantry component had also swelled, bringing the total forces under his command for the move inland to 13 000 men – a force three times the size of the one that had attacked Riet. Extending the infantry component is difficult to understand, given the scarce logistical resources. The footslogging infantry, performing fatigue and garrison duties, and also undertaking strenuous marches in the wake of the mounted infantry, saw minimal action throughout the campaign.

Botha's forces resumed their advance and the Germans were forced to retreat towards Karibib. They were psychologically overwhelmed not only by the speed of the South Africans' advance, but also by their numerical strength and the distance they had covered. The Germans abandoned Karibib on 5 May, which effectively allowed the UDF to cut the railway line to the north. Consequently, the Germans abandoned Windhoek on 12 May.

Smuts and Botha could now claim to have achieved the British objectives as requested: they had occupied the coast and rendered the German wireless stations, especially the one at Windhoek, inoperable. After Windhoek's occupation, Smuts disbanded the Southern Force and Botha could at last command a leaner, more fit-for-purpose army that relied on the art of manoeuvre rather than brute force to overcome the enemy.

At this point, the German governor, Theodor Seitz, sought an armistice and a negotiated settlement. German military prospects in South West Africa looked bleak, even if the news of the German advance on Paris brought a ray of hope to Seitz and Victor Franke, the commander of the *Schutztruppe*.

Seitz sent Botha a letter on 13 May, calling for a meeting on 21 May at Giftkuppe during a temporary armistice. At the meeting, Botha demanded the unconditional surrender of the Germans. He also brushed aside Seitz's suggestions for the establishment of a demilitarised neutral zone between the two forces, with the Germans occupying the northern part of GSWA. Given their expansionist agenda, Smuts and Botha would be satisfied with nothing less than the occupation of the entire territory.

Botha tried to discern Seitz's mood at the conference. He believed that the German forces, still mostly unscathed and intact, would not attempt a last stand. He was also influenced by the German reluctance to stand fast and enter a pitched battle up to that point in the campaign. The Germans had retired north and any attempt to hold fast would invite an enveloping movement by the South Africans, with Botha's force enjoying the advantages of overwhelming numbers and greater mobility. However, Botha underestimated German resolve.

The Germans were unwilling to surrender unconditionally and believed they could hold nearly half the remaining territory north of Windhoek. They were encouraged by the undeniable sluggishness of the South Africans in the eight months of campaigning thus far. The Germans also retained the more hospitable portion of the territory, with its water supplies, good grazing, plentiful wild game and 160 km of railway line. There was also the possibility of waging a guerrilla campaign from southern Angola. Holding out until favourable news arrived from Europe was a sound strategy for the Germans to adopt.

The Germans took up positions to the west and east of Omaruru, while the South Africans, with 20 000 troops, held the Usakos–Karibib line. The two sides skirmished on this line, and on 12 May Union forces launched an attack on a German forward position just to the north. Franke, conscious of Botha's penchant for envelopment and knowing that his position lacked natural defences, withdrew his force 65 km to the Kalkfeld–Osire–Waterberg Mountain line on 17 May. There he established a long defensive line to preclude a flanking manoeuvre by the UDF. The Germans intended to withdraw to the line 'Kilometre 514' after resisting at the Kalkfeld line.

Botha had received information from the local population about the likely German intention to defend Kalkfeld and he had detailed knowledge of the German defences there. After putting up a show of resistance, the Germans could continue the fight through guerrilla warfare, flee to Angola or even make a dash for German East Africa. Botha was again hamstrung by having to wait for his supply columns to catch up with his main force holding the Usakos–Karibib line. Engineers had partially rebuilt and extended the railway network, but the mixture of German and standard Cape railway gauges necessitated much unloading and reloading to bring supplies forward.

Manoeuvre warfare restored

After the decision to disband the Southern Force soon after the capture of Windhoek, the remaining UDF field forces were reorganised with 32 artillery pieces and a complement of 13 000 men divided into six brigades, of which one was regular infantry. Interestingly, the German official history overestimates the numerical superiority of the UDF during the final push at 20 000–35 000 men.

Botha was ready to resume his offensive on 18 June, having at last dispensed with the superfluous forces, and he set forth with a leaner, better supplied and more agile force. He conducted the final phase of the campaign using the deep roots of operational manoeuvre-type warfare within the UDF's binational doctrine. The double envelopment used by Botha at Otavifontein – the final battle in GSWA –would be replicated to good effect by Smuts when commanding veterans of the Afrikaner Rebellion and the GSWA campaign in East Africa in 1916.

Meanwhile, Botha fielded a force of 5 250 mounted infantry, 4 750 regular infantrymen and 32 guns against Franke's 4 750 men. This represented a 2:1 numerical superiority – relatively modest in the context of the campaign thus far. The brigades were cut down to 1 500 men and the wings each had 750 men, the previous larger units being too large for the relatively untrained staff. There was a real risk that the Germans could concentrate superior numbers against Botha's divided force during his advance. But for the first time in the campaign, Botha would rely on superior mobility, enabling a higher tempo and unleashing his penchant for manoeuvre warfare, rather than sheer numerical superiority.

Using combined-arms operations, Botha finally managed to find a combat role for his footslogging infantry: they were to safeguard the rear areas vacated by the mounted infantry. This configuration made the UDF force much nimbler. Secure supply lines in the rear emboldened Botha to risk cutting the advancing columns off from their logistical constraints and letting them live off the land. He appointed Col PCB Skinner as the General Officer Commanding (GOC) Lines of Communication and, together with Sir William Hoy, who energetically directed work on the railways, there was a marked improvement in logistics – no doubt aided by the drastic reduction in the numbers of troops earmarked for the final assault. Each of the six advancing brigades now had sufficient wagons to ensure supplies for two to three weeks. The supply wagons would carry a minimum of provisions and meat was to be procured in the country covered by the advance. Each mounted brigade would be allocated 100 supply wagons, a vast improvement compared to previous operations in the campaign. A small and highly mobile force such as this was perhaps what Smuts had originally envisaged in August 1914.

Botha's plan, as was his penchant, involved a wide turning movement. Brits would lead his mounted units on the left flank well to the west of the railway line, making his way through Outjo to the south of the Etosha Pan. He would then proceed in an easterly direction to Fort Namutoni, where the Germans kept the majority of the 600 South African prisoners of war, placing him well in the rear of the German defences at Kilometre 514. Myburgh's advance, using highly mobile mounted infantry, would move in an easterly arc tracking east of the railway line with the objective of capturing Grootfontein and, beyond that, advancing further to Tsumeb. Each wing would cover more than 300 km in a matter of days – a stark contrast to the trench warfare in Europe, where movement was measured over months and in metres. The closing of the Brits/Myburgh pincers to the west and east of Tsumeb would cut off the German defenders facing Botha, with the infantry in the centre.

The speed and distance of the flanking manoeuvres would mean that Brits and Myburgh would have to exercise their initiative in the absence of reliable communication with Botha. The location of Brits's and Myburgh's flanking forces was often ascertained by aerial reconnaissance. The sheer tempo of the advance on both flanks outpaced logistical support, forcing the commandos to live off the land. Botha was left with Lukin's 6th Mounted Brigade and Beves's 1st Infantry Brigade to advance up the railway line and distract German attention from the enveloping wings. The entire operation bore the hallmarks of the Boer way of war.

Although outnumbered, the Germans enjoyed some advantages of concentration, having a numerical advantage in artillery and machine

Generals Jan Smuts and Louis Botha in the field in
German South West Africa, 1915

guns and being familiar with the territory. Still, Botha's advance met with little resistance and the 3 000 Germans holding the Kalkfeld line, facing 12 000 South African advance troops, beat a retreat to Kilometre 514 on 21 June, reaching Otavifontein on the night of 26–27 June. Botha learned of the hasty German withdrawal from local informants and his air reconnaissance.

The Brits/Myburgh advance on the flanks achieved the desired result of unnerving Franke, who had no desire to be surrounded. The northward advance of Brits's force remained undetected until Franke learned of their presence west of Etosha. Realising his predicament, he decided to defend Otavifontein and its wells. This would deny water to Botha's central forces, who had to cross a 65 km arid stretch from Omarassa. If Franke could inflict a tactical defeat on the UDF at Otavifontein and deny them the water in the immediate vicinity, he would force Botha to retreat to the start line at Omarassa. This was Franke's opportunity to deliver a decisive tactical defeat, which in turn would strengthen the German hand at the negotiating table.

Furthermore, by forcing a South African retreat before Otavifontein, he could engage Brits and Myburgh in sequence with overwhelming numerical superiority. His forces enjoyed the advantages of internal lines of communication and proximity, which allowed him to concentrate rapidly on Otavifontein, where he could achieve near numerical parity with Botha's forces. Botha was aware that the Germans operating on interior lines had ample opportunity to concentrate against any one of his advancing wings.

Judging by an appeal made to his troops on 28 June, Franke had every intention of making a last stand. He justified his evasive tactics in the campaign up to that point, and his avoidance of pitched battles, by the need to preserve German fighting power. Now he called for the preservation of the *Schutztruppe* until the conclusion of peace in Europe. He appealed to his troops to deliver a final, powerful blow to the South Africans. However, the constant retreat in the face of the relentless, albeit ponderous UDF had taken its toll on German morale.

Otavifontein: The battle commences

Whereas Otavifontein offered Franke strong natural defences, Botha's rapid advance threw the Germans off balance, rendering their defensive preparations insufficient. Furthermore, the Germans realised too late the strategic importance of Otavifontein. The German official history reveals the poor state of the German defences, explaining that effective defences would have required several more weeks of preparation.

Without waiting for the infantry, Botha decided on an immediate attack with his mounted units. He intended to distract German attention from the two rapidly advancing mobile columns under Brits and Myburgh. Botha's conduct of the operational manoeuvre thus far was a delicate balance of advancing on the flanks and either delaying or expediting the centre, and then pinning the German centre to enable the flanks to envelop them.

Botha launched his attack on Otavifontein on 1 July. He deployed a double tactical envelopment with Commandant Manie Botha and the 5th Mounted Brigade on the left of the railway line and Lukin's 6th Mounted Brigade on the right. Their rapid and at times instinctive advance, at an unexpected tempo, managed to dislodge the Germans from their strong positions. The Germans were awed by the speed of Botha's advance, which they described as 'extraordinary' and attributed both to excellent horses and supplies of fodder and to the rear-area logistical network built by Botha over the preceding month.

On-the-spot decisions driven by the commanders' initiative unsettled the German defenders, who could not dispose of their main force as they had planned. The German reserves remained undeployed during the battle, as Franke, immersed in the fog of war and distracted by the enveloping manoeuvre, had no idea of the extent of the direct attack on Otavifontein nor of the course of the battle.

Using his initiative, Manie Botha pressed the attack with all his forces in close country covered in dense bush, which reduced visibility. Maj Hermann Ritter, who commanded the German forces in the field, retreated to Grootfontein, allowing Botha to secure the wells at Otavifontein. Some would ascribe the South African success to luck; however, rapid manoeuvre often offers opportunities that a wily commander can exploit to his benefit.

The Germans lacked resolve, and Franke only committed a fraction of his available forces. According to Louis Botha, the Germans had an opportunity to make a proper defence. Their mediocre performance is ascribed to low morale and marginal leadership. The German official history describes the low casualties suffered by both sides as 'out of proportion to the importance of the task' of defending Otavifontein. The Germans failed to identify the importance of the position in time and their constant retreat undermined their resolve to fight aggressively. Had they held Otavifontein and repulsed the South Africans as planned, they would have inflicted a substantial tactical defeat. In fact, a South African southward retreat back to their water sources would have given Franke a few weeks' respite to deal with the enveloping wings of Brits and Myburgh or to retreat even further north.

The threat of Brits and Myburgh enveloping his entire force worried Franke, who requested a meeting with Seitz on 2 July 1915. Franke was pessimistic about German prospects in the face of a numerically superior enemy advancing on three fronts against his tired, worn-out troops, in addition to the German troops' morale being at its lowest point by this time. Furthermore, their horses were malnourished and unable to exert themselves, and food and clothing were in short supply.

Franke did not believe the Germans could escape encirclement fast enough because of the proximity of Botha's pressing forces in the centre. This effectively meant that Franke had failed to deliver the tactical victory Seitz had sought to allow them to negotiate from a position of strength. The sheer speed of Botha's enveloping forces destroyed Franke's will to resist, despite some of his junior officers' wanting to attack one of the enveloping wings by mustering superior numbers. There was also an opportunity to counterattack in the centre and recapture Otavifontein, with all its supplies and abundant water, and even to capture Botha, the biggest prize of all. Botha was aware of his vulnerability in the centre but he was content to wait for the slow-moving infantry to reinforce his position. However, Franke did not believe his demoralised *Schutztruppe* were up to the task.

Botha rejected Seitz's first attempts at a parley on 4 July by demanding unconditional surrender as he wanted a more favourable position to develop. A meeting was set for 6 July at Kilometre 500, just north of Otavi station. The ceasefire excluded Brits and Myburgh, which allowed them to complete their encirclement. Botha was at pains to explain that the truce involved only his local forces and not the Brits/Myburgh wings that were rapidly closing the gap to the north of the Germans.

The garrison of 110 Germans at Fort Namutoni surrendered to Brits on 6 July, while Myburgh reached Tsumeb on the same day, a mere 32 km north of the main German force at Khorab. Taking full advantage of the fog of war, they occupied Tsumeb while Botha negotiated with Seitz and Franke at Kilometre 500. The Germans, surrounded and demoralised, signed the final surrender on 9 July, ending the GSWA campaign.

The UDF conquest of GSWA was conducted with fewer casualties than during the Afrikaner Rebellion. More importantly, the GSWA campaign and the final battle at Otavifontein cemented a new South African way of war. Botha successfully combined infantry and mounted infantry components in a double enveloping manoeuvre. This combination would become the hallmark of the manoeuvre warfare Smuts would practise and build on in German East Africa.

The most important consequence of the invasion of GSWA and the operations during the Afrikaner Rebellion was that the UDF came of age. The GSWA campaign had revealed some profound doctrinal flaws in the UDF. Initially, the command structure was messy, with Botha and Smuts having an ambiguous command–subordinate relationship. The lack of properly trained staff at all levels and problems with the railway gauge hampered the UDF's advance. Effectively fielding two armies with different doctrines and command-and-control structures posed problems in implementing combined-arms operations. The infantry component was rendered ineffective and ultimately unnecessary for the campaign's success.

Instead, Botha and Smuts came to rely heavily on the old commando brigades as the cutting edge of their offensive. These formations remained unchanged in doctrine and composition from the old republican days, and, in this form, they carried much of the genetic make-up of yester-year. The Battle of Otavifontein reversed this trend somewhat and began the melding of Boer and English formations and doctrine. Many of the commanders who served with Smuts and Botha in GSWA would serve again under Smuts in German East Africa, which served to ensure the continuity of the lessons learned during that campaign.

Interestingly, and unlike in German East Africa, both sides in the GSWA conflict failed to deploy black troops fully in a combat role. Smuts believed the political situation did not lend itself to such an approach. The Germans in GSWA were unwilling and incapable of using indigenous black troops as a force multiplier, unlike in German East Africa, where the vast majority of *Schutztruppe* were indigenous Askaris. The real prospect of a black uprising in GSWA, owing to the *Schutztruppe*'s murderous history, precluded the use of black troops to any significant level. Had the Germans been able to field well-trained black combat troops in anything like the numbers deployed in German East Africa, the UDF would have faced an enormous challenge.

Despite the shortcomings at the operational and tactical levels, the GSWA campaign was ultimately successful at the strategic level, in several respects. Smuts achieved his aim of ridding South Africa of a hostile force on its borders. He opened the way for territorial expansion and realised his dream of a Greater South Africa. His actions and loyalty to the United Kingdom elevated South Africa's status and demonstrated his unbending loyalty to the Empire at a time of its greatest need. He achieved this at much political but little human cost. It was a remarkable accomplishment in a global war renowned for the scale of its cost in human life.

The British press lauded Smuts and Botha, even suggesting that

GSWA be renamed 'Bothaland'. In 1915, the South Africans delivered a victory at a time when the Allies were experiencing nothing but reversals. The alacrity and proficiency with which Botha and Smuts, former sworn enemies of the Empire, came to the aid of the United Kingdom cemented their positions as major players within the British Empire and Commonwealth and secured them their seats at the peace conference in 1919.

The GSWA campaign and the Afrikaner Rebellion were also fundamental in providing Smuts with valuable experience in conducting warfare with large formations under difficult conditions. Smuts would continue to build on the doctrinal foundation the UDF had set in the latter stages of the GSWA campaign.

For its part, the UDF underwent a doctrinal transformation and would present a far more homogeneous fighting force during the campaign in GEA. The opening battles of the GEA campaign in 1915 proved to be the zenith of South African manoeuvre warfare at the operational level. These battles were some of the largest ever conducted by the South African military, and the Battle of Kilimanjaro in 1916 was an example of the South African penchant for double and single envelopments to overcome a well-entrenched enemy.

4

KILIMANJARO, 1916

South Africa's successful conclusion of the South West African campaign in 1915 encouraged Britain to ask the South African government for help in East Africa, where British East Africa (present-day Kenya) bordered on German East Africa (GEA), a territory that included present-day Burundi, Rwanda, the Tanzania mainland and Zanzibar.

Meanwhile, back in the Union, the October 1915 election returned the ruling South African Party to power, though with a much-reduced majority of 54 out of 130 seats. The election result forced the South African Party to seek support from the pro-British Unionist Party on the opposition benches to form a minority government. This delivered a mandate that cleared the way for a South African military contingent to be sent to GEA.

The British Cabinet sanctioned the use of 10 000 South Africans for the campaign and asked Smuts to take command of the imperial forces in East Africa. Initially, though, he turned down the offer because of concerns about the volatile political situation in South Africa before the election.

Up to that point, British endeavours in East Africa had been a failure. Col Paul Emil von Lettow-Vorbeck, the capable commander of the *Schutztruppe* in GEA, had inflicted a devastating defeat on the British at Tanga in November 1914. Since then, Lettow-Vorbeck and his troops had been safely ensconced on British territory, holding the Taveta Gap, where he spent 18 months profitably fortifying his position. From there he adopted a raiding strategy, interdicting the Mombasa–Uganda railway line.

Out of desperation, the British appointed Gen Sir Horace Smith-

43

The Battle at Kilimanjaro, 1916

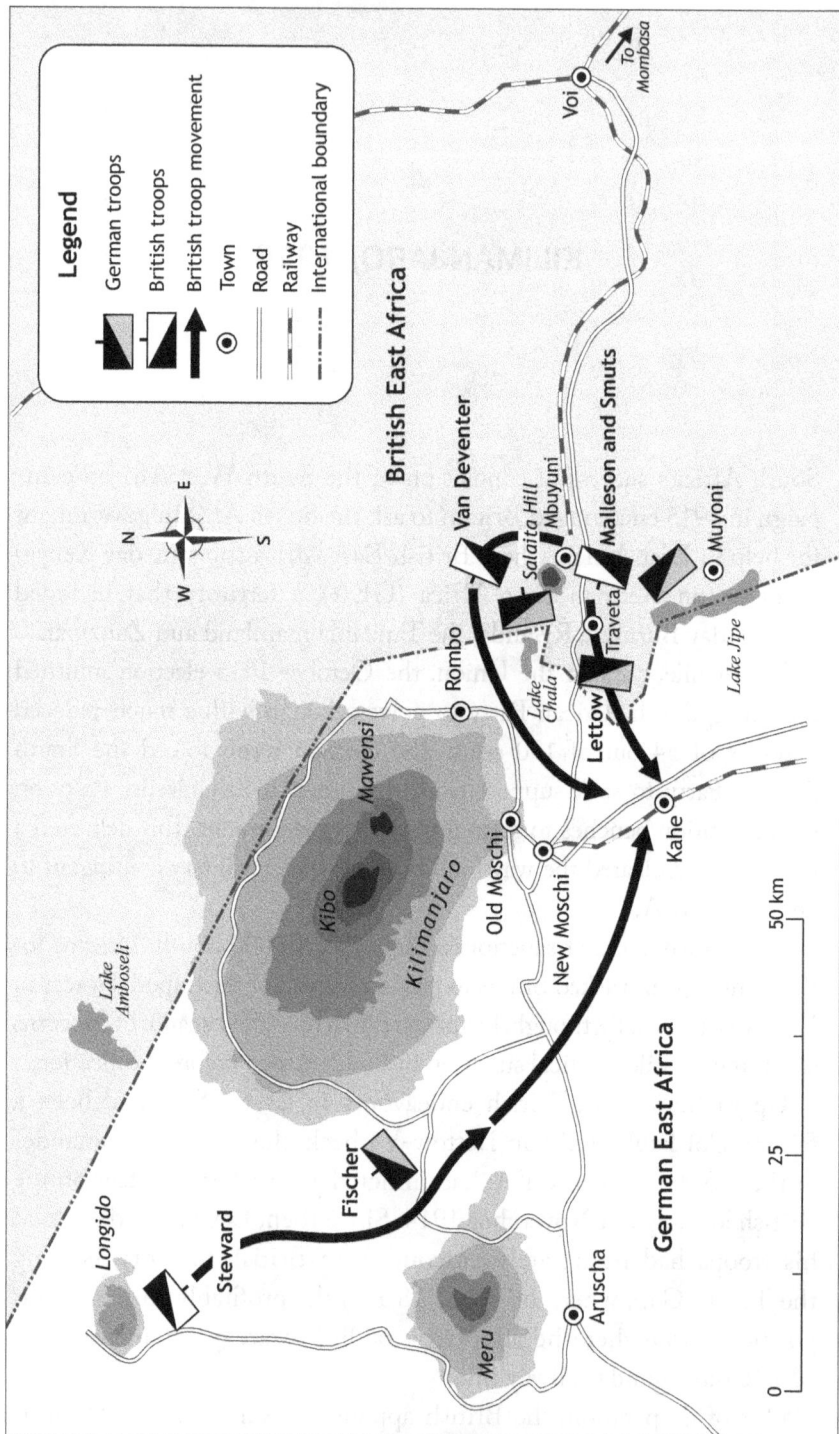

Legend

German troops
British troops
British troop movement
Town
Road
Railway
International boundary

To Mombasa

Voi

British East Africa

Van Deventer

Salaita Hill
Mbuyuni
Malleson and Smuts

Muyoni

Lake Jipe

Rombo

Lake Chala

Traveta

Lettow

Kahe

Old Moschi

New Moschi

Mawensi

Kibo

Kilimanjaro

Lake Amboseli

Longido

Steward

Fischer

Meru

Aruscha

German East Africa

N

0   25   50 km

44

Dorrien to take command of the East African Force in December 1915, hoping that he could evict Lettow-Vorbeck from British territory. However, Smith-Dorrien's health started to fail, and when the position of supreme commander of the East African Force was again offered to Smuts in January 1916, he could not refuse it a second time.

Smuts would command imperial formations in which a large part of his leader group and troops would consist of veterans of the GSWA campaign. The UDF was now also a somewhat sounder and less fractured organisation. Political fissures seemed to have become subdued, if not healed, and Afrikaner and English soldiers, once bitter rivals, fought side by side as mounted infantry and regular infantry for a common cause.

However, the 11-month GSWA campaign had revealed worrisome operational and tactical shortcomings in an organisation that had not yet fully integrated British and Boer doctrines into a single coherent doctrine or implemented a combined-arms approach to incorporate both mounted and regular infantry in combat operations. Nevertheless, as witnessed at Otavifontein (see Chapter 2), the UDF had embraced Boer operational and tactical manoeuvre doctrine and started to master the use of mounted and regular infantry in a combined-arms fashion. Smuts, as an innovator and founding member of the defence force, and an enthusiastic military moderniser, remained a product of the Boer way of war. The GEA venture would provide him with an opportunity to practise his uniquely South African craft in a way that still leaves contemporary critics nonplussed.

Smuts assumed his command on 12 February 1916 and set sail for East Africa on the same day. He arrived in Mombasa on 19 February and immediately met with Brig Gen Michael Tighe, the former East African commander. The latter briefed him on the preparations for an operation in the Mount Kilimanjaro area before the onset of the seasonal rains at the end of March, after which operational manoeuvres would become extremely difficult. The British generals and officers whom Smuts was to command were not charmed at the prospect of having a 'colonial' in charge. Despite their apparent reservations, though, Smuts's appointment was a relief to his fellow South Africans, who had started arriving in GEA in December 1915, and to the European colonial volunteers already deployed in the theatre. The ordinary soldiers respected his knowledge of the military operating environment and his willingness to share in the hardships and dangers of combat.

Taveta-Salaita (in present-day Kenya) was the only British territory the Germans occupied in the First World War, as it was close to the border with German East Africa. But the political necessity of removing the Germans from British territory placed immense pressure on the military. It would not be an easy task, particularly since the German forces had been strengthened by successful Askari recruitment drives. Their reported numbers had swelled to 20 000 and they were adequately supplied with arms, ammunition and equipment from blockade runners and the guns salvaged from the light cruiser SMS *Königsberg*, which had been scuttled on 11 July 1915. They had many modern rifles, eight Maxim guns, six field guns and enough ammunition to last for the duration of the campaign. If Smuts succeeded in removing the German threat, it would earn him the admiration and gratitude of the British government.

Before Smuts's arrival, any campaign objectives beyond the eviction of the Germans from British territory were vague. Smith-Dorrien had outlined two different objectives: occupy as much German territory as possible to have something as a negotiation lever or secure British territory and bottle up the Germans in their colony for the duration of the war. He insisted on having at least three months to prepare for the 'thorough organisation of the transport'. This would have taken the launch date beyond April and well into the rainy season, which would have meant deferring operations until the rains ceased, in June or July. Smith-Dorrien could not envisage decisive military success before August 1916. As it happened, though, Smuts had already conquered two-thirds of the territory by that date.

Smuts wasted little time, launching his first attack on 5 March, a mere three weeks after his arrival. Smith-Dorrien had identified the German-occupied Kilimanjaro–Taveta area as the most profitable objective. A measure of success there would remove the fear of a German invasion of British East Africa and restore the damaged prestige of the British forces. Victory would also boost flagging Allied morale and lower the morale of the Germans. Historians have recorded the low morale of the troops prior to Smuts's arrival, due mainly to months of inactivity and remaining on the defensive.

The Germans were naturally aware of the military buildup and were expecting an offensive in the Kilimanjaro area. They had correctly discounted the possibility of a seaborne landing at Dar es Salaam. Therefore, there was little chance of Smuts achieving a strategic surprise. However, by launching the offensive in the teeth of the rainy season, he hoped to achieve an operational surprise.

Planning the attack: 19 February to 4 March

Smuts deployed his operational art with little knowledge of his enemy and the capabilities of his forces. We should judge his initial move against Lettow-Vorbeck as a first battle, one on which Smuts was shrouded in ignorance and uncertainty, lacking the luxury of a realistic appreciation of his adversary's calculations, predictions, hopes and aspirations as a commander.

Smuts did benefit from a report produced by Lt Col Dirk van Deventer and Lt Col AM Hughes, who had conducted a military mission to East Africa in November 1915 in anticipation of the South African contingent's arrival. Their first meeting was with Maj Gen (Sir) Wilfrid Malleson, who commanded the Voi area, and later with Tighe, then commander of the East African Force. They learned that the Germans had entrenched themselves in the Taveta Gap, the only viable route into the interior, which was flanked by two impassable obstacles: Mount Kilimanjaro in the north and the Pare Mountains in the south.

The Germans had strengthened their defences considerably in the Taveta Gap and also the road and railway infrastructure that would have to support the logistics for a protracted defence. Presupposing a frontal attack on the German positions, the British noted a need for howitzers to dislodge the well-entrenched enemy: the Germans had put the guns salvaged from the *Königsberg* to good use. Tighe also reported that the Germans had trebled their manpower through local recruitment drives and he estimated their strength at between 15 000 and 20 000 men by the end of 1915.

Van Deventer and Hughes concluded that the territory was suitable for mounted infantry operations, primarily in the high country, which was less disease-ridden and generally more friendly to the animals. In contrast, the regular infantry were better suited to operations in the low country, where malaria and tsetse flies were lethal to both man and beast. They insisted that the operational aspects of the campaign would be practical only with a strong mounted component. Smith-Dorrien backed their point of view and spoke of 'the necessity of using considerable bodies of Mounted Troops for the subjugation of German East Africa'. Their reported underestimation of the abilities of the 'native' enemy was equalled by an underestimation of the deadly diseases that awaited man and beast. They declared that 'horse sickness is not as bad [as in] the low-lying districts of the Transvaal', that 'mule transport is suitable to that country' and that animals could work a further six to eight weeks after being bitten by the tsetse fly.

Among Smuts's substantial list of challenges, besides an inhospitable climate and disease, was the considerable experience and skill of his opponent. The Germans had put the 18 months before Smuts's arrival to good use in preparing their defences, especially in the Taveta Gap. Their knowledge of the climate and terrain was unrivalled. Lettow-Vorbeck would be operating on interior lines of communication and possessed a railway network that would greatly aid his troop movements and allow him to swiftly reinforce areas under threat and capitalise on opportunities. The Germans were familiar with the tactics Smuts would use against them, Lettow-Vorbeck having gained first-hand experience of them when fighting side by side with the Boers during the Herero Wars (1904–1908).

At the beginning of March 1916, the Germans were able to field a force comprising 3 007 white troops and 12 100 Askaris, including administrative staff. Not included in these numbers were several thousand auxiliaries, who were used for border, railway and coastal protection, and also as scouts and messengers. Significantly, the *Schutztruppe* made use of thousands of porters in their logistical supply chain. Porters were an integral part of a *Schutztruppe* company, providing a ready source of fighting replacements, whereas the British initially relied on unwieldy 1 000-man porter units that were separate from the fighting forces.

Traditionally, Boer forces often operated without transport and supplies, living off the land as they had during the South African War and the last stages of the GSWA campaign. But in East Africa Smuts was somewhat on the back foot. While the Germans, who recruited from local tribes, were able to gather intelligence and live off the land, depleting local food supplies as they retreated before Smuts's force, the South Africans depended on long, tenuous supply lines, as the British had during the South African War.

Besides the two railway lines, the few developed roads ran almost exclusively in a west–east direction following the territory's old caravan paths. Constructing railway lines lessened the importance of road networks. However, crisscrossing the territory were many paths and trails whose use depended on the impact of the rain season. The rivers were not much used as waterways owing to the many rapids.

The Germans possessed few motor vehicles: at the outbreak of war, they had only nine cars, eight trucks and eight motorcycles. The use of ox-wagons was limited to an area in the eastern highlands because of the prevalence of the tsetse fly, which meant that only mules and donkeys could be used for transport. Notably, the Germans did not use horses, the mainstay of the South African mounted infantry, as horses were too susceptible to disease. Instead, they made almost exclusive use of African porters for their transportation. East Africa was indeed 'the land of carrier transportation', as Ludwig Boell wrote in his semi-official history of the campaign, *Die Operationen in Ostafrika* (1951).

The Germans organised their structure around a self-contained company with an integral logistical organisation. On average, a company consisted of three officers, one medical officer, two sergeants, one medical sergeant and 159 Askari troops. The Germans were almost self-sufficient in fuel for their vehicles, ersatz whisky, boots and cloth for their uniforms; more importantly, they had munitions factories producing both artillery and small arms ammunition. They were also able to manufacture quinine.

A rampart of formidable mountain ranges buttressed the German frontline, which ran for 200 km from the coast to Kilimanjaro. As mentioned, in the eight-kilometre-long Taveta Gap – the gateway to the interior – the Germans had fortified their entrenchments around Taveta and Salaita Hill against attack. Piet van der Byl, who was appointed staff captain to General Smuts, described Salaita Hill as an almost impregnable fort, with an extensive trench system and machine-gun positions with well-prepared tactical fields of fire.

Further back, and constituting another formidable defensive bastion, were the twin hills of Latema-Reata. Gen JM 'Jimmie' Stewart held the northwestern sector of the British line in the Longido area. This force faced a gap between Kilimanjaro and Mount Meru guarded by Maj Eric Fischer and 1 000 Askaris. The plan was for Stewart to force the Kilimanjaro–Meru gap and take the enemy positions at Kahe from the rear.

Tighe's plan involved advancing from two directions – one arm from Longido and the other from Mbuyuni, converging on Kahe to the south of Kilimanjaro. The distance to Kahe from Longido was 130 km as the crow flies, as opposed to 50 km from Mbuyuni to Kahe. It would be possible to cut off the German forces with this strategic encircling movement. However, this depended on the westerly arm reaching Kahe before the Germans retreated in the face of the easterly arm.

Tighe gave Stewart's westerly arm a two-day head start to reach Kahe by 11 March and trap the Germans. The operation aimed to encircle the German forces via a pincer movement and eliminate them once the pincers snapped shut. On 25 February 1916, Smuts received permission to conduct the operation before the start of the April rainy season. This decision to launch an attack so close to the onset of the rainy season, with so few good campaigning days left, has attracted vociferous criticism from military historians.

Before Smuts's arrival, Tighe had ordered Stewart, who commanded the 1st Division, to occupy Longido on 15 January and Malleson, who commanded the 2nd Division, to occupy Mbuyuni on 24 January. Securing the jumping-off points for the offensive's two wings coincided with extending the railhead inland and improving logistics to support the attack. Smuts was generous in his praise for Tighe's efforts in preparing for the operation. However, the attempt to rid Salaita Hill of the Germans in the weeks before Smuts's arrival showed the futility of conducting a frontal assault against prepared German positions.

On 12 February, Malleson had launched an ill-fated attack on Salaita Hill using the newly arrived 2nd South African Infantry Brigade. The Germans had repelled the uninspired attack, with great loss to the South Africans, even though the East African Force had enjoyed an overall numerical advantage. Malleson had fielded 6 000 troops, 41 machine guns and 18 guns against a German force of no more than 1 400 troops,

Union Defence Force Mounted Infantry in German East Africa

12 machine guns and two small guns. The whole incident was played down by Tighe, who described it as an advance to ascertain the enemy's strength. The 133 South African casualties caused great consternation and Botha used his influence to keep news of the reverse out of Parliament.

Smuts adopted Tighe's plan, but with a significant modification: he removed Jaap van Deventer's 1st South African Mounted Brigade from Stewart's right wing and transferred it to the left wing, which placed it directly under his command. He was able to complete the transfer by rail on 4 March. Smuts was determined to avoid costly frontal attacks against entrenched enemy positions hidden in the dense bush. Notably, he was concerned with maintaining the tempo of the operation and the speed of the advance, which he saw as fundamental to success.

The Germans assumed, based on incorrect intelligence, that the bulk of the South African mounted troops would operate from Longido, allowing Smuts to achieve operational surprise with his switch. They failed to identify that Van Deventer had switched from Longido to Mbuyuni, despite capturing ten South African mounted infantrymen in the vicinity of Lake Jipe on 1 March. Reports from patrols confirmed the presence of South African mounted infantry in the Mbuyuni region, but the Germans mistakenly concluded that Longido was yet to be reinforced.

Stewart complained that the transfer of 'the purely Dutch elements' of his command had stripped him of all but a small mounted contingent. He believed that the objective and terrain allotted to his command were more suited to cavalry action. A reading of the German official history suggests that the Germans had a good idea of the mechanics of Smuts's plan. They correctly identified the direction and intent of the east and west pincers and witnessed the buildup of troops through intelligence and reconnaissance. The Germans, who intended to concentrate their forces and defeat each flank consecutively, would not be completely surprised, although Smuts's switch of Van Deventer's mounted infantry to the east flank would remain unknown to them.

Adding Van Deventer as a force multiplier to the east pincer unhinged the German positions at Salaita and the defenders withdrew without firing a shot. Van Deventer's advance threatened Salaita's only supply of water, situated deep behind the lines. Lettow-Vorbeck did not take the decision to abandon hard-won territory lightly, but had he not done so, the German forces would probably have faced destruction.

Van Deventer's flanking attack had the same effect on the strong German positions at Latema-Reata. The threat of a flank attack by the South African mounted infantry forced the Germans to abandon their position despite their rebuffing a strong Allied frontal attack.

The mounted brigade was to execute a turning movement on the Germans holding Salaita and Taveta by taking a northerly route. With Salaita Hill still fresh in Smuts's mind, the objective of this manoeuvre by the mounted brigade was, first, to avoid frontal attacks in the dense bush and, second, to secure the rapidity of the advance before the onset of the rains at the end of March. Smuts also created a reserve force to follow Van Deventer to a central position on the Lumi River, where it would then be available to reinforce either Malleson or Van Deventer as the situation required.

Smuts's plan to outflank Salaita Hill rather than engage in a frontal assault was grounded in sound reconnaissance of the area. Before the operation, he had consulted with Maj Piet Pretorius – the scout who had famously located the SMS *Königsberg* in the Rufiji Delta – about the best course of action. Pretorius revealed the fatal chink in the German armour: there was no water in the vicinity of the hill. This forced the Germans to transport all the water for the Salaita garrison from Taveta, some 13 km away. Whoever controlled the Taveta area would control Salaita without having to fire a shot.

Lettow-Vorbeck correctly identified the threat of a two-pronged attack and anticipated Van Deventer's flanking manoeuvre in good time. He opted to attack each prong in turn, using the classic advantage of concentrating in space using interior lines of communication. During the South African advance, Lettow-Vorbeck looked for opportunities to concentrate his forces and overwhelm vulnerable, isolated South African units pressing forward. However, when the battle unfolded, he could not concentrate his forces in this fashion, for reasons not fully explained by him.

Smuts enjoyed a 3:1 numerical superiority in manpower and artillery but only 2:1 in the all-important area of machine guns. The machine gun dominated the battlefield, especially in the dense bush, and the Germans crewed them with the more skilled white troops – they considered the Askari marksmanship to be inferior – with most of the casualties inflicted on the Allied troops attributed to machine-gun fire. Thus, the force ratio favouring Smuts was not overwhelming: it was the bare minimum required at the tactical level to overcome an enemy occupying a strong and well-prepared defensive position.

The Germans, going on the operational defensive, could conceal themselves in the dense bush. They had strengthened their defensive positions in the months before the attack, gaining maximum cover and creating excellent fields of fire. The *Schutztruppe* were also eminently familiar with the terrain they defended, having occupied the positions for more than two years.

In contrast, Smuts was new to the job and possessed little knowledge of the commanders who reported to him, their capabilities under fire or the capabilities of the forces they commanded. He was also unfamiliar with the extreme nature of the East African terrain, climate and diverse ecology and the effects these would have on his campaign. However, it seems that Smuts and Smith-Dorrien were not far apart in determining the importance of mounted troops in defeating Lettow-Vorbeck. But in considering the fundamental role of mounted troops, both men severely underestimated the debilitating impact of tropical diseases on men and horses.

The attack on the Kilimanjaro position, 5 March 1916

Stewart, commanding the western pincer, completed the concentration of his forces at Longido on the morning of 5 March 1916. His advance began two days before that of the 2nd Division, which would place his division well in the rear of the German defences by the time the 2nd Division launched their attack. He set off for the Sheep Hills and halted there to avoid crossing the arid area stretching in front of him during the heat of the day. Dusk saw the resumption of his advance and the 1st Division reached Engare Nanyuki by 08:00 on 6 March, having covered some 50 km.

After this cracking start, the pace of the advance slowed considerably. Stewart did not reach Garangua before 8 March, even though he encountered little opposition. The Germans responded to Stewart's advance by reinforcing Maj Eric Fischer with four more companies, bringing his strength to 250 white troops and 1 450 Askaris. This reinforcement reduced the reserves available to Lettow-Vorbeck for his eastern front and could help to explain why his vigorous counterattack never took place.

Stewart adopted an over-cautious approach, sending his mounted troops on 9 March to reconnoitre the route ahead. He was unwilling to commit himself to a blind advance through unknown territory covered in bush. Smuts began to suspect that Stewart's hesitancy would be the ruin of his encirclement strategy at this early stage. At 15:00 Stewart received a telegram from Smuts urging him forward with speed. Ignoring Smuts's impassioned pleas, Stewart waited on the return of his mounted reconnaissance, who duly reported that impenetrable bush covered the way ahead. On the morning of 10 March, he set off cautiously without his exhausted mounted troops and managed to advance five kilometres short of the Mbiriri River.

The German official history is scathing in its criticism of Fischer for his failure to attack the over-cautious Stewart, despite the reinforcements sent to him at a considerable cost to Lettow-Vorbeck's reserve. Boell believes that Fischer, despite suffering a numerical disadvantage, had sufficient modern weapons, including artillery and machine guns, to overcome Stewart's larger force. What Lettow-Vorbeck needed from Fischer was for him to launch an aggressive attack on Stewart and seize the initiative, but it became evident that Fischer lacked the determination to do so. Instead he divided his forces and undertook several evasive manoeuvres that yielded extraordinarily little on the battlefield.

On 8 March an exasperated Lettow-Vorbeck issued a direct command to Fischer to launch an immediate and concerted attack on Stewart, by which time Fischer's troops were exhausted from all the marching and countermarching along the front. When Fischer eventually attacked, on 10 March, he intercepted a screening force of only 300 men as the main body of Stewart's troops had already passed. Smuts was fortunate that Fischer was as incompetent as Stewart; a more resolute German commander could have inflicted a severe reverse on the British force.

After escaping unscathed from Fischer's attack, Stewart received a further message from Smuts at 07:45 on 11 March urging him forward. Supposedly spurred on, he set out and reached the intact road bridge at Boma Ngomba. However, his sluggish progress had set him a full four days behind the planned timetable. During his advance, he had seen little of the enemy, but that was about to change.

The day before, on 10 March, the mounted units, carrying the lion's share of the artillery, set out to catch up with the main body at 16:00. On the way, they encountered the Germans under Fischer, where the main body had passed unscathed some hours earlier. A short, sharp exchange ensued, which convinced the mounted units to retreat into a defensive position for the night. The proximity of the Germans induced the mounted units to retreat to Garangua. Stewart retrieved his mounted units on 12 March, delaying the 1st Division by another day.

Smuts was convinced that there had been practically no opposition to Stewart's advance, which to him indicated that the main German forces were facing him at Latema-Reata. The advance from the east set off a full two days after Stewart launched his advance. The two-day delay was at Stewart's request as his line of advance was longer and more difficult.

Van Deventer left Mbuyuni with the reserve force on the evening of 7 March to initiate his flanking manoeuvre to the north of Malleson's main thrust on Salaita. On the morning of 8 March, he occupied positions near Lake Chala, forcing the Germans to abandon their positions at Salaita and retreat. Boell's account reveals that, although Lettow-Vorbeck was prepared to trade territory for time, it was a tough call to sacrifice territory when confronted with Smuts's flank attack.

Further reconnaissance established that the Germans held Taveta in some strength. Malleson's force began to bombard Salaita Hill, which he captured at 14:30 on 9 March. The Germans abandoned the position after Lettow-Vorbeck had concluded that its defence was untenable in the face of Van Deventer's flanking movement. The German forces at Salaita, which a few weeks before had inflicted many casualties on the British, fell back without a fight.

Van Deventer, continuing the advance, inserted himself in the rear of Taveta on 9 March. The Germans retreated from Taveta on 10 March after a sharp skirmish, no doubt wary of Van Deventer's forces in their rear. The bulk of the German forces withdrew to the hills of Latema and Reata, where they were determined to offer stubborn defence.

Smuts decided to launch an immediate attack on Latema-Reata after he had conducted a reconnaissance in person. He chose a frontal attack without the aid of a turning movement owing to the difficulty of the terrain. In this respect, he proved his versatility as a commander by not shying away from a frontal attack when the situation demanded it.

The 1st East African Brigade launched its attack in the afternoon of 11 March. The assault took them to the foot of the hills before heavy enemy gunfire held them up. Malleson, suffering from dysentery and perhaps a dose of déjà vu, chose to report sick. Tighe took over his command at 16:00 and ordered more units forward into the fray. The Germans pinned down the British for five hours, with casualties mounting, and subjected them to numerous counterattacks. Lettow-Vorbeck, although determined to defend the position, was keenly aware of Van Deventer and the threat to his left flank.

Tighe attempted a night attack with fixed bayonets at 20:00, judging that the Germans were not holding the hill in strength, but a determined German counterattack flung the attack back. All that remained on the hill as night fell were pockets of British soldiers doggedly clinging on to the ground they had held for hours.

More importantly, Van Deventer managed to advance to Spitz Hill after a brisk skirmish, placing him to the flank and rear of the German positions at Latema-Reata. Smuts, fearing a German counterattack and preferring to wait for the results of his turning movement, ordered Tighe to withdraw his whole force before daybreak. At dawn, Smuts realised that British units still occupied positions on the hill. He ordered an immediate advance to reoccupy, only to find that the Germans had abandoned their positions during the night.

Once again, the threat of Van Deventer's turning movement at Spitz Hill forced the Germans to abandon a powerful defensive position. Smuts thought Van Deventer's operational–tactical flanking movement so crucial to the outcome of the battle that he placed himself 'in close touch' with him at the expense of remaining in continuous contact with general headquarters. It is worth pondering the far more important strategic outcome if Smuts had placed himself in closer proximity to Stewart and been able to influence the latter's sluggish tempo positively.

A sign of the ferocity of the battle was the loss of nerve suffered by Maj Georg Kraut, one of Lettow-Vorbeck's most experienced officers, who commanded the German forces defending Latema-Reata and later Kahe. He managed to recover after a month's rest and later served with great distinction in the campaign.

The hasty German retreat was an opportune moment for the two prongs to snap shut and entrap the hapless foe, but Stewart's tardiness put paid to what would have been a strategic victory. He saw his mission as twofold: first, to draw off as many of the enemy as possible – a task he failed at miserably, as the Germans ignored his advance – and, second, to threaten the German line of retreat, which would have been better served by an early occupation of Kahe. Smuts intended for Stewart to reach Kahe on 11 March, cutting off the German retreat into the interior. Contrary to Smuts's expectations, however, Stewart languished at Boma Ngombe, 50 km from his destination. He revealed his state of mind when he admitted to an 'uneasy feeling' at receiving news on 7 March that the main force was to the east of Salaita instead of near Taveta. He felt vulnerable, stripped of his mounted units, deep inside enemy territory to the tune of 96 km and some 240 km from the nearest railhead. In a disastrous change of plan, Stewart, feeling vulnerable and isolated, linked the pace of his advance to the successes of the main force.

Smuts grew increasingly frustrated at Stewart's hesitancy and sensed that the narrow opportunity to encircle Lettow-Vorbeck's forces was fast disappearing. He sent a message on the afternoon of 12 March, urging the timid Stewart forward to Kahe. Instead of making a concerted effort towards Kahe, Stewart sent most of his force towards New Moshi, well to the north of the intended target. Heavy rain halted his faltering advance at 01:30 on the morning of 14 March.

Ironically, Lettow-Vorbeck grew equally disenchanted with the performance of Fischer, the commander facing Stewart. Fischer, presented with several opportunities during Stewart's bumbling advance, had failed to grab the chance to inflict damage. Lettow-Vorbeck severely reprimanded Fischer and his lack of aggressive action, which resulted in the latter's suicide by gunshot to save his honour.

Despite Stewart's renewed advance, Van Deventer was first to arrive in Moshi, early on 14 March. Smuts described Stewart's conduct of the operation as lamentable. He had managed to cover an average of only 6.5 km per day over a period of six days in the face of little opposition. Van Deventer finally closed the pincer when he sent a motorcyclist to Boma Ngombe to contact the hesitant 1st Division. Van Deventer also found Moshi abandoned. The Germans had quickly retreated south along the railway out of harm's way.

Smuts's intention of encircling Lettow-Vorbeck was frustrated by Stewart's lethargic advance. His own flanking manoeuvre, executed deftly by Van Deventer, managed to dislodge the Germans from their prepared defensive positions at little cost. If Stewart had executed his enveloping manoeuvre with the same zeal as Van Deventer, he could have reached his objective of Kahe between 10 and 12 March and the Germans would have found themselves encircled and in a precarious position.

Smuts had good reason to be irate at Stewart's lacklustre performance: it robbed him of a decisive strategic victory. Shortly after the battle, Smuts relieved Malleson and Stewart of their commands, barely concealing his contempt at their poor performance. He also ensured that Tighe was reassigned but was at pains to acknowledge his excellent preparation for the offensive.

Lettow-Vorbeck, operating on internal lines of communication, posed a constant danger to the Allied manoeuvre wings. Had he been able to concentrate his forces into a powerful counterattack against any one of the three – Stewart, Tighe or Van Deventer – there was a good chance of inflicting a defeat on each of them in turn. It was his plan all along to attack each force in quick succession.

Smuts's simultaneous advance on exterior lines was enough to unsettle the defenders and reduce their chances of concentrating an attack. In response, Lettow-Vorbeck was unable to conduct a successful defence of Latema and Reata, robbing himself of the chance to concentrate his forces against Van Deventer or Stewart. Nevertheless, he came within a hair's breadth of launching an attack on Van Deventer after the first successful defence of the Latema-Reata hills on the night of 11 March. The constant threat of outflanking and Van Deventer's threat of encirclement dissuaded Lettow-Vorbeck from launching an attack. On the contrary, Van Deventer's flanking movement dislodged the Germans from their defences and kept them constantly off balance, making a concentrated counterattack impossible.

Smuts's lightning operational manoeuvre failed to encircle the enemy, but it unhinged them psychologically. He managed to reclaim all the British territory held by Lettow-Vorbeck and opened a gateway to the interior of GEA. By doing so, he gained much strategic territory with relatively little loss of life: the Germans suffered 334 casualties against 800 for the British. Smuts received a well-deserved congratulatory letter from Louis Botha via Governor General Buxton in which he recognised that 'These successes have obviously only been attained by the gallantry and determination of the troops and by skilful leading of their commanders'.

The way the South Africans conducted their operational and tactical affairs in GEA was very different from the way the war was being fought on the Western Front in Europe. The open spaces of East Africa and the low density of military manpower in the theatre of war lent themselves to a manoeuvre-type warfare that was not possible on the Western Front until the later stages of the war.

Smuts's interpretation of a particular South African brand of man-oeuvre warfare yielded an impressive amount of territory in a short space of time, with relatively few casualties. This would not be the case for the South African contingent that fought at Delville Wood in 1916, where the troops manned trenches in static positions and were subject to incessant artillery bombardment and brutal frontal attacks. Gains of territory were measured in metres instead of kilometres and in the lives of thousands of men. The pointless sacrifice of thousands of South African men in France was anathema to a South African way of war that frowned upon the pursuit of victory at any cost.

The Battle of Delville Wood, 1916

Tactical symbols

II	Batallion
X	Brigade
⊠	Infantry

Legend

- ▬ ▬ Attack boundary
- ▭ ▭ ▭ Brigade boundary
- ➤ Advance of Allied troops
- ⊠ South African troops
- ⊠ British troops
- ⊠ German troops
- ➤ Advance of German troops
- .... Trench
- Village
- Wood
- Road
- Railway

Delville Wood (inset map)

0   0,5   1 km

5

DELVILLE WOOD, 1916

Following the successful conclusion of the German South West Africa campaign in 1915 and with the German East Africa campaign well under way, South Africa decided to raise an infantry brigade for deployment to France. The 1st South African Infantry Brigade (1 SA Inf Bde), commanded by Brig Gen (Sir) Henry Timson Lukin (of Sandfontein fame), numbered some 160 officers and 5 648 other ranks, organised into four regiments. In November 1915, the brigade arrived in England and began training in earnest for deployment to the Western Front. However, it soon became necessary to divert Lukin and his brigade to Egypt.

In Egypt, a tense situation had developed. The British were wary that Turkish forces could threaten the Suez Canal from their bases in Syria, while rebellious Senussi nomads posed a serious threat on Egypt's western frontier. The Senussi, under the command of Gaafer Pasha, were armed by the Turks. In mid-December, the Western Egyptian Force, commanded by Maj Gen Alexander Wallace, suffered heavy losses against a strong enemy force at Beit Hussein, near Mersa Matruh. In January, Gaafer's forces once more threatened Mersa Matruh.

In early January 1916, Lukin and his brigade disembarked at Alexandria. Between January and April, 1 SA Inf Bde, as part of the Western Egyptian Force, fought in the largely successful actions at Hazalin (23 January) and Agagia (26 February) in which Gaafer's forces were routed and defeated. Moreover, at the strategic level, the Battle of Agagia secured Egypt's western frontier. After occupying Barrani and Sollum without meeting any further resistance, there was no further noticeable fighting in this sector. In mid-April, Lukin and his now somewhat battle-hardened brigade sailed for France.

Into the line

On 20 April, 1 SA Inf Bde disembarked at Marseille. While 4 South African Infantry Regiment (4 SAI) and a part of 1 SAI were placed in quarantine, the remainder of the brigade travelled to the frontline in Flanders. After arriving in Steenwerck on 23 April, Lukin established his headquarters at Bailleul, with 1 SA Inf Bde now attached to Maj Gen WT Furse's 9th (Scottish) Division. During their first three weeks near the front, detachments from 2 SAI and 3 SAI received instruction in trench warfare. On 11 May the rest of the brigade joined their compatriots in Flanders.

April 1916 proved to be a critical month for the Entente Powers on the Western Front. By 9 April, the relentless German attacks on the French positions at Verdun had failed. Despite suffering heavy losses, Gen Philippe Pétain's forces had held their ground, although the Battle of Verdun would go on until December. Moreover, the German hope of inducing a British counteroffensive came to naught. Instead, the French commander-in-chief, Gen Joseph Joffre, decided to wait for the German forces to spend their strength at Verdun, after which the British and French armies could launch a combined offensive against the weakened enemy. The Entente Powers therefore decided to wait it out. This decision proved extremely costly in men, and the inactivity and lack of an overall strategic objective directly affected the morale of the frontline troops. However, this period provided the British commander-in-chief, Gen (Sir) Douglas Haig, with ample time to replenish arms and ammunition and train up his troops for future offensive operations.

For the next two months, 1 SA Inf Bde underwent rigorous training in the methods of trench warfare, which was completely different to the large-scale manoeuvre-type operations conducted by their compatriots in the African theatres of operations. During May the South Africans held a portion of the frontline, moving to the training area near Steenbecque and Morbecque at the beginning of June. There, further battalion and brigade training was conducted until 14 June, when 9th Division was ordered to move to the Somme sector. Lukin and his brigade were quartered at Ailly-sur-Somme, near Amiens, and groups of officers and non-commissioned officers visited the frontlines near Maricourt. At this stage, 2 SAI and 3 SAI were detached for service with the 30th Division as it prepared for the upcoming Somme offensive. On 23 June, 1 SA Inf Bde moved to Corbie and Sailly-le-Sac, located a few miles from the frontline.

To understand the events that would unfold at Delville Wood in July 1916, it is pertinent to reflect on the purpose of the larger Battle of the Somme. By mid-1916, the Central Powers, and Germany in particular, had suffered a few reverses – principally at Verdun and during the recent Brusilov Offensive on the Eastern Front. However, despite these setbacks, the German forces on the Western Front were still numerous and occupied strong defensive positions in depth. The strongest parts of the defence were at Arras and along the Somme River, where the Germans occupied the main high ground. They also controlled several fortified woods and villages in the immediate rear area, which provided for a defence in depth through a series of reserve trench lines.

By this stage of the war, the Allied forces had learned valuable lessons from their experience on the Western Front. The Allied commanders acknowledged the fact that they could not break through the German frontline due to its defence in depth. They thus accepted that any future offensive should occur in stages and only after massive preparatory artillery fire. Moreover, to maintain momentum, and cognisant of the protracted nature of such action, the Allied high command maintained that fresh troops would be required for each successive stage of offensive operations. Undeniably, this was grand attritional warfare with limited tactical and operational objectives. In hindsight it is easy to level criticism, but at the time, and despite its uninspired nature, the plan for the Somme offensive seemed reasonable.

On the South Africans' immediate front, the plan was to roll up the German defensive positions on the Bapaume Ridge, which, with no alternative course of action, would compel the enemy into open warfare. For the ensuing attack, the British front extended from Gommecourt in the north to Maricourt in the south, with the French responsible for the sector across the Somme River to a point near the village of Fay. Haig intended to focus the main effort of his attack between Ancre and Maricourt.

The Battle of Delville Wood

On 30 June, shortly before the battle commenced, 1 SA Inf Bde moved to Grove Town on the outskirts at Bray. At this stage, the 9th Division was held in the general reserve of the British XIII Corps. In the early hours of Saturday 1 July, the British infantry went over the top and the Battle of the Somme began in earnest. On the first day, the British results were favourable, with the German line pushed back from Ancre southwards. The results in the area of operations of XIII Corps were also noteworthy, since it captured Montauban and advanced to the edge of Bernafay Wood. Over the coming days, XIII Corps worked with French forces to try to clear the German positions in the woods around Trônes and Bernafay. Despite Allied successes, the Germans held their positions at Trônes Wood, dominated in the south by the Maltz Horn Ridge and by Longueval in the north. In due course, British and French forces took most of Trônes Wood but struggled to hold on to it. This was the general situation on 13 July, shortly before Haig commenced the second stage of his offensive operations.

At the beginning of July, the South African troops became incrementally involved in the first stage of the Battle of the Somme. On 2 July, 1 SA Inf Bde moved forward to Billon Valley, where it relieved two brigades in the Glatz sector of the front over the coming days. Then 1 SAI and 4 SAI held the line to Briqueterie Trench, east of Montauban, while 3 SAI occupied frontline trenches immediately to the northwest of Maricourt in support. The remaining South African battalion, 2 SAI, was kept in divisional reserve at Talus Boise. During this period, British and French forces attacked along the immediate front, specifically towards Maltz Horn Farm and Trônes Wood. On 7 July, 1 SAI came out of the line. That evening, Haig's headquarters issued general orders for the second stage of the battle to commence; for the 9th Division, this meant an attack on the German line at Longueval.

On 8 July, the only South African unit in the line was 4 SAI, still holding the Briqueterie Trench and a section from Dublin Trench to Dublin Redoubt. Having left Talus Boise, 2 SAI moved forward and relieved British units holding part of the line at Bernafay Wood. Two days later, they were relieved by 4 SAI. During the brief deployment to the frontline, the South African troops were heavily shelled and suffered some 200 casualties.

The remaining South African unit in the frontline, 4 SAI, soon became drawn into the battle for control of Trônes Wood. After a series of strong German counterattacks, an order was issued on 10 July for Trônes Wood to be cleared. The night before, a company and platoon from 4 SAI were detached to support 30th Brigade and garrison Briqueterie, while 3 SAI was held in reserve. The attack at Trônes Wood commenced at dawn on 10 July, with a company from 4 SAI joining the troops from the 30th Division, which advanced through and cleared the southern half of the wood. However, the sector would prove extremely difficult to hold. German artillery positions were situated around Trônes Wood, which threatened Allied communication with the rear and the forward movement of men and supplies. That afternoon, the Allies had to concede their recent gains after a strong German counterattack.

Fighting around Trônes Wood continued throughout 11 July. The 4 SAI companies deployed near Glatz Redoubt and Bernafay Wood experienced heavy enemy shellfire during further counterattacks. During the day, the Officer Commanding (OC) 4 SAI, Lt Col FA Jones, was mortally wounded and Maj DM MacLeod assumed command. On 13 July, 4 SAI was relieved. The entire 1 SA Inf Bde then concentrated at Talus Boise as the divisional reserve of the 9th Division. The week-long deployment to the frontlines had taken a heavy toll on the South Africans, with casualties amounting to at least 537 men.

The attack commenced on the morning of 14 July against a 6 km section of the German line stretching from southeast of Pozières to Longueval and Delville Wood. XIII Corps was tasked with capturing the area around Bazentin-le-Grand, Longueval and Delville Wood and with clearing Trônes Wood to form a defensive flank. During the day's fighting, the objectives from Bazentin-le-Petit to Longueval were captured, but the German positions at High Wood were only penetrated. In this sector of the line, comprising the British right flank, the 9th Division and 18th Division were deployed against Longueval and Trônes Wood respectively. An attack on this section of the frontline, forming a salient of sorts, would be extremely difficult. Any attack would draw fire from three sides, with communications to the rear being extremely difficult. Moreover, the terrain also proved difficult, with the land sloping upwards from Bernafay and Trônes Wood to the village of Longueval.

Delville Wood was located to the immediate east and northeast of Longueval. A series of trench lines ran throughout Delville Wood, with the main German positions, comprising strong entrenchments covered by machine guns, to the north, northeast and southeast. The occupation of Longueval was thus ultimately dependent on securing and holding Delville Wood.

On 14 July, the main attack on Longueval was entrusted to the 26th Brigade, with the 27th Brigade following in their wake. Unrealistically, the operational intent was, if practicable, to capture Longueval and Delville Wood that day. Early that morning, Lukin was ordered to detach 1 SAI to the 27th Brigade to help clear Longueval, while a decision to detach 3 SAI to the 26th Brigade was cancelled. The attack by the 26th Brigade made some initial gains as the German trenches were rushed and desperate hand-to-hand fighting broke out in Longueval. Despite the tenacious German defence, and the fact that the entire west and southwest part of Longueval was taken by noon, it transpired that the occupation of Delville Wood was a prerequisite to capturing and holding Longueval. Shortly after midday, Furse indicated to Lukin that as soon as Longueval was taken, 1 SA Inf Bde had to capture and consolidate the outer edge of Delville Wood. Based on this information, Lukin drew up his order for the subsequent attack, scheduled to commence on 15 July. His orders were clear: Delville Wood must be taken at all costs, even if further attacks on Longueval failed.

Shortly before dawn on 15 July, 2 SAI and 3 SAI left Montauban and advanced towards Delville Wood, with 4 SAI following in their wake. Lukin had ordered Lt Col WEC Tanner, the commander of 2 SAI, to base the plan of his attack on the Allied progress in Longueval, which at that stage was still unclear. As the South Africans advanced towards Delville Wood, two companies from 4 SAI were detached to the 26th Brigade. As 1 SAI Inf Bde advanced forward across broken ground, they drew sustained fire that cleared only once they reached the southern edge of Longueval. At this point, Tanner visited the 26th Brigade in Longueval to try to ascertain the position on his immediate front. His reconnaissance confirmed that the northern part of Longueval, and the wood adjoining the village along the line of Buchanan Street, were strongly held by German forces. Moreover, while the overall situation

Cheery South African Jocks serving with the 9th Scottish Division – wounded but happy

The pet baboon of the South African Scottish – it has been through the fighting with the men

The Delville Wood Cemetery showing the scarred battlefield and surroundings

in the greater part of Delville Wood remained uncertain, a company of British troops had advanced and dug themselves in along the southwestern corner of the wood. Tanner therefore decided to launch his attack from the position along the line of Buchanan Street, which offered a somewhat covered approach to the objective.

With the assistance of a guide, the South Africans advanced in single file from the south end of Longueval, across the fields towards the Buchanan Street trench, which they reached at 06:00. Tanner decided to systematically clear the area south of Princes Street, after which his troops would advance north and occupy the Strand. In principle, the South Africans would then occupy the perimeter of Delville Wood from the northeastern end to the southwestern corner – leaving only the northwestern corner, bordering on Longueval, in enemy hands.

The initial South African attack proved extremely successful. By 07:00, 3 SAI, supported by a company from 2 SAI, held everything south of Princes Street. Tanner ordered the remaining three companies of 2 SAI to advance and occupy the Strand and northeastern perimeter of Delville Wood. However, this advance proved far more difficult and taxing for the men. Upon reaching their objective, the three weak 2 SAI companies had to hold a front approximately 1 200 metres long. No sooner had the South Africans started to dig in than they were subjected to heavy shelling, with machine-gun and rifle fire breaking out from the German defensive positions elsewhere in the wood. Meanwhile, in the eastern sector, 3 SAI had some success when it captured three German officers and 135 other ranks.

By mid-afternoon, Tanner reported that he had captured the whole of Delville Wood, apart from the German strongpoints in the northwestern corner bordering Longueval. However, the South Africans then faced the daunting task of holding on to their gains. Lukin planned to thin his line of defensive troops once the perimeter was reached, which meant that the long South African frontline was now thinly held by small infantry detachments supported by machine guns. Strong German counterattacks soon threw his plans into disarray. At 15:00, elements of the 10th Bavarian Division attacked from the east but were driven back. At 16:40 and 18:30, Tanner reported enemy troops massing for an attack at the northeastern end of the wood. He also informed Lukin that he had suffered heavy casualties during the fighting and requested reinforcements to bolster his defences. In due course, companies of 4 SAI and 1 SAI were sent forward to reinforce the defenders of Delville Wood. Despite battle fatigue setting in, 2 SAI and 3 SAI were ordered to dig in since renewed counterattacks were expected the next morning. While reserve troops of 1 SAI ferried ammunition into the wood, a series of machine-gun nests were established at the southwestern corner of the wood.

Throughout the night of 15–16 July, sustained enemy artillery fire engulfed Delville Wood. The South African troops, numbering 12 weakened infantry companies supported by machine guns, were holding on to a portion of Delville Wood less than a square mile in area. A semicircle of German trenches surrounded the South African positions and German artillery fire was accurately ranged on Delville Wood. The South African troops found themselves in a perilous position, with only one company of 1 SAI in reserve and a further two 4 SAI companies due to return from their detachment to the 26th Brigade soon.

At 02:35 on Sunday 16 July, Lukin was ordered to block the northern entrance into Longueval, a route the Germans were using to reinforce Longueval and the northern part of Delville Wood. The South Africans were therefore ordered to capture the northern perimeter of the wood and then to advance westwards and northwards until they linked up with the 27th Brigade in the vicinity of Flers Road. Owing to the tactical situation, the target area could not be prepared by artillery bombardment, but preparatory fire from trench mortars preceded the infantry attacks. The subsequent advance, which started at 10:00, failed completely, with no headway being made against the strong German defensive positions. Instead the South African troops fell back on their former positions and were subjected to steady fire throughout the day – preventing replenishment and the evacuation of the mounting casualties. That afternoon, Lt Col FS Dawson, commanding 1 SAI, requested Lukin to relieve the exhausted South African troops in Delville Wood. However, Lukin could do nothing since his orders were to hold on to Delville Wood at all costs. The overall situation proved precarious: Longueval and Delville Wood remained strongly held by German forces, and without adequate reinforcements moving forward, the 9th Division could not capture its immediate objectives. Moreover, success at Longueval or Delville Wood remained interdependent: failure to capture either would continue the stalemate.

It was decided to make another effort against the northwestern corner of Delville Wood on Monday 17 July. Prior to the commencement of the attack, British and South African troops were withdrawn from Longueval and Delville Wood to a line south of Princess Street and the Strand, so that the objective could be saturated by artillery fire. The barrage ceased at 02:00, at which time the Allied attack commenced. But this attack, too, failed, with strong German defences preventing any advance from the south and east. Once more the attackers had to fall back on their previous positions without gaining any ground or dislodging the German defenders. Lukin then visited Delville Wood to discuss the overall situation with his officers. The situation was dire: his troops had been in combat for nearly 48 hours; they had been subjected to intense artillery bombardment and machine-gun fire; battle fatigue was growing among the men; and they had failed to dislodge the German defenders. Despite Lukin's general concern for his men and his forlorn attempt to obtain relief or reinforcements, higher headquarters remained steadfast in their conviction: Delville Wood had to be held at all costs.

During the afternoon the situation remained unchanged, apart from Tanner being wounded and replaced by Lt Col EF Thackeray. However, that night Lukin was informed that the 3rd Division would attack Longueval imminently from the west. By 19:30 Lukin received orders that 1 SA Inf Bde was to attack the German positions in the southeast edge of the wood before dawn on Tuesday 15 July. However, when the two companies of 3 SAI facing that part of the German line confirmed that it was strongly held, and that at least 200 men would be needed for the action, Maj Gen Furse cancelled the operation. At 22:30 Lukin was informed that as soon as the 3rd Division occupied Longueval, it would establish strong positions to the northwest edge of Delville Wood, from where they could help to protect the South African positions. The renewed attack on Longueval was scheduled for Friday 18 July.

During the night of 14–15 July, all available South African reinforcements moved forward to shore up the strength of the perimeter amid strong German counterattacks. The Germans breached the perimeter and advanced as far as Buchanan Street and Princess Street. A South African counterattack managed to win back the lost ground but in doing so suffered heavy casualties. By 03:45 on 15 July, the 76th Brigade had advanced through Longueval to a point between Flers Road and North Street. At 08:00, on the fourth day of the battle, Thackeray sent forward South African patrols that made contact with the 76th Brigade without meeting any serious opposition. However, the South African arrival at the edge of Delville Wood was the signal for the Germans to unleash a strong bombardment that smothered the entire area. The Germans drove back the 76th Brigade into Longueval, which exposed the South African left flank and allowed the enemy to enter the wood in numbers. At 09:00, limited reinforcements were moved forward and, despite relentless German attacks, the South African defenders clung to their positions.

At 14:00, the dire situation changed to desperate. Dawson was ordered to take 150 men from 1 SAI forward to relieve some of the troops in the line. However, these men had also been in action for nearly four days without any rest. The South Africans were nearing exhaustion. They occupied a trench in the southeast corner of Longueval. At this point, Dawson moved forward into the wood, where he found Thackeray, and the remainder of his troops, barely holding the southwestern corner of Delville Wood. The South African garrison had nearly been destroyed; scores of wounded men filled the trenches and could not be evacuated to the rear since all the stretcher-bearers were casualties.

That night, news was received that the 26th Brigade would relieve 1 SA Inf Bde. The relief, occurring under trying conditions, was slow and intricate. By midnight the withdrawal had been partly carried out, with two companies each from 1 SAI and 4 SAI moving out of the line. Throughout the night, fresh troops from the German 8th Division continued their attacks on the Buchanan Street line. The remnants of the South African troops under Thackeray doggedly held the southwestern corner of Delville Wood. They survived three determined attacks on the night of 18–19 July, inflicting heavy losses on the German attackers. A gallant handful of South Africans held on to their positions throughout 19–20 July, despite incessant shelling and accurate fire. At 18:00 on Sunday 20 July, the 76th Brigade took over the remnants of the positions in Longueval and Delville Wood. Thackeray marched out of Delville Wood with the remainder of his men, numbering only two officers and 140 other ranks. The troops spent the night at Talus Boise before joining the rest of the South African brigade at Happy Valley the next day. Delville Wood was only successfully taken, by the 14th (Light) Division, on 25 August.

Over the period 14–20 July, a total of six days and five nights, 1 SA Inf Bde held on to one of the most difficult parts of the British front. The South Africans were subjected to intense, concentrated German fire throughout. Moreover, the vastly superior German positions were continually reinforced with fresh troops, which allowed them to break through the South African lines, only to be driven back time and again. The protracted South African defence was similar in ferocity to the fighting at Verdun and in the Ypres salient. When the South Africans went into the line at Delville Wood on 14 July, 1 SA Inf Bde numbered some 121 officers and 3 032 other ranks. By the time Thackeray marched out of the wood with the remnants of the defenders on 20 July, only 143 men were left. Moreover, the total number of troops mustered at Happy Valley on 21 July was roughly 750 men. Throughout July, 1 SA Inf Bde suffered 2 815 casualties, comprising 502 killed, 1 735 wounded and 578 missing.

At Delville Wood, despite the overwhelming odds, unfamiliar terrain and a determined enemy, the South African infantrymen conducted themselves well while putting up a gallant defence. Within the space of six months, Lukin and his brigade had deployed to two vastly different operating environments. The Egyptian campaign largely favoured manoeuvre warfare and combined-arms operations, while the deployment to the Western Front was a static affair dominated by massive artillery barrages, trench warfare and near-suicidal infantry assaults. Moreover, between these deployments the nature of the enemy also drastically changed, with the result that the deployment to Egypt did not prepare the South African troops for the experience of the Western Front. Once deployed to the static frontline in Flanders, the infantrymen of 1 SA Inf Bde bore the brunt of the fighting, and casualties steadily increased. There was a disconnection between the training that the

South African infantrymen had received in trench warfare and their actual experience at Delville Wood.

The South African defence of Delville Wood remains noteworthy. During the battle, the understrength brigade, suffering mounting casualties, without adequate artillery support and with little to no reserves moving forward, followed orders and held on to their isolated positions against overwhelming German forces and sustained counterattacks from 14 to 20 July. The evident gallantry and resolve of 1 SA Inf Bde at Delville Wood, along with the numerous accolades conferred on Lukin's men after the battle, showed that the South Africans could hold their own under extremely trying operational conditions.

The South African deployment to the Western Front continued until the cessation of hostilities in 1918; it would would be characterised by further gallantry, battlefield successes and reverses, and mounting casualties. However, following the end of the First World War, the UDF was demobilised and underwent a period of rationalisation that affected threat perceptions, force design and its budget. By the early 1920s, the Union faced with the increasing threat of internal unrest, the defence force would be called upon to defend the legitimacy and security of the state.

The Rand Revolt, 1922

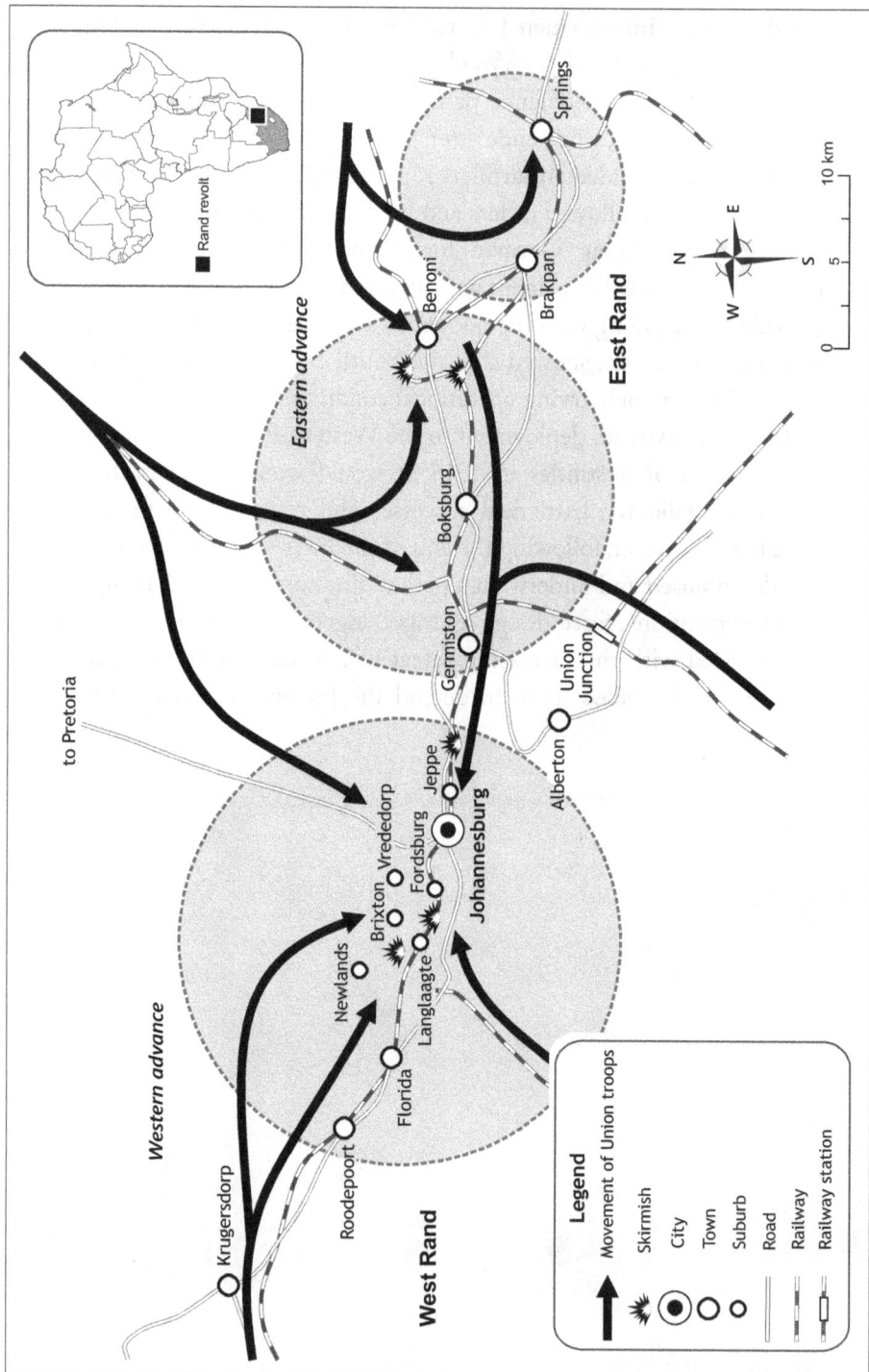

Legend

Movement of Union troops	
Skirmish	
City	
Town	
Suburb	
Road	
Railway	
Railway station	

6

RAND REVOLT, 1922

Despite emerging from the First World War with an admirable military record, which included deployments to the African, European and Middle Eastern theatres of war, South Africa after 1918 was a deeply divided and war-weary nation. Along with a growing preoccupation with domestic concerns, the Union government had to reorder its national priorities drastically. These included reconsidering the country's foreign and defence policies, especially regarding matters of post-war strategy and evolving threat perceptions. Shortly after the Great War, the reigning political debate in South Africa mainly focused on the morality and wisdom of future military interventions in foreign imperial wars. It was generally agreed that intervention in European wars had to be avoided at all costs, in no small part due to the heavy losses suffered by the South Africans during the attritional warfare on the Western Front (1916–1918). Instead, South Africa would focus its military and political power on future interventions closer to home in sub-Saharan Africa.

Perceptions of threats to South Africa, historically speaking, considered three divergent scenarios: a seaborne invasion launched by a European power that could exert its power intercontinentally; a landward invasion by a European colonial power in Africa; and the threat of an internal uprising by African nationalists, along with the outbreak of industrial strife. These were considered to be the main threats to the state's security and legitimacy at the time. But while the threat of seaborne and landward invasions existed in theory, and contingency plans were in place to deal with these, it was acknowledged that the main threats were the potential outbreak of industrial unrest and uprisings by the African population.

During the post-war period, the UDF also underwent drastic reorganisation and rationalisation, principally driven by fiscal constraints and the need for demobilisation. Three broad principles underpinned the reorganisation of the defence force. First, and probably due to 'Delville Wood syndrome', it was accepted that the UDF would deploy only for the immediate defence of South Africa and where it would have a distinct advantage over would-be adversaries in weapons, equipment and force structure and design. The UDF also had to change from a conventional force to one organised to conduct low-intensity warfare in southern Africa. Second, the UDF would have to be able to carry out its mandate in line with prevailing threat perceptions. Built around a nucleus of mounted infantry and a small air force, it would conduct highly mobile and mutually supportive operations. Finally, the UDF needed to be sufficiently lethal to deal rapidly with any internal unrest threatening the security and legitimacy of the state, without incurring unnecessary casualties.

Since 1910, the UDF had been deployed on several occasions to deal with internal conflict within the borders of the Union. Before 1918, these actions included quelling the wave of strikes in 1913–1914, dealing with the Afrikaner Rebellion in 1914 and suppressing the growing black resistance to white rule. Regarding the last of these, the most prominent deployment was the so-called Ovamboland Expedition to South West Africa in 1917, which dealt with the rebellious Chief Mandume Ya Ndemufayo of the Ovakuanyama.

Following the end of the Great War, the UDF and the SAP had to deal once again with outbreaks of internal unrest that challenged the authority and legitimacy of the state. However, the UDF faced severe fiscal, political and manpower constraints that adversely affected its nature, organisation and operability.

The Israelite Rebellion of 1921 caught the Union government and the security forces off guard. While the Israelite Rebellion clearly demonstrated the effectiveness of modern weaponry and the use of overwhelming force in asymmetrical warfare against an irregular opponent, it also revealed several inadequacies within the UDF and the SAP – particularly regarding conducting rural counterinsurgency operations. First, no budgetary provisions existed for the deployment of the military in case of internal emergencies where it had to deploy to support policing actions. Second, the small Permanent Force of the UDF could deploy a maximum of only 200 South African Mounted Riflemen in support of the SAP during the Israelite Rebellion. In fact, apart from the small SAMR complement, the UDF had no excess troops available in the Permanent Force at the time to assist in the suppression of internal unrest and the maintenance of order. However, more serious problems were on the horizon.

Suppressing the revolt

During the interwar period, the South African General Staff prepared several contingency plans for the use of the defence force in the event of serious industrial disturbances on the Witwatersrand. To offset manpower limitations, they planned for the large-scale mobilisation of reserves, in particular the ACF units and several Defence Rifle Associations, comprising former commandos, from the military districts adjoining the Witwatersrand.

In January 1922, and in striking similarity to the 1913–1914 industrial strikes discussed in Chapter 1, coal miners in the then Transvaal went on strike to protect white jobs from the employment of lower-paid black labour. They were soon followed by gold miners on the Witwatersrand. The violent turmoil that ensued became known as the Rand Revolt. This prompted the Chief of the General Staff, Brig Gen AJE Brink, to hold an urgent conference at Defence Headquarters in Pretoria. During the meeting, the defence schemes discussed above were revised, the necessary proclamations calling out the reserves finalised and the required regulations for the proclamation and imposition of martial law prepared.

On 22 February, the first request from the SAP for military reinforcements was received: which was met by the dispatch of six machine-gun sections from the Permanent Force to the Witwatersrand. On the morning of 28 February, Prime Minister Jan Smuts, at the urgent request of the Commissioner of Police, Col (Sir) Theo Truter, ordered a further portion of the Permanent Force to move to the East Rand.

However, during the night, an intense firefight occurred between the police and a group of strikers in Boksburg. As a result of this incident, Truter pressed for further UDF reinforcements to reach Boksburg and

Benoni by daybreak on 1 March to bolster the police and help restore order. That same night, orders were issued for the remainder of the Permanent Force to proceed to the East Rand, with all available men leaving by special train during the early morning hours.

By the evening of 1 March, therefore, the whole of the SAPF was concentrated on the East Rand between Boksburg, Benoni and Germiston. The deployed force was placed under the overall command of Lt Col NHM Burne and would be used by Truter only when needed. For the following week, beyond complying with periodic requests from Truter, Burne and his men took no active part in operations, while the industrial unrest on the Witwatersrand spiralled out of control.

After the declaration of a general strike on Tuesday 7 March, the industrial disturbances took a more serious turn. On Wednesday 8 March, conflict also broke out between the strikers and segments of the black population in various areas across the East Rand, which resulted in several deaths. Concurrently, many railway workers also joined the general strike. Smuts then sought and obtained the necessary authority from the Governor General, Prince Arthur of Connaught, to mobilise a number of ACF units for active service. However, it would take some time for the ACF units to mobilise and deploy to the Witwatersrand.

On the morning of 9 March, conditions on the Witwatersrand deteriorated further. So-called striker commandos became particularly aggressive and more daring in their actions. Moreover, railway communications between Johannesburg and surrounding centres were disrupted. With matters going from bad to worse, the necessary authority was granted to call out two complete infantry battalions, from the Railways & Harbours Brigade and the Durban Light Infantry, to help restore order. The Durban Light Infantry was at full strength, fully armed and equipped, and had recently conducted a training camp.

At this stage, martial law had not yet been proclaimed, which meant that the UDF was still only acting in aid of the civil power. On the morning of 10 March, the unrest reached a climax when strikers attacked several police stations across the Witwatersrand (see map). The situation developed into a state of semi-revolution. Furthermore, at Benoni, a pitched battle took place between strikers and police in the vicinity of the Trades Hall. Martial law was declared on the

Witwatersrand and adjoining magisterial districts on 10 March.

The General Staff took over the conducting of operations on the Witwatersrand. Additional ACF units and 26 Defence Rifle Associations (DRAs) were also mobilised from the adjoining magisterial districts. This greatly bolstered the strength of the UDF forces converging on the Witwatersrand. On Friday 10 March, the heaviest fighting occurred on the East Rand, particularly around Benoni and Brakpan. The fledgling South African Air Force (SAAF) conducted reconnaissance sorties over these locations to gauge the extent of unrest and the general dispositions of the revolutionary forces. These flights drew heavy fire, which damaged one aircraft and fatally injured an observer. By mid-morning, the situation in the Benoni–Brakpan area became critical. In response, a detachment of the Transvaal Scottish was sent by train to bolster the strength of the government forces in the area. As soon as this force arrived in the vicinity of Benoni, it was heavily engaged by a strong revolutionary force.

At this stage, the SAP in Benoni urgently requested Defence Headquarters to dispatch aircraft to bomb and, if possible, destroy the Trades Hall. The police had already suffered numerous casualties from the incessant heavy fire from revolutionaries occupying the building. Moreover, by mid-afternoon, Defence Headquarters had received further reports that the Transvaal Scottish were being forced back from Benoni by the revolutionary forces. As a result of the critical nature of the situation at hand, the bombing of the Benoni Trades Hall was authorised. During the subsequent bombing, the Trades Hall was damaged but not destroyed.

A further centre of revolutionary activity during the day was in the central sector, specifically the suburb of Fordsburg and its environs. In this sector, a squadron of policemen from Marshall Square were ordered to relieve the policemen who had earlier been overpowered at Newlands. On their way through Fordsburg, they were engaged by strong revolutionary forces concealed in the built-up terrain, and ultimately surrounded and overpowered. At mid-morning another SAP squadron was ordered to move from the Show Grounds to strengthen the police in the direction of Newlands. This squadron reached Brixton Ridge shortly before midday, where their progress was halted and they were surrounded by a strong force of approximately 1 200 revolutionaries.

By the evening of 10 March, despite the precarious position of the government forces and the reverses suffered, the revolutionary forces in the Vrededorp–Mayfair–Fordsburg area had been effectively hemmed in. However, central Johannesburg was still threatened. The general situation was serious. Nevertheless, if the lines of communication between Pretoria, Johannesburg and the Witwatersrand were to remain largely intact, the rapidly concentrating government forces could gain control of the operational situation.

At daybreak on Saturday 11 March, the revolutionary forces resumed operations. Heavy sniping and sustained fire were reported in the vicinity of Brixton, Vrededorp, Old Cemetery, Braamfontein and Fordsburg. Large groups of revolutionary forces were also reported to be active between Germiston and Johannesburg. In the eastern sector of the Witwatersrand, the SAAF conducted 15 reconnaissance flights during the day. At this stage, most aircraft were fully armed so as to engage any revolutionary forces that they might discover. The reconnaissance flights proved somewhat successful, and large bodies of revolutionary forces were successfully engaged. In the central sector, a revolutionary force surprised and attacked a 130-man detachment of the Imperial Light Horse at Ellis Park. The soldiers were busy cleaning their rifles and kit when the revolutionaries opened fire on their camp at close range. After the first onslaught, the soldiers reinforced their positions and took the offensive. In doing so, they drove off the revolutionary forces from the vicinity of Ellis Park, killing and wounding many.

Elsewhere on the Witwatersrand, government forces made no progress in Fordsburg during the day. The Trades Hall and Sacke's Hotel had been converted into veritable revolutionary strongholds. In a ridge of hills near Rietfontein, located along the crucial Germiston–Pretoria railway line, a revolutionary force of approximately 500 men were located and bombed by aircraft.

By the evening of 11 March, the incremental mobilisation and con-centration of government forces on the Witwatersrand had taken shape. However, it would be at least another day before these forces could actively take part in offensive operations. During the night, plans were made to take the offensive in the eastern and central sectors the next day. The focus of effort would be Brixton in the central area and Boksburg in the eastern area.

Fordsburg policemen captured by strikers during the 1922 Rand Revolt, after their release

Burghers passing the Trades Hall upon entering Benoni on Monday 13 March 1922

Burghers under the command of Lt Col AHM Nussey at the Auckland Park Racecourse

At daybreak on Sunday 12 March, aircraft located the revolutionary force responsible for blowing up the railway line at Driefontein the previous evening. This group was successfully intercepted by aircraft along a ridge near New Kleinfontein. However, throughout the day this group twice succeeded in causing further damage to the Germiston–Pretoria railway line. On both occasions, railway repair parties succeeded in restoring the line, which was effectively secured following the occupation of Rietfontein station.

Meanwhile, in the central sector, government forces under the command of Brig Gen PS Beves started their advance on Brixton Ridge to relieve the besieged police squadrons. Aircraft were again used to bombard the revolutionary forces, while food and ammunition were dropped on the police positions. The aerial bombardment caused a few casualties among the enemy and in due course the tactical situation on the ground changed. The police squadron on Brixton Ridge was successfully relieved and many revolutionaries surrendered. A further force under the command of Lt Col EF Thackeray also cleared the area between Parktown, Cleveland, Melville and the Auckland Park racecourse. The government forces were slowly regaining the operational initiative in the central sector.

In the eastern sector, a portion of Lt Gen (Sir) Jaap van Deventer's force under the command of Burne engaged a strong revolutionary force near Benoni. Van Deventer, like many of the other key role-players in the UDF during the Rand Revolt, was one of Smuts's trusted lieutenants. The subsequent counterattack near the Standard Brass Foundry was supported by artillery fire from two 13-pounders, which forced the revolutionary forces to abandon their positions and retire. Shortly before mid-afternoon, the first batch of DRA members arrived at Boksburg. Van Deventer then consolidated his immediate position.

In the western sector, a large force under the command of Lt Col AHM Nussey reached the vicinity of Krugersdorp and pushed on towards Roodepoort. With the proverbial noose tightening around the enemy throughout 12 March, the stage was now set for the final operations to dislodge the remaining revolutionary forces in the central and eastern sectors.

At daybreak on Monday 13 March, Van Deventer's forces resumed operations in the Boksburg–Benoni area. At mid-morning, his forces advanced into the heart of Benoni without meeting any serious opposition and took up positions at the Trades Hall. Van Deventer continued his advance in the direction of Brakpan, where his forces relieved a besieged police garrison. Meanwhile, forces under the command of Brig Gen CJ Brits and Col JJ Alberts advanced towards and occupied Springs.

In the western sector, Nussey's forces had pushed towards Maraisburg, meeting only very slight opposition. In doing so, Nussey's force established contact with Beves's men in the central sector, opening up the possibility for further cooperation against the revolutionary stronghold at Fordsburg.

Throughout 13 March, there was close cooperation between ground troops and aircraft during offensive operations. The government forces succeeded in completely enveloping the Witwatersrand area. Because of these tactical and operational developments, considerable numbers of troops – notably those under Van Deventer, Beves and Nussey – were now available to concentrate in and clear the Fordsburg area. Plans were made for the final assault on Fordsburg, to take place the following day.

During the early hours of Tuesday 14 March, aircraft dropped leaflets over Fordsburg and the surrounding areas calling upon women, children and government supporters to leave the area before the commencement of operations. Thousands of women and children soon left Fordsburg, but it appeared that the remaining men were determined to resist. Nevertheless, the mounting pressure prompted the revolutionaries to send forward an envoy and ask for conditions of surrender. Beves, unwilling to enter into lengthy negotiations, demanded an unconditional surrender by 11:00 or else offensive operations would start.

With no unconditional surrender forthcoming, final offensive operations in the central sector duly commenced. The government forces steadily applied pressure on the revolutionary positions around Fordsburg as government troops completed the encirclement of the area. A Whippet tank and three 13-pounder field guns were also deployed to bolster the attack. By early afternoon the revolutionary forces in Sacke's Hotel and the Market Hall had capitulated. At 15:00, Lt Col R Godley's police force met strong opposition in the southwest corner of Fordsburg. Beves reinforced Godley's force, and at 16:20 the last redoubt of revolutionary Fordsburg was overcome.

With the fall of Fordsburg on 14 March, organised resistance on the part of the revolutionary forces was broken. Most of the troops were employed in rounding up prisoners and conducting cordon-and-search operations over the following days. By 18 March these operations had been completed, and the demobilisation of government forces began.

The deployment in retrospect

A more nuanced and critical appraisal of the UDF operations provides several insights. At the outbreak of the Rand Revolt, the operational initiative lay with the revolutionary forces, and they achieved several minor tactical successes owing to their superior numbers and tactics. However, the tide turned from 12 March, when UDF reserves were deployed in large numbers. Over the following days, the government forces regained the operational initiative and achieved several tactical and operational successes across the Witwatersrand. As a result, the Rand Revolt was suppressed in a mere five days.

Soon after the demobilisation of forces, the General Staff started a process of reflecting critically on the recent operations. This process, it was hoped, would influence the doctrine, force design and operations of the UDF to suppress any future internal unrest. In terms of professionalisation, the UDF had come of age in 1922. Gone were the days when the prime minister and minister of defence personally led troops on operations, as Botha and Smuts had done during the First World War.

The General Staff agreed that the prevailing threat perceptions should remain unchanged. However, the UDF also had to ensure that it had sufficient forces available for rapid mobilisation and deployment and, above all, that it could safeguard essential government infrastructure and services in the event of unrest. It was thus suggested that at least five ACF units should undergo peacetime training and be maintained as organised units on the Witwatersrand, with a minimum of 50 per cent of wartime strength. Second, and to respond to the concerns regarding the rapid mobilisation of forces and the protection of essential services, it was argued that the preliminary mobilisation of reserves should be decentralised. This would allow units to respond immediately to any local attacks, reinforce local security forces and secure vital government, economic and industrial infrastructure.

However, it was also evident that it was the SAAF that had prevented the revolutionary forces from achieving further operational successes during the disturbances. In fact, the Rand Revolt highlighted the necessity of close and intelligent cooperation between ground and air forces. The Director of Air Services, Col (Sir) HA (Pierre) van Ryneveld, argued that the air force could have played an even more pronounced role if he had been allowed to concentrate the aerial bombing on the nucleus of the revolutionary forces earlier. Thus, instead of the gradual commitment of aircraft and incremental aerial bombing efforts, Van Ryneveld advocated timely, concentrated aerial bombardments and interdiction in the event of future internal unrest.

While Van Ryneveld argued for close cooperation between land forces and aircraft, in practice such cooperation had proved difficult to realise. For one thing, an extremely short-sighted policy, partly driven by fiscal constraints, meant that wireless communication between ground forces and aircraft was non-existent. Thus, for the sake of saving a paltry £2 000 per annum of the defence budget, ground troops had to make use of an intricate, and largely flawed, system of ground signals to communicate with aircraft during operations. Moreover, pilots and observers found it extremely difficult to distinguish between government troops and revolutionary forces and were therefore forced to descend to unreasonably low altitudes to identify forces on the ground. Only if they were fired upon could they be sure of hostile intent and engage the enemy.

Clearly, the operations conducted by the UDF to suppress the Rand Revolt represented warfare by trial and error. This was not surprising, given the UDF's experience in suppressing internal unrest. Moreover, its wartime experience had been dominated, on the one hand, by highly mobile operations, and, on the other, by largely static trench warfare. While arguably capable of conducting rural counterinsurgency operations, the UDF had no real operational experience or institutional memory of urban warfare.

Fortunately for the UDF, despite the initial successes of the revolutionary forces, and their apparent high morale, their use of the urban terrain was poor. In some instances, the revolutionary forces tried to build roadblocks, dig trenches and fortify buildings, but they failed to use the cover and concealment, and the sheer scale and complexity, of the urban environment to their advantage.

Despite their overall success in suppressing the Rand Revolt, the government forces suffered heavy casualties. However, this is unsurprising, since it is generally accepted that urban warfare entails heavy casualties: a few determined men, armed with modern weapons and skilled in their use, and operating in a built-up environment, can inflict terrible losses on an adversary.

During the Rand Revolt, the UDF conducted high-tempo manoeuvre-type operations instead of the methodical firepower-driven approach sometimes associated with urban warfare. In doing so, they deprived the revolutionary forces of the luxury of time and prevented them from further strengthening their hold on large areas of the Witwatersrand. Once sufficient forces had been mobilised and deployed, the UDF managed to outmanoeuvre the revolutionaries. By using counterviolence and high-tempo operations, especially from 12 March onwards, the UDF kept the revolutionary forces off balance, interrupting their organisational framework and forcing them to continuously give ground and retreat.

Ultimately, however, the UDF managed to locate, isolate and neutralise the revolutionary forces in a piecemeal fashion. Once the centre of gravity of the revolutionary forces was located, the UDF isolated the pockets of resistance and prevented any further cooperation between them. After that, the military forces executed a large pincer movement across the eastern, western and southern sectors of the Witwatersrand before concentrating all forces for a final decisive showdown with the revolutionary forces in Boksburg and Fordsburg. The UDF was thus able to concentrate overwhelming force in space and time to suppress the revolt.

During March 1922, in the wake of the declaration of martial law, the UDF conducted high-tempo manoeuvre-type operations to suppress the large-scale violent industrial unrest that had broken out across the Witwatersrand. However, the UDF had not been caught totally unprepared by the crisis. Two separate mobilisation schemes drafted as early as 1919, and updated in 1921, allowed military reserves to be mobilised and deployed rapidly in the event of serious industrial disturbances. Following the deployment of the small Permanent Force, several ACF and DRA units were mobilised and deployed to the affected areas in early March. While the government forces suffered some initial setbacks, the operational initiative soon shifted to the UDF once enough troops moved in and restored law and order across the Witwatersrand. Moreover, the overall UDF operations were designed to envelop the revolutionary forces completely, which allowed the government forces to deal with the isolated pockets of resistance piecemeal. The deployment of the UDF's infantry, artillery, armour and aircraft in high-tempo combined-arms operations gave the government forces a definite edge over their adversaries.

The UDF's success in suppressing the industrial unrest also raised several concerns. The deployment to the Witwatersrand highlighted more than ever that the UDF needed to change from a conventional force to one organised to conduct low-intensity counterinsurgency operations across any possible terrain where and when called upon. Considering the increasing threats to the state's security and legitimacy during the interwar period, it was argued that a more sophisticated defence force would be required. Such a defence force would need to be appropriately structured, sufficiently staffed and adequately armed and equipped and have the appropriate doctrine to respond to any of the prevailing threats. While the UDF was quite capable of conducting large-scale rural counterinsurgency operations, the Rand Revolt was its first real test in an urban environment. It did not yet have the required institutional expertise or the appropriate doctrine or force design for urban warfare. However, for the foreseeable future, the UDF would be preoccupied with rural counterinsurgency operations, such as the Bondelswarts Rebellion of 1922.

The Bondelswarts Rebellion, 1922

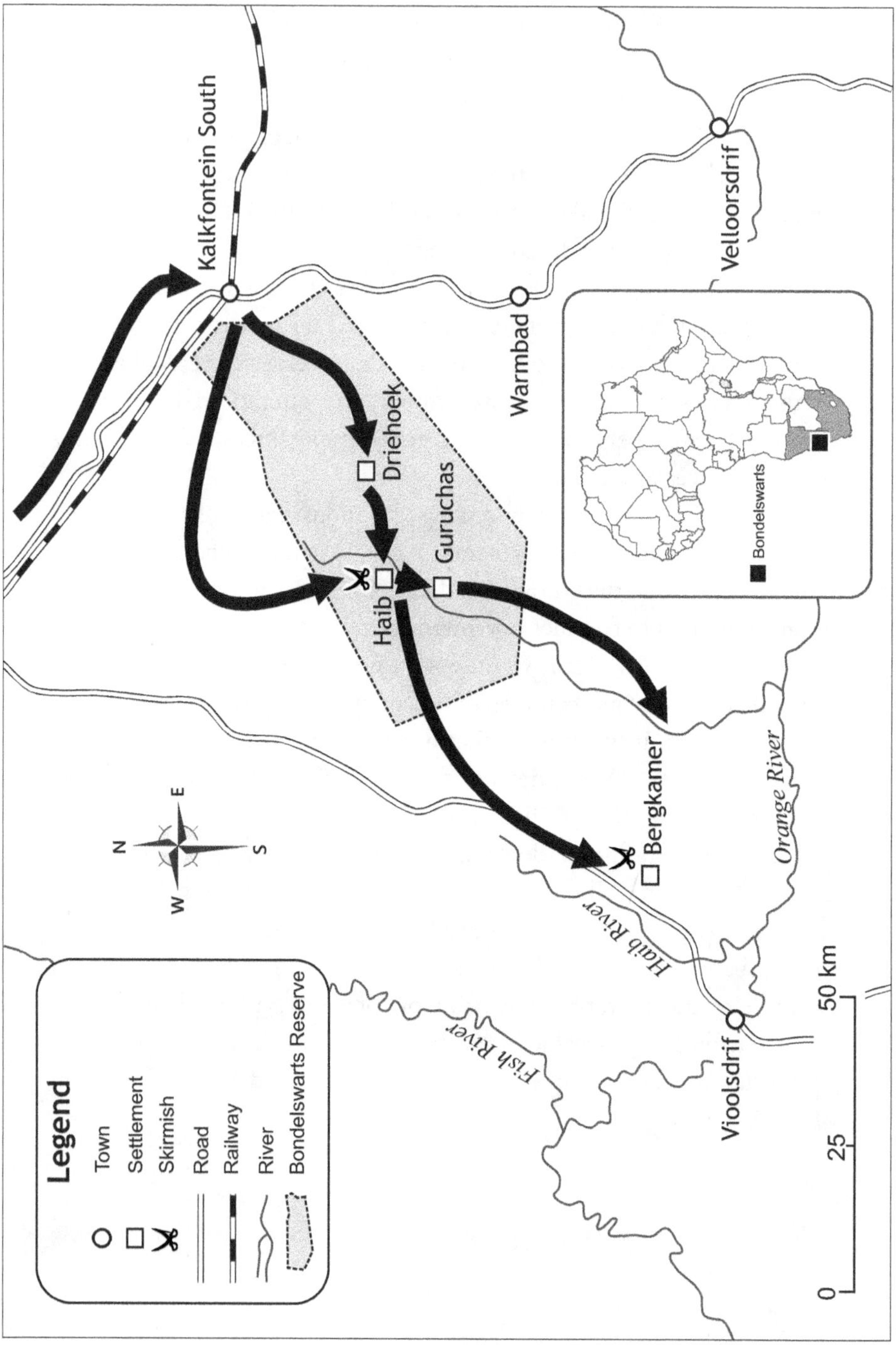
Kalkfontein South
Velloorsdrif
Warmbad
Driehoek
Guruchas
Haib
Bergkamer
Orange River
Haib River
Fish River
Vioolsdrif
Bondelswarts
N
E
S
W
Legend
Town
Settlement
Skirmish
Road
Railway
River
Bondelswarts Reserve
0
25
50 km

7

BONDELSWARTS REBELLION, 1922

Since Union in 1910, the nascent UDF had been deployed on several occasions to deal swiftly with internal conflict within the country's borders. Before 1918, these military actions, which today we would call 'counterinsurgency operations', included quelling industrial unrest, the Afrikaner Rebellion of 1914, and growing black resistance to white rule. In the case of the latter, the most prominent deployment was to South West Africa in 1917 during the Ovamboland Expedition, when a small contingent of the UDF was deployed to dispose of the rebellious Chief Mandume Ya Ndemufayo of the Ovakuanyama.

During the post-war period, the UDF and the SAP would again be called upon to deal with several outbreaks of internal unrest that challenged the authority and legitimacy of the state. But, as we have seen, fiscal, political and manpower constraints adversely affected the nature, organisation and operability of the UDF. Both the Israelite Rebellion of 1921 and the Rand Revolt of 1922 caught the Union government and the security forces by surprise. Despite the success of these operations, several issues relating to command and control, training, administration and discipline were noted.

It was against this backdrop, mere months after quashing the Rand Revolt, that the SAP and elements of the UDF were called upon to quell the so-called Bondelswarts Rebellion in SWA. The tough and proud Bondelswarts people, dissatisfied that their political and economic grievances were going unheard, embarked on limited offensive actions. They were accustomed to the arid terrain, and although the uprising did not gather overwhelming support, it certainly got the attention of the authorities. The Union government was keen to maintain control and, fearful of the rebellion escalating, quickly deployed the military and the police. The security forces had to shift their attention rapidly from the high-intensity urban operations used in suppressing the Rand Revolt to low-intensity rural counterinsurgency operations conducted in unfamiliar broken terrain and against wily and reputable guerrilla fighters.

Background to the rebellion

South Africa had claimed South West Africa following the successful campaign of 1915 (see Chapter 3). At the end of the First World War, the territory was formally placed under Union governance and the Class C mandate granted by the League of Nations allowed South Africa to administer SWA as part of its territory. However, the people of SWA wanted their independence – something that would test the Union's willingness to engage in 'small wars'. It was against this backdrop, and in the vast territory of SWA, that several groups, with differing identities and interests, sought greater political representation and possible independence.

One such group were the Bondelswarts, a nomadic pastoral people who mainly practised transhumance. Since the early 19th century, the Bondelswarts had inhabited an arid and inhospitable part of the southern Warmbad district near the South African border. They had had a complicated relationship with the German colonial government following the German occupation of the territory in the 1880s. Relations between the Germans and the Bondelswarts were strained – especially after the German-Herero Wars (1904–1908). The influx of large numbers of European farmers also pushed the Bondelswarts further from their traditional pastoral areas. As a result, a large group of Bondelswarts fled to the Union to escape German rule. The Bondelswarts therefore viewed the First World War as an opportunity to regain some measure of independence and the restoration of their status and lands under the Union government.

During the campaign in GSWA, the Germans forcibly removed and relocated the Bondelswarts to Tsumeb in the north of the territory. The forced removal of the Bondelswarts resulted in considerable loss of cattle and other livestock. Following the conclusion of the military campaign, the Union government resettled the Bondelswarts in their reserve in the Warmbad district in August 1915. There they would suffer further deprivations. The loss of their livestock, ill-treatment of farm workers and low wages, coupled with the lack of industry and other economic opportunities, increased their dissatisfaction. This was in addition to several unanswered grievances related to rampant poverty and boundary disputes, and this tense and volatile situation was further aggravated by significant oppressive legislation.

These were some of the underlying causes of the Bondelswarts Rebellion. But the more immediate cause was the desire of the Bondelswarts residing in South Africa to return to their reserve in SWA. Their request was turned down by the Union authorities at Warmbad. So, in August 1919, the heir apparent, Jacobus Christian, along with some followers, disregarded the authorities and returned to the territory without the necessary permits. After coming into conflict with the authorities, Christian surrendered himself to the local magistrate in Warmbad and was fined for breaking the law. However, Christian and his followers were allowed to settle in the reserve on condition that they surrendered their arms and ammunition, did not interfere in the administration of the reserve and respected the authority of the nominal headman, Timotheus Beukes. The successful return of Christian prompted a further group of exiled Bondelswarts to return. Tension soon followed when Christian wanted to be recognised as the official hereditary chief of the Bondelswarts. While the Union government would not entertain this matter, it was apparent that the real influence and power over the Bondelswarts rested with Christian.

Towards the end of April 1922, the exiled guerrilla fighter Abraham Morris, along with some followers, also crossed back into SWA to return to the Bondelswarts reserve. Unsure of his motives, the Union authorities speculated that Morris had been invited to join the Bondelswarts drive for improved living conditions. His return was immediately detected by the Union authorities, with the police at Raman's Drift reporting his crossing to Fleck, the magistrate at Warmbad, on 24 April. Evidence suggests that Morris was aware that he needed to report to the authorities at Warmbad to obtain the necessary permit and approval for his return. On

28 April, Christian reported to Noothout, the Location Superintendent at Driehoek, in the reserve, that Morris was on his way to Haib and that it was his intention to report to Fleck. Fleck asked Noothout to write to Morris and instruct him to report to Warmbad immediately. In the meantime, large numbers of Bondelswarts started congregating at Haib to welcome back the legendary Morris. By 5 May he had not yet reported to Fleck and two policemen were sent to determine whether Morris had the necessary permits and, if not, to arrest him.

The first sparks of the rebellion flared on Monday 8 May. The prelude to this encounter took place the weekend before, when Sergeant JA van Niekerk and Constable Gert Kraai met with Morris at Haib. During the meeting, Morris handed over his rifle and ammunition and agreed to pay the nominal fine for not having the correct permit. On the Sunday, Van Niekerk informed Christian that he had instructions to arrest Morris unless he voluntarily presented himself to Fleck. Eventually it was agreed that Christian would escort Morris to Warmbad. However, on the Monday the Bondelswarts, who had grown increasingly suspicious, were unwilling to allow Morris to travel to Warmbad. Van Niekerk became aware of the situation and, keen to regain control, gave the Bondelswarts four hours to reconsider their decision. Later, when he arrived at Guruchas, events began to run out of control. When Van Niekerk attempted to arrest Morris, the Bondelswarts indicated that they would forcibly oppose such a move. Van Niekerk warned the Bondelswarts that in such a case force would be used against them. The Bondelswarts, considering this a declaration of war, began military preparations.

Once Fleck was informed of what had transpired in the reserve, he contacted Christian and instructed him to report immediately to Warmbad. Christian ignored the message, assuming that he would probably be arrested. Fleck informed Gysbert Hofmeyr, the Administrator of SWA, of the deteriorating security situation and requested the deployment of a strong police force. Hofmeyr dispatched Maj Van Coller, the head of the police force in the territory, to conduct an initial investigation, explain the laws of the country to the Bondelswarts and arrest Morris and his followers.

On 13 May, Van Coller and a small detachment of police arrived at

Kalkfontein South. Van Coller immediately tried to open negotiations with Christian and requested a meeting at Driehoek. Christian refused to attend, citing Van Niekerk's apparent declaration of war as a reason. The SWA administration was keen to open dialogue with the Bondelswarts, and on 15 May Hofmeyr ordered Fleck to continue with negotiations. Van Coller instructed Noothout, along with Monsignor Krolikowski – the head of the local Catholic mission – to travel to the reserve on 17 May and deliver the government's demands, specifically that it had no intention of declaring war on the Bondelswarts and that all that was required was for Morris to report to Fleck.

During the subsequent meeting at Guruchas, the Bondelswarts, including several armed members, demanded a written assurance from Hofmeyr that if the men surrendered themselves, no further action would be taken against them. While Noothout agreed to wire a letter from the Bondelswarts to Hofmeyr officially requesting such assurances, he cautioned that if they remained uncooperative, drastic measures would be taken against them.

On 19 May, Hofmeyr instructed Van Coller, along with Krolikowski, to meet with Christian and to bring the Bondelswarts to reason and prevent unnecessary bloodshed. However, Krolikowski refused to accompany Van Coller, as he was wary of being identified with the authorities. On 20 May, Krolikowski compromised and delivered a message that Van Coller was acting on behalf of the government, but that none of the Bondelswarts' demands could be met. This message was met with suspicion and the Bondelswarts countered with a request to meet Hofmeyr in person. Before leaving for Keetmanshoop, Krolikowski advised Van Coller and Fleck not to visit the reserve since it would aggravate the already tense situation.

On 21 May, and disregarding Krolikowski's warning, Van Coller, Fleck and Noothout travelled to the reserve to deliver Hofmeyr's original message. Upon their arrival, Van Coller delivered the unchanged demands and indicated that if these conditions were not met, there would be serious repercussions. He also re-emphasised that Van Niekerk had no authority to declare war on behalf of the Union government and that the Bondelswarts would have two further days in which to comply with Hofmeyr's conditions. Despite the overtures, Van Coller was convinced that the Bondelswarts would resist any attempt to arrest Morris and his companions.

On 22 May, the Bondelswarts met to discuss Hofmeyr's conditions and agree on the way forward. While there were internal divisions, the motion to resist carried the day. The next day the Bondelswarts delivered their written reply to Hofmeyr's conditions to Noothout, who relayed it to the Administrator. This letter signalled the start of hostilities. Hofmeyr extended a final invitation to Christian to meet him in person to find a solution to the problem and avoid conflict, but the invitation was completely ignored.

Suppressing the rebellion

Owing to the rapidly deteriorating situation in the Warmbad district, Hofmeyr sanctioned a limited operation to put down the rebellion. The subsequent rural counterinsurgency operation, designed to restore law and order, was characterised by the use of local volunteers and by mounted and dismounted infantry acting in cooperation with aircraft.

Hofmeyr ordered the magistrates in the Keetmanshoop, Warmbad and Gibeon districts to proceed with the recruitment of local volunteers to serve as special constables for the duration of operations. His decision to use local volunteers was based on two reasons. First, Hofmeyr did not want to place a further burden on the Union's security apparatus following the recent conclusion of the Rand Revolt. Second, he believed that the local settler population had a vested interest in ensuring safety and security within the territory. Only later, once he acknowledged the inadequacy of his volunteer force, did he request support from the UDF – especially in the form of aircraft, machine-gun sections and an artillery component.

The volunteers, envisaged to total some 200 mounted men, were to report to the various railway centres in their districts before travelling to Kalkfontein South. By 19 May, Hofmeyr's initial call to arms had failed to secure the required volunteer numbers. The authorities even considered the possibility of declaring martial law and relying on commandeering to bolster the numbers. Hofmeyr, leading from the front with a force of 60 men comprising his staff and civil servants, left Windhoek and made his way south. This had the desired effect, with more volunteers answering the call to arms. Thus, when Hofmeyr arrived at Kalkfontein South on 23 May, his force numbered some 100 men. Over the coming days, further volunteers from the Keetmanshoop and Warmbad districts reported for duty. By 25 May, nearly 400 mounted infantrymen were available.

Once Hofmeyr's force had concentrated at Kalkfontein South, the next phase of the operation commenced. Hofmeyr, a civil servant with limited military and policing experience, assumed the temporary rank of colonel and took personal command of the operations despite the availability of more experienced officers such as Van Coller. The rationale behind this decision appears to have been his insistence that any delay in dealing with the rebellion could ultimately lead to further uprisings.

In planning for the operation, Hofmeyr acknowledged that Morris had an intimate knowledge of the operating environment and that he was a reputable guerrilla fighter with vast experience of irregular warfare. He therefore planned to completely envelop the Bondelswarts reserve, and then systematically clear the Bondelswarts out of their strongholds – particularly at Haib and Guruchas. Then his forces would occupy the reserve and take possession of all livestock and property. Hofmeyr further planned to prevent the Bondelswarts from leaving the reserve and moving into their traditional mountain strongholds along the Fish and Orange rivers. He therefore accelerated the mobilisation of local volunteers, oversaw the rapid deployment of government forces, occupied strategic positions and tried to strike a quick and decisive blow to restore control within the territory.

However, the Union authorities had not been caught off-guard by the deteriorating security situation. From 1915 onwards, they had been aware of both the current and the historic grievances harboured by the Bondelswarts. In fact, when writing up his official report on the Bondelswarts Rebellion in June 1922, Hofmeyr identified both the remote and the immediate causes of the unrest. The Union authorities therefore had a good grasp of the human elements that underpinned the Bondelswarts Rebellion in all its complexity.

The location of the Bondelswarts Rebellion in geographic space and time was relatively straightforward and was made possible by timely intelligence reports received from the local authorities – especially Noothout, Fleck and Van Coller. The intelligence-driven approach allowed the authorities to identify, track and monitor the rebellion while it was still in its infancy and to implement the appropriate counter-response. Thus, once the actors and institutions of the Bondelswarts Rebellion were located in practical and conceptual terms, Hofmeyr and his administration could orchestrate their physical and political isolation.

The Union authorities feared that the Bondelswarts Rebellion could ignite a more general uprising among the black population in SWA. Their concern was not unfounded. On 19 May, Hofmeyr received reports of considerable unrest brewing among the black population in the Keetmanshoop and Gibeon districts. Hofmeyr was particularly wary that these groups would offer military support to the Bondelswarts in the event of armed conflict. The government's concerns were intensified by reports of armed Bondelswarts forcibly collecting arms and ammunition from isolated farmers in the Warmbad district. Collectively, these events created a state of general panic among the local settler population as the security situation continued to deteriorate. It was against this backdrop that Hofmeyr had to act decisively and effectively isolate and neutralise the threat at hand.

Hofmeyr and his staff implemented several measures to physically isolate the Bondelswarts Rebellion to the Warmbad district alone. Hofmeyr relied on Col De Jager and Andries de Wet to hold the central position at Windhoek and closely monitor the unfolding situation within the territory – particularly in the central and northern districts. In the event of an emergency, they could call up additional volunteers and rapidly deploy these forces to any flashpoints. Across the border in the Union, Lt Col HF Trew, the head of the SAP in the Western Districts, instructed police reinforcements in the Steinkopf region to assist with border patrols along the Orange River. These forces were to prevent any Bondelswarts or sympathisers from crossing the border. The deployment of a military contingent under the command of Lt Col AHM Nussey to support the police and act as a blocking force was also sanctioned. Nussey and his force were therefore ordered to prepare for rapid deployment should military intervention become necessary.

With the Bondelswarts located and isolated in physical space and time through a combination of local intelligence and aerial reconnaissance,

Hofmeyr positioned his forces for a swift operation to neutralise Morris's force. The capture or killing of Morris also remained a key tactical objective throughout the operation. Moreover, with the noose steadily closing on the Bondelswarts fighters, the government forces also occupied the waterholes at Wortel, Driehoek, Dawigabis, Neuwfontein, Auputs and Norachas. In doing so, they surrounded and cordoned off the Bondelswarts reserve. However, during the early course of operations, the Bondelswarts retained the tactical initiative, ambushing Union forces between Driehoek, Wortel and Us. Nevertheless, by 28 May, Morris's forces were in complete retreat, fully aware of the government pincers closing in on them.

A Union force received information from local farmers as to the whereabouts of the Bondelswarts fighters deployed in and around Neuwfontein. Morris and his followers set up an ambush in which there was an exchange of gunfire with the government forces. Following this limited tactical engagement, the Union forces went into defensive positions while the Bondelswarts withdrew across the inhospitable terrain. On 29 May, however, a combined air and ground assault was launched on the Bondelswarts' central position between Haib and Guruchas. The combined attack, which culminated on the morning of 30 June, completely enveloped the rebel positions. This resulted in the surrender of 90 men and approximately 700 women and children, as well as the confiscation of 1 400 head of cattle and other livestock. It was learned that Morris and a group of armed men, between 50 and 200 strong, had escaped the area under cover of darkness and were headed in the direction of the Orange River. After the attack on Haib and Guruchas, Hofmeyr believed the rebellion to be over and returned to Neuwfontein.

The fact that Morris and a large group of armed Bondelswarts had escaped was a concern for Defence Headquarters. They estimated that, without his capture or neutralisation, the potential for further uprisings within the territory remained. Moreover, Hofmeyr's claim that the rebellion was over was met with disbelief. Pretoria expressed a clear lack of confidence in Hofmeyr, stating that they would continue to monitor the situation and, if need be, replace him with a 'first class' commander.

Defence Headquarters was right to be suspicious of Hofmeyr's premature claim of victory, especially since the Bondelswarts proved to be crafty opponents. Union forces struggled to pursue Morris and his armed followers in the difficult terrain, and it was only through a combination of aerial reconnaissance and local guides that police units were able to track Morris's force.

A strong force under Acting Inspector Prinsloo set out from Haib in pursuit of Morris and his followers. Operating in a dispersed fashion over a wide geographical area, there were definite concerns about the ability to reinforce individual units and maintain their lines of communication. The lack of waterholes in the area also made the situation even more difficult. In due course, aircraft located the Bondelswarts fighters moving in the direction of Vioolsdrift and a force under Lieutenant Jordaan pursued them through a gorge, driving them in the direction of Prinsloo and his men.

But Morris and his followers escaped from the gorge and made their way to a tributary of the Orange River. On 2 June, they were spotted by aircraft, which strafed them with machine-gun fire and dropped 40 bombs in their proximity. The pilots provided coordinating instructions and pinpointed the new location of Morris's group to the ground forces. With the updated information, the pursuers set out to locate and engage Morris's fighters at a spot between Haibmund and Vioolsdrift, some 16 km north of the Orange River. It was also later claimed that Morris, Beukes and Christian were all injured during the airstrike.

Morris and his followers became increasingly desperate as they traversed the difficult terrain along the Orange River. The terrain also made it extremely difficult for the aircraft to observe their movements. But aerial reconnaissance managed again to locate the Bondelswarts fighters near Vioolsdrift on 3 June and reported their positions to Prinsloo, who proceeded in the direction of Vioolsdrift from Goodhouse, while Jordaan and his men travelled from Haibmund to reinforce Prinsloo.

On 4 June, Morris ambushed Prinsloo's force near Vioolsdrift, but Prinsloo and his men were able to extricate themselves. Aerial support then established that Morris and his guerrilla fighters had moved towards Tsavisis. The Union forces reported significant rebel casualties after the engagement, while sustaining only four injuries themselves.

Captain Balt and his force made further contact with a group of

Bondelswarts fighters near Gams on 5 June, forcing them to retreat in the direction of Haibmund. Informed of the Bondelswarts' new positions, the Union forces cooperated closely in tracking the fleeing fighters. With Trew setting up camp close to Jakkalswater, approximately 40 km from Viooolsdrift, the Union forces once more tightened the noose around Morris's group, forcing them into further difficult terrain. At the same time, prisoners confirmed that Morris himself had died of wounds sustained during one of the earlier attacks.

The Bondelswarts finally surrendered at Uhabis on 7 June. Both Beukes and Christian were among the group of 120 men – armed with only 50 rifles. It was reported that approximately 200 more men had fled into the hinterland. Beukes and Christian were treated in hospital, along with more than 800 women and children. Displaced civilians were also fed, and Hendrik Mentz, the minister of defence, ordered that no further action be taken against the Bondelswarts. Beukes and Christian laid the blame for the rebellion squarely at the feet of Morris. Reports from prisoners also claimed that the rebellion had ultimately collapsed following the death of Morris.

The operations to suppress the Bondelswarts Rebellion can mainly be classified as a rural counterinsurgency policing action with very limited involvement by the UDF. The Union and SWA authorities reacted to a perceived breach of authority and with the personalities involved, and the ever-present fear of further uprisings in the territory, events in the Warmbad district quickly got out of control. In hindsight, if the Union authorities had responded to the underlying and immediate grievances and made concessions through further diplomatic overtures, the Bondelswarts Rebellion could have taken a different shape and form. However, this is mere speculation.

Viewed through a cold military lens, the operations to suppress the Bondelswarts Rebellion were entirely successful, despite evoking strong condemnation from the international community at large and the League of Nations in particular. Although the operations were brief, there were several notable developments. The rapid mobilisation of a part of the local population as a paramilitary reserve proved to be a definite force multiplier within the territory. Hofmeyr's decision to recruit local volunteers with a vested interest in ensuring the rule of law and stability within SWA directly correlates with contemporary counterinsurgency theory, which advocates the recruitment and deployment of local troops in regional security operations. Moreover, the operations highlighted the crucial role of reserves to both the police and the defence force. The timely deployment of aircraft also provided the Union forces with an unsurpassed advantage in the form of aerial reconnaissance, liaison duties and close air support. Despite some tactical challenges, close air-to-ground cooperation provided a definite measure of success to the government forces during the final pursuit of the Bondelswarts along the Orange River. In future, South Africa would rely increasingly on airpower, and especially on the notion of 'air policing', to supress internal unrest within the Union and SWA.

However, for the remainder of the interwar period, the state of South African defence deteriorated. The UDF, infrequently called upon to assist with the suppression of internal unrest, entered a downward spiral. Amid further post-war rationalisation, a change of government in 1924 and a shrinking defence budget, the UDF became characterised by a severe state of unpreparedness and questionable force design. The dire state of South African defence would be rectified only with the coming of the Second World War.

8

SOUTHERN ETHIOPIA, 1941

Throughout the interwar period, the UDF was affected by muddled thinking about future trends in warfare, modernisation and innovation. During this period, JBM Hertzog and Oswald Pirow – prime minister and minister of defence respectively – maintained that the Union had no immediate threat to its sovereignty. However, Italy's annexation of Ethiopia (then Abyssinia) and parts of Somalia (then Italian Somaliland) in May 1936 soon displaced this notion. Despite these events, a firm belief remained that the sole purpose of the UDF was to protect the Union's neutrality. Politically, it was also felt that South Africa should remain neutral in the event of a European conflict. By the latter half of the 1930s, with tensions mounting in Europe and a changing geo-political landscape in Africa, the Union's preparations for the looming global conflict were entirely inadequate.

The South African declaration of war against Germany on 6 September 1939 was the catalyst needed to transform the UDF into a modern defence force capable of projecting offensive power across Africa. From the outset, Jan Smuts, the new prime minister, advocated active participation in the war at the behest of Britain. Throughout the 1930s, Smuts had argued that the Union's first line of defence was further afield in Africa and not simply beyond its immediate borders. On 7 September, Smuts approached the British War Office and proposed to send a South African contingent to Kenya as a vanguard, with further troops earmarked for deployment once trained.

The Chief of the General Staff, Lt Gen Sir Pierre van Ryneveld, also warned Defence Headquarters of Italy's possible belligerence on the

101

The Offensive Operations in Southern Ethiopia, 1941

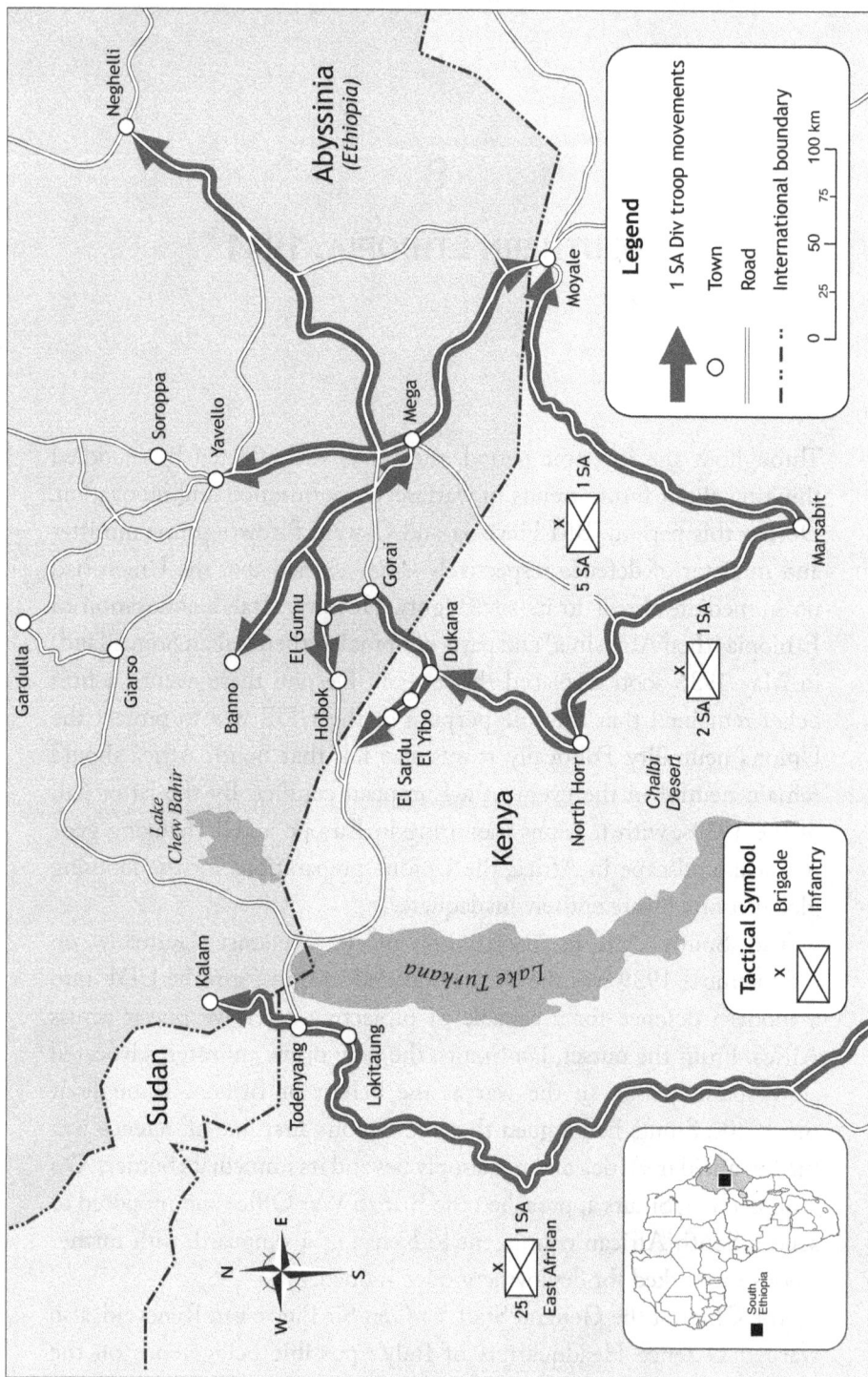

Legend

1 SA Div troop movements

○ Town

International boundary

Road

0 25 50 75 100 km

Abyssinia
(Ethiopia)

Neghelli

Soroppa

Yavello

Mega

Moyale

Gardulla

Giarso

Banno

El Gumu

Gorai

Dukana

Marsabit

1 SA
5 SA

Hobok

El Sardu
El Yibo

North Horr

1 SA
2 SA

Chalbi
Desert

Lake
Chew Bahir

Kenya

Kalam

Lake Turkana

Sudan

Todenyang

Lokitaung

25 1 SA
East African

Tactical Symbol

x Brigade

Infantry

South
Ethiopia

side of Germany. He argued that Italian armies could simultaneously overrun Sudan and Egypt, threatening British possessions in East Africa. During December, Anthony Eden, the British Secretary of State for Dominion Affairs, informed Smuts that the Italian presence in East Africa was in no way threatening. Britain also wished not to provoke Italian aggression by deploying large numbers of troops to this theatre. On 20 December, the British government thus indicated that the deployment of UDF troops to Kenya might become necessary only if the geopolitical situation changed drastically.

However, by January 1940, the Commander-in-Chief of the Middle East, Lt Gen Sir Archibald Wavell, advocated that Britain should defend her possessions in East Africa in the event of a war with Italy. He even contended that with sufficient troops the Allies could launch an offensive in this theatre and drive Italian forces from Ethiopia, Eritrea and Somalia. Smuts received a telegram from London in February, reminding him of his suggestion to deploy South African troops to Kenya as a precautionary measure. Smuts duly accepted the British proposal and on 7 February informed the Union Parliament that UDF operations would now extend as far north as Kenya. The first South African soldiers arrived in Kenya at the start of June 1940 to help protect the territory. This was a remarkable feat, given that, in a mere ten months, Smuts managed the complete turnaround of the defence force and succeeded in raising nearly two full field divisions of volunteers.

On 10 June 1940, Italy declared war on Britain. The Union followed suit and declared war on Italy, which meant that the nearest military threat to South African sovereignty was now located in East Africa. Towards the end of June, the supreme commander of the Italian forces in East Africa, Prince Amadeo of Savoy, the Duke of Aosta, ordered tentative thrusts into British territory to gauge the Allied defences. During the first week of July, Italian forces attacked Moyale in Kenya, Kassala in Sudan and Gallabat on the Sudan–Ethiopia border. These offensives, albeit limited in scope, highlighted the numerical inferiority of British troops in East Africa and caused some concern at the War Office. However, Winston Churchill, the new British prime minister, believed that the possibility of an all-out Italian invasion of Kenya was inconceivable.

A steady stream of South African units continued to arrive in East Africa throughout the latter half of 1940. In mid-August, the 1st South African Division (1 SA Div) was established under the command of Maj Gen George Brink, comprising the 1st, 2nd and 5th South African Infantry Brigades (SA Inf Bde) under the command of brigadiers Dan Pienaar, Ferdinand Buchanan and Frank Armstrong respectively. By the beginning of December, the entire 1 SA Div was in the theatre and took over the defence of the Marsabit area in northern Kenya. The South African troops soon undertook intensive patrols from Isiolo towards the border of Ethiopia and Somalia in search of the Italian vanguard.

Strategic and operational considerations

At a strategic meeting held at Khartoum, in Sudan, towards the end of October 1940, it was decided that the Italians could be driven from East Africa by a series of coordinated attacks launched from Kenya and Sudan. Operations in East Africa were dependent on rainfall, so the period between December and March would offer the best weather conditions. The meeting therefore decided that the offensives in East Africa would start early in 1941. At the end of the meeting, Lt Gen Alan Cunningham was appointed as the new GOC East African Force. He replaced Maj Gen Douglas Dickinson, who was recalled after an apparent disagreement with Smuts over the overall strategy and employment of South African troops under his command.

During the first week of December, Wavell held a further conference with Cunningham and Maj Gen William Platt, GOC Sudan Defence Force, to decide on an overall plan of action for the East African offensives. Wavell emphasised the importance of synchronising the respective offensive operations across the theatre. He and his staff were convinced that the Massawa–Asmara area, Djibouti and Addis Ababa represented the strategic nerve centre of Italian East Africa and, if they were threatened in unison, resistance would crumble piecemeal. The combined offensives thus rested on three pillars. First, from Sudan, Platt's forces were to capture the Kassala–Sabdarat–Tessenei triangle on the Sudan–Eritrea border. Second, from Kenya, Cunningham would capture Kismayu and threaten the area around Lake Rudolf. Finally, a patriotic Shifta revolt needed to be sparked in Ethiopia to harass the Italian forces and make the countryside ungovernable.

Upon his return to Nairobi in December 1940, Cunningham decided to postpone the capture of Kismayu, designated Operation Canvas, to May–June 1941. His decision, contrary to Wavell's plan, was based on several considerations: a shortage of water supplies, a belief that Italian morale was high, insufficient numbers of trained troops and inadequate motor transport to move and provision his forces. Cunningham instead decided to advance on the frontier with Ethiopia and Somalia and establish a defensive line. These movements, known as 'cutting-out' operations, culminated in the establishment of a series of administrative facilities and supply depots to secure sufficient stockpiles before the main Allied offensive began in January 1941.

Cunningham expressed his wish that operations in the vicinity of Lake Rudolf were to start as soon as possible. The southern Ethiopian province of Galla-Sidamo was to be attacked by Brink's 1 SA Div, and Wavell instructed Cunningham to employ these troops on irregular lines. He argued that small mobile columns should be used to harass and occupy Italian outposts, attack their lines of communication and foment a Shifta revolt. This style of warfare, it was argued, suited the UDF's penchant for manoeuvre-type operations, largely considered to be South Africa's strength. Despite the Somalia operations receiving priority, Cunningham realised that Brink and his division could actively threaten Addis Ababa before the arrival of the rainy season.

On 15 January 1941, the Allies launched combined offensives across East Africa. Cunningham and his staff had allotted several pertinent objectives to Brink and his division. They were to secure the area around Dukana, Hobok and Gebel Affur, and protect and develop communications in this sector to assist in the eventual invasion of Ethiopia. Brink was furthermore tasked with using flying columns, invariably drawn from the South African Tank Corps units under his command, to support the Shifta rebellion forming in the general area north of Banno. Finally, the 25th (East Africa) Infantry Brigade, attached to 1 SA Div for this period, was ordered to capture Namaruputh, Todenyang and Kalam.

On 12 January 1940, Cunningham visited Brink at his headquarters at Marsabit to discuss his upcoming offensive operations. The attachment of Pienaar's 1 SA Inf Bde to the 12th (African) Division remained a bone of contention. Brink suggested to Cunningham that 1 SA Inf Bde revert to his command, since this would allow him to secure the Moyale–Mega–El Dokelle area, and even capture Neghelli and Yavello before the arrival of the 'long' rains. Moreover, this could then open an alternative route of advance to Addis Ababa via central Ethiopia. However, Brink had to do without Pienaar's brigade, since Cunningham had earmarked them for the offensive operations in Somalia. Regrettably, the British tended to break up Allied units and disperse them among other British units. This would happen to the South African forces in North Africa too. Such a course of action not only affected cohesion and fighting power but also led to friction between British and South African leaders.

The 'cutting-out' operations

In January 1941, Brink manoeuvred his division into the no-man's-land of the Northern Frontier District, ready for the start of Allied offensive operations on 15 January. At this stage, Buchanan's 2 SA Inf Bde occupied Dukana, while Armstrong's 5 SA Inf Bde was at Marsabit. Cunningham, realising that a direct frontal attack on the Moyale escarpment would be impossible, ordered Brink to conduct a wide flanking envelopment on the Mega–Moyale escarpment. Brink decided to conduct the envelopment through a series of tactical and operational bounds. In doing so, he would first rid the Northern Frontier District of the Italian presence by capturing El Yibo, El Sardu and the Turbi Hills, after which the heavily defended Italian garrisons at El Gumu, Gorai, Hobok, Banno, El Sod, Mega and Moyale would be taken in turn.

Brink realised that water, and access to it, would be the single most important factor in the coming offensive operations. To sustain the needs of his army, and to deny water to the Italians, 1 SA Div would have to capture and control all the water sources along the Kenya–Ethiopia frontier. This would also relieve the pressure on the already stretched lines of communication. It was decided to first clear the area around the wells at El Yibo–El Sardu and then active patrols to the Ethiopian frontier would be undertaken along the Dukana–Gorai road. This would give the South African Engineer Corps (SAEC) the necessary time needed to develop water supplies in the Dukana and North Horr areas to such an extent that they could support the South African advance into Ethiopia.

Brink's division fought their first battle between 16 and 18 January, when 2 SA Inf Bde was ordered to capture the wells at El Yibo and El Sardu. The Battle of El Yibo, however, was no more than a staccato affair despite problems with extreme heat, inadequate maps and a shortage of water. The plan was to envelop the Italian forces occupying the area around El Yibo by infantry and armour acting in a mutually supportive role. However, at the tactical level, unity of action and command between the armoured cars and the infantry remained an issue, negating the effective deployment of fighting patrols. Success at El Yibo was achieved with limited casualties – one man killed and three wounded, whereas the Italians lost 22 killed, 40 wounded and two taken prisoner. The capture of El Yibo and El Sardu, along with the actions fought by 5 SA Inf Bde in the vicinity of the Turbi Hills and Sololo during this period expelled the last Italian outposts from the Northern Frontier District and further secured valuable water sources. In fact, these actions convinced Brink that the nature and speed of their operations called for the rigid doctrine to be modified owing to tactical and operational requirements. This would become a hallmark of the South African offensive operations during the campaign, with the motorised infantry being used in the same way mounted infantry were used during the campaign in GSWA in 1915 (see Chapter 3).

The operational envelopment

On 31 January, the lead elements of Brink's division crossed the Kenyan frontier into southern Ethiopia. The next morning, the two South African brigades formed up in battle order to advance on the Italian outposts at Gorai and El Gumu, which directly impeded their advance. Brink had tasked Buchanan with attacking towards the vicinity of the Gorai crater, while Armstrong was to capture the fort at El Gumu.

Buchanan's 2 SA Inf Bde immediately made for the Italian fort at Gorai, which, at first glance, appeared difficult to attack due to the nature of the terrain. A diversionary attack by six armoured cars on an Italian outpost encountered only slight resistance, which was quickly brushed aside, and the fighting column continued their advance. In late afternoon the main attack on Gorai developed after an initial aerial bombardment by the SAAF. Two infantry companies conducted the main attack, with four armoured cars offering mobile fire support. The rapid advance of the armoured cars managed to breach the outer perimeter of the fort, and the Italian machine-gun emplacements were silenced one by one. The swift and sharp armoured attack caused a general retreat, with the infantrymen merely consolidating the position at Gorai. The South African casualties included two men killed and seven wounded, while the Italian losses were much heavier, with 28 men killed and a further 49 wounded. The South African attack was a well-executed affair which included a mutually supportive attack by infantry, armour and the air force.

At roughly the same time, the lead elements of Armstrong's 5 SA Inf Bde broke through the dense scrubland before El Gumu. Reminiscent of a cavalry charge of old, the armoured cars overran the Italian positions, causing the remaining defenders to flee in the direction of Hobok and Kunchurro. The entire contact lasted no longer than an hour and bore testimony to the offensive capabilities of the South African Tank Corps. The accompanying infantry only secured the village and rounded up prisoners.

The South African advance was next directed towards the Italian fort at Hobok on 2 February. After the defeats the day before, the routed Italian defenders had retreated towards Hobok, hoping to consolidate their defensive position. Brink decided that Armstrong's brigade would lead the advance on Hobok. The good visibility and openness of the country during the approach march lasted until only about 5 km from the fort, where the open ground changed to dense, broken scrubland. Italian troops set fire to the surrounding bush to force the armoured cars to return to the narrow confines of the road, in so doing channelling the fighting column into a predetermined Italian ambush.

Approximately three kilometres from Hobok, the lead armoured cars encountered an Italian roadblock. While the armoured cars engaged the defenders, the SAEC cleared the obstruction. Then the armoured cars executed an aggressive reconnaissance towards the outpost's defences and immediately came under sustained fire. Armstrong decided to precede the final attack on Hobok with a combined aerial and artillery bombardment, then his infantry and armour would advance towards

South African armoured cars leading the advance into Southern Ethiopia, January 1941

Springbok motorised infantry, the backbone of the South African offensive operations in East Africa

The Italian fort at Mega

the heart of the Italian defensive positions. The main attack developed under the blanket of a supporting aerial bombardment and artillery barrage; when the armoured cars surged forward, they drew an immense volume of defensive fire. The advance was so rapid that the artillery barrage had to be called off for fear of hitting the advancing armour and infantry. The dash and tenacity of the infantry and armour brought about the desired effect, for the Italian defenders broke cover. The fort was soon surrounded and cleared of its defenders, with a large quantity of equipment and ammunition being captured. While the South African casualties included three wounded, only five defenders were captured during the battle. The attack on Hobok was once more a textbook affair that demonstrated the advantages of the combined-arms approach.

To secure the western flank of his area of operations, Brink needed to capture the Italian fort at Banno. This was necessary before an attack on the fortress at Mega could be launched. Occupying Banno would also help to establish contact with the Shifta leaders in the Yavello area. The planned assault comprised a double envelopment by two fighting patrols drawn from the South African brigades. According to aerial reconnaissance, their path of advance lay across an open plain. However, the actual terrain encountered slowed down the advance considerably – a problem compounded by poor terrain intelligence and inadequate maps, a recurring issue throughout the campaign.

After the brigades had laagered for the night, the approach march on Banno resumed at dawn on 9 February, with the Italian outpost sighted at mid-morning. The armoured cars moved ahead and reconnoitred the defences unopposed. By noon, the South Africans had reached the fort without drawing fire and with no visible signs of defenders. Aerial reconnaissance and a low-level attack also yielded no results. Some armoured cars even advanced inside the fort, without any reaction. The Italian defenders, showing great tenacity and tactfulness, successfully lured the South Africans into a predetermined killing area. As the South African infantry arrived at the fort, the Italian defenders, hidden in well-sited defensive positions on the high ground, laid down an immense volley of accurate fire. But the attack had fortunately been misjudged, and the South African infantry were able to debus and take over the brunt of the fighting after two sections of armoured cars delivered a sustained fire-belt action, and by firing all their weapons at a specific target they managed to silence the Italians temporarily.

By midday, the full weight of the South African attack materialised when elements of the South African Artillery arrived and joined the battle. The combined firepower of the infantry, armour and artillery managed to silence the Italians during the late afternoon, and the defenders later retreated. The poor state of the vehicles and the difficult terrain prevented a pursuit, and during the night the Italian forces reoccupied the positions around Banno and harassed its occupiers. South African casualties amounted to one man killed, while Italian losses were difficult to gauge as their casualties had been removed. After the capture of Banno, Brink ordered long-range reconnaissance patrols towards Yavello to aid the Shifta leaders in fomenting a rebellion.

Throughout the actions at El Yibo, El Sardu, El Gumu, Gorai, Hobok and Banno, the South Africans showed immense courage and dash. Despite meeting only token resistance, they inflicted more than 300 casualties on the Italian colonial and irregular defenders of southern Ethiopia while outflanking the Mega–Moyale complex. The strongest remaining Italian bastion was the fort at Mega, which dominated the surrounding plains from a position high on a mountain plateau. Defended by experienced Blackshirt and colonial infantry battalions, along with heavy artillery and a series of minefields, Mega would be a challenging objective.

The plan for the assault was twofold: first, to cut the Italian line of retreat northwards; and, second, to prevent Italian reinforcements from Yavello, Neghelli and Moyale interfering with the attack. Brink thus tasked Buchanan with occupying El Sod, which served to secure the Mega–Neghelli road. A detachment would also hold Medaccio, giving them complete control over the Mega–Yavello and Mega–Kunchurro roads. Then 2 SA Inf Bde would advance to the south and east to cut the Mega–Moyale road and prevent interference from the south. Armstrong was tasked with moving from El Gumu via El Gobso and threatening Mega from a northerly direction. Once these moves were complete, 1 SA Div would have effectively enveloped the Italian defences, allowing the launch of coordinated attacks on the stronghold.

On 14 February, 2 SA Inf Bde advanced and successfully cut the

Mega–Yavello road as planned, and Medaccio was occupied. Choosing to leave an infantry company and two armoured cars astride the Mega–Yavello and Mega–Neghelli crossroads for protection, Buchanan occupied El Sod, where the rest of 2 SA Inf Bde laagered for the night. Armstrong's brigade had reached its staging area at El Gobso without interference and bivouacked for the evening. Lulled into a false sense of security due to recent battlefield successes, the South African stopper group at the crossroads failed to adhere to the appropriate defensive standing orders. During the early hours of 15 February, two Italian supply trucks, destined for Mega, drove unopposed into the undefended laager. In the ensuing confusion the Italian soldiers debussed and opened fire. The two armoured cars drew most of the fire and proceeded to engage the Italians with their guns. The attackers soon withdrew, and, in anticipation of a counterattack, the armoured cars advanced to a position further up the road.

At daybreak, a strong Italian fighting patrol, which included 15 light tanks, once more attacked the South African position. The Italian armoured attack succeeded in surrounding the South Africans and causing the infantry to flee towards El Sod. Content at having caused the South Africans to flee, the Italian patrol returned towards Yavello. The South African losses during the morning's skirmish amounted to two killed, four wounded and a further 11 taken prisoner. Buchanan ordered a fighting patrol to pursue the Italian force. The patrol soon closed in on the attackers and, along with aerial interception by the SAAF, hampered the Italians' progress. The pursuit, however, soon petered out and Buchanan recalled his men to El Sod. Despite suffering losses, the Italians had been prevented from reinforcing Mega with a strong complement of armour and infantry from Yavello.

The main attack on Mega was, primarily, a South African infantry affair, with the accompanying armour only conducting long-range reconnaissance patrols and rearguard and flanking duties. Brink scheduled Buchanan and Armstrong to start their attacks simultaneously on 16 February. Soon after Armstrong started his advance, he was forced to halt and consolidate his position along a ridge of hills because Buchanan's brigade had reached the starting line for the attack only by late afternoon. Buchanan's advance was hampered by a shortage of water, adverse weather, poor lateral communication and a general state of confusion regarding Brink's orders. However, by nightfall 2 SA Inf Bde managed to cut the Mega–Moyale road. Further patrols south also established that the Italian garrison at Moyale had withdrawn towards Neghelli. Both brigades were forced to bivouac for the night and resume their attacks the following morning.

The South African attack on Mega developed throughout the morning of 17 Febuary. To the south of Mega, Buchanan's infantry worked their way along the high ground but directed their attack at the wrong sector of the defences. Towards the northwest, Armstrong's men made some progress towards the central Italian defensive lines despite the presence of extensive minefields and accurate artillery fire. In the early afternoon, Armstrong brought his artillery forward, which resulted in effective counter-battery work. By the end of the day's fighting, the South African infantry had advanced to within striking distance of the Italian defences.

The attack on Mega resumed the next morning, with renewed promises that Buchanan's troops would support the final push on the Italian positions. His infantry launched a surprise attack on the Italian artillery positions from the east over rough terrain, and in doing so silenced them. To the north, Armstrong's men managed to capture Mega Hill and Fort Hill after a successful bayonet charge. Armstrong then ordered his infantry forward for the final assault in the late afternoon, and the Italian garrison soon surrendered. This yielded about a thousand prisoners and large quantities of materiel and equipment. The South African losses were eight killed, nine wounded and a further eleven missing.

With its fighting role essentially over, Brink's division moved to Nanyuki for a period of rest and refit – ready to revert to an offensive role if called upon. Between the end of April and June, the various elements of 1 SA Div embarked for Egypt to reinforce the Allied forces in the Western Desert.

The South Africans executed their offensive operations in southern Ethiopia between 15 January and 18 February 1941, a mere 34 operational days. The operations were a complete success, and the objectives set by Wavell and Cunningham were all met. A high degree of tactical and operational mobility underpinned these actions. The South African belief in manoeuvre warfare found expression through the offensive operations aimed at outflanking the Mega–Moyale complex, and by 18 February 1 SA Div had attained all their objectives. Throughout the offensive operations, Brink had manoeuvred to fight and had used the combined-arms approach, along with his division's mobility, to obtain complete mastery of the southern Ethiopian battlespace. In doing so, he attacked the Italian outposts and severed their lines of communication piecemeal, proving to Cunningham that the Italian defence of southern Ethiopia was wavering.

The combined-arms approach, as practised by Brink and his sub-ordinates throughout the offensive, became a hallmark of South African operations in southern Ethiopia throughout 1941. Although limited in scope, these operations afforded Cunningham the option of an alternative route of advance towards Addis Ababa. The capture of the important ports of Kismayu and Mogadishu and the arrival of the rains, however, convinced Cunningham that the most viable route of advance on Addis Ababa was from the north, through Somalia. This decision made the further deployment of the bulk of 1 SA Div unnecessary and led to its redeployment to the Western Desert.

The offensive operations in southern Ethiopia, though a resounding success, failed to prepare 1 SA Div adequately for the Western Desert. In fact, the lessons learned by Brink and his men in East Africa would have to be relearned in North Africa, where the nature of the enemy, and his weapons and tactics, drastically changed.

The highly mobile phase that characterised the southern advance into Ethiopia ended after the occupation of Addis Ababa in April 1941. The remaining combat operations of 1 SA Inf Bde in the theatre can at best be described as a tedious infantry slog in the mountains of central and northern Ethiopia. Without specialised troops, training and equipment, and lacking experience, institutional expertise and an accompanying doctrine for mountain warfare, Pienaar and his men had to adapt quickly to the demands of combat at high altitude. In time, the battles of Combolcia and Amba Alagi would prove to the South Africans that combat operations at high altitude were extremely taxing on men and equipment alike.

9

COMBOLCIA AND AMBA ALAGI, 1941

The South African deployment to East Africa during the Second World War was, for the most part, characterised by highly mobile operations across deserts and scrubland, where infantry, armour and artillery deployed in a mutually supportive role. The penultimate battles of the campaign, fought in the mountains of northern Ethiopia, were, however, largely static in nature and took place in extremely trying terrain under adverse weather conditions. For the South African troops this would be their first real experience of mountain warfare since the establishment of the defence force in 1912. Without specialised troops and training, and lacking both actual experience and institutional expertise, the UDF would have to adapt quickly to new demands.

The experiences of 1 SA Inf Bde, which served with the 11th (African) and 12th (African) divisions through Somalia and into central and northern Ethiopia, were quite different from those of 1 SA Div, as described in the previous chapter. Following the initial success of 1 SA Inf Bde at El Wak in the Northern Frontier District in December 1940, the remaining Italian forces in that sector of Kenya fell back to the main Italian defensive line in Somalia, situated on the Juba River – the only real defensible feature in the territory. While planning for the Allied advance into Somalia, Gen Alan Cunningham realised that swift, sharp action to capture the water supplies at Afmadu, Jelib, Gobwen, Jumbo and the coastal port of Kismayu would be of the essence. Without these water sources, the Allied advance would be severely hamstrung.

The advance into Somalia effectively began on 12 February. Allied troops captured Afmadu, Gobwen and Kismayu in quick succession.

The Juba River was successfully forded by troops of 1 SA Inf Bde at Yonte on 17 February, ensuring the capture of Jumbo, Margherita and Jelib by the end of the month. The successful crossing of the Juba River before the arrival of the 'long' rains meant that the hinterland of Somalia was now open for a rapid advance.

The new route of advance negated the active employment of the South African cars and light tanks because of sudden, drastic changes in the terrain. The dense bush and open desert flats of the coastal belt of Somalia gradually gave way to the sweeping mountainous terrain that dominates central and northern Ethiopia. As a result, the South African armour and motorised infantry were confined to roads and tracks, effectively losing their freedom of operational movement. The South African infantrymen would now bear the brunt of the fighting. Nevertheless, the Allied advance was extremely rapid despite the changing terrain and, after the capture of the Marda Pass (21 March), Harar (25 March) and Diredawa (29 March), Addis Ababa was occupied on 6 April. From this point, open flanks disappeared completely and the highly mobile phase of the southern advance became a tedious infantry slog through the mountains.

The occupation of Addis Ababa did not mark the end of hostilities; instead, it was largely overshadowed by a host of serious problems that were unfolding in the Middle East. The German invasion of Greece and Yugoslavia, a tense situation in Syria and Iraq, and several reverses in the Western Desert prompted Wavell to redeploy the entire 1 SA Div to Egypt as soon as possible. Cunningham was ordered to advance north with the remainder of East African Force, which opened the road from Addis Ababa to Asmara in Eritrea and the Red Sea ports of Massawa and Port Sudan, both of which were held by British forces. However, the Italian commander in East Africa, the Duke of Aosta, and his Eritrean and Central armies, barred the way, having fallen back on a series of well-established mountain defences in the Dessie–Amba Alagi sector. Brigadier Dan Pienaar and his men would spearhead the southern operations against this sector, which would be primarily infantry affairs, supported by artillery and fought under some of the harshest conditions of the entire campaign.

On 11 April, Cunningham ordered Pienaar to move northwards with 1 SA Inf Bde on Dessie, which marked the southern boundary of the Dessie–Amba Alagi sector. The occupation of Dessie would be the first step for the South Africans towards their ultimate objective of Asmara. The 5th Indian Infantry Division (5 Ind Div), which included several Indian Army units with training and experience in mountain warfare, along with support elements from the Sudan Defence Force, simultaneously advanced on the Italian defensive positions from the north. By 13 April, the South Africans had made rapid progress along the tarred Strada Vittoria highway, gradually becoming accustomed to the mountainous terrain and climate. However, their lack of experience with the cold at high altitude, and the fact that they were still in summer field dress, meant that the adverse weather conditions severely plagued them.

Between 14 and 16 April the Duke of Edinburgh's Own Rifles (Dukes) operated as the vanguard of 1 SA Inf Bde during the advance northwards to the Italian stronghold at Dessie. To their astonishment, the road tunnels they encountered along the way had been neither mined nor destroyed by the retreating Italian forces. However, the Italians used the terrain to their advantage by triggering rockfalls across hairpin bends in the twisting passes. Hampered by heavy mist and driving rain, the sappers of the SAEC were often called upon to clear the road or construct makeshift bridges. The rate of advance slowed accordingly and the South African troops covered only about 56 km in two days.

The Battle of Combolcia

On the morning of 17 April, the Dukes found themselves in the Karramarra Gorge, in the approach to the Combolcia Pass. Because of their rapid advance, the Dukes, along with a complement of armoured cars and field artillery, had become separated from the main body of 1 SA Inf Bde. At mid-morning, the leading armoured cars started drawing heavy, accurate mortar and artillery fire from well-sited Italian defensive positions hidden in the mountains along the Combolcia Pass. The Dukes immediately deployed two companies of infantrymen forward and took up defensive positions while awaiting reinforcements. The accompanying field artillery soon deployed and returned fire, despite their lack of suitable gun positions.

The South Africans had in fact happened upon the vanguard of the

The Battle of Combolcia, 1941

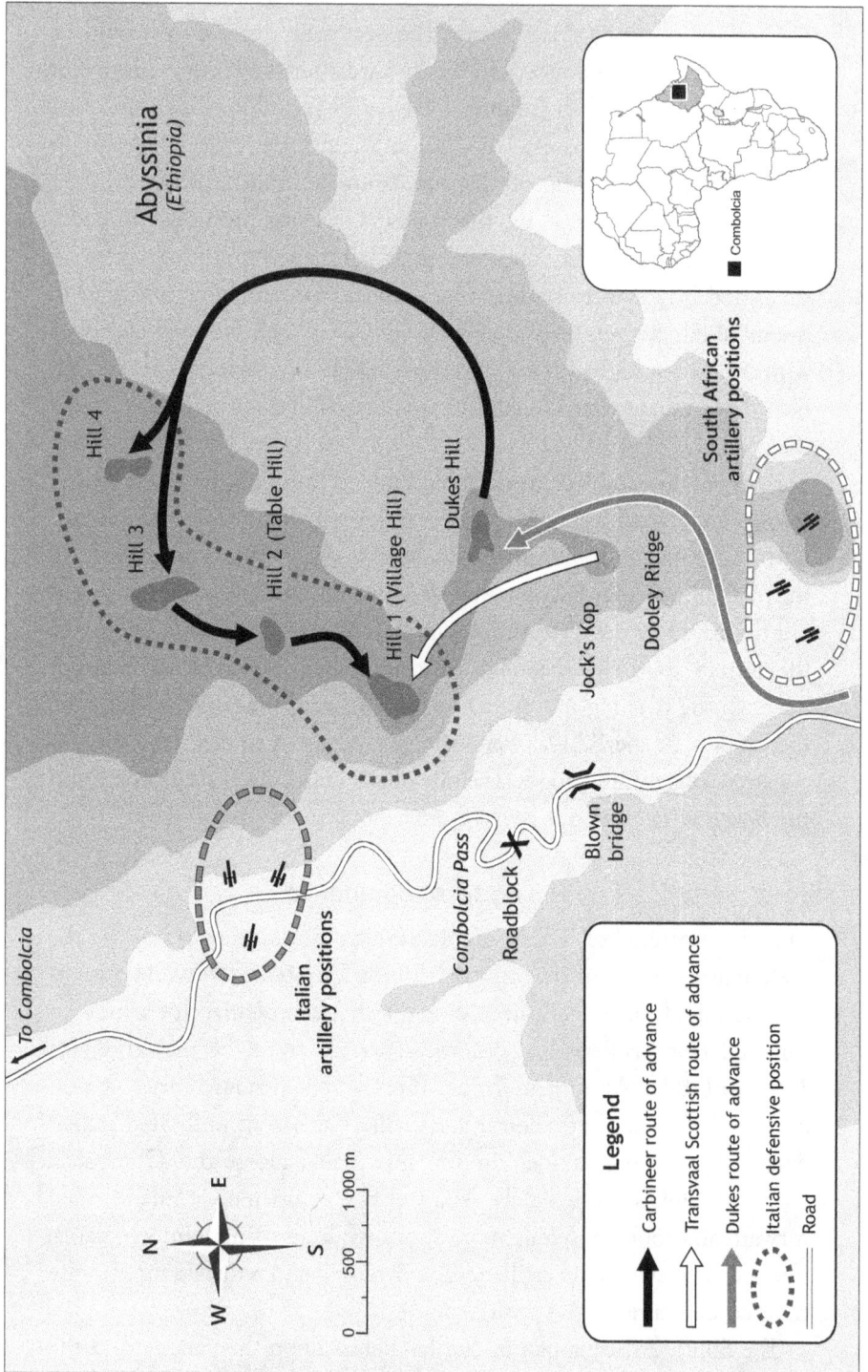

Legend

Carbineer route of advance

Transvaal Scottish route of advance

Dukes route of advance

Italian defensive position

Road

Abyssinia
(Ethiopia)

Hill 4

Hill 3

Hill 2 (Table Hill)

Hill 1 (Village Hill)

Dukes Hill

Jock's Kop

Dooley Ridge

South African artillery positions

Combolcia Pass

Roadblock

Blown bridge

Italian artillery positions

To Combolcia

Combolcia

N
E
S
W

0   500   1 000 m

Italian forces in the Dessie area – estimated at more than 10 000 men and supported by 52 artillery pieces. The Italian defenders had also blown up the road bridge and blocked the road beyond Combolcia with abandoned vehicles. Their right flank was secured by the Borchenna River and an adjacent marshland, which prevented the South African troops from deploying off-road. The Italian left flank was fixed on a series of fortified positions on steep mountain slopes which dominated the approaches to Combolcia. Despite the trying terrain, Pienaar, who in the meantime had arrived on the scene, decided to focus his attack on the Italian left flank. While the terrain seemed unfavourable to an operational envelopment, Pienaar, true to the roots of South African manoeuvre doctrine, favoured just this kind of battle.

During the initial engagement, the field artillery received the bulk of attention from the Italian gunners. Despite the poor quality of the Italian shells, two South African guns were damaged. Consequently, Pienaar redeployed his artillery to less exposed positions and the South African gunners soon initiated retaliatory fire and scored direct hits on the enemy guns. By nightfall, though, the South Africans found themselves in a rather precarious position. While still unsure of the extent of the Italian defensive positions, Pienaar consolidated his position for the night and planned for a detailed reconnaissance the following morning.

During the night, the Dukes occupied forward defensive positions situated on some of the dominant terrain features. Conditions were uncomfortable, with bitter cold, incessant rain and icy squalls taking a toll on the men. Moreover, reconnaissance could be conducted only on foot. The next morning, the Transvaal Scottish moved forward, which allowed the Dukes to continue their advance further with the aim of probing the Italian left flank. Unable to secure new observation positions, the South African guns soon engaged the Italian positions with speculative fire. Meanwhile, a group of Abyssinian patriots under Lt AG Campbell captured an Italian observation post towards the west, which immediately blinded the Italian long-range guns.

Progress throughout 19 April was extremely slow. Despite the difficulties encountered, though the Dukes managed to press forward and occupy Dukes Hill, which offered concealed positions overlooking the Italian left flank. During the afternoon, the Dukes beat off a large but ill-prepared attack by a mixed force of Italian and colonial troops. For the remainder of the afternoon the South Africans fortified their forward positions and readied themselves to spend another night out in the open. Fortunately, the Royal Natal Carbineers (Carbineers), initially held in reserve, arrived with supplies of rations, water, ammunition and warm coats for the Dukes and Transvaal Scottish.

On 20 April, Pienaar ordered the Carbineers to relieve the Dukes the following night, with the final assault on the Italian defensive positions planned for 22 April. Forward patrols had also established that the Italians occupied a strong defensive line along four dominant peaks across a valley that offered virtually no cover. The four peaks were designated (from north to south) Hill 4, Hill 3, Hill 2 and Hill 1 (see map). The strongpoint, Hill 3, could be approached only by a wide flanking movement from the east. In finalising his plan for the assault, Pienaar ordered the Carbineers to move around the Italian left flank and take Hill 4 – believed to already be in the hands of Abyssinian irregulars. Then they would shift the focus of their attack and systematically work their way towards Hill 1. Once the Carbineers were in control of the high ground, the Transvaal Scottish would launch a frontal attack on Hill 1.

In the early hours of 22 April, the Carbineers approached the saddle between Hill 3 and Hill 4. Shortly before dawn, the South African infantrymen managed to advance towards the steepest part of Hill 3 without trouble. In fact, the lead elements progressed to within 10 m of the Italian perimeter before the alarm was raised and a full-scale attack developed. With visibility rapidly improving, the Carbineers delivered accurate small arms and mortar fire on the Italian defenders – many of whom were still scrambling to occupy their defensive positions. The South African infantrymen pushed ahead with their attack and soon routed the remaining defenders. Shortly after daybreak the Carbineers were in full control of Hill 3, even though the Italian artillery were now focusing their fire on them. The initial success had been swift, and although casualty numbers were fortunately low, the OC, Lt Col Jock McMenamin, had been killed.

The focus of the South African attack next shifted to the Italian defensive positions on Hill 2 and Hill 1. Meanwhile, the South African gunners began engaging several predetermined targets on the high ground. The Carbineers soon attacked the remaining Italian positions on the opposite hills with their small arms and mortars. The Transvaal Scottish now also started their advance on Hill 1, but before long became bogged down in the open by accurate Italian artillery, mortar and small arms fire. By now, the Italian defenders had realised that a major attack was developing on their front and left flank. After successfully occupying Hill 2 by midday, and despite having expended nearly all their first-line ammunition, the Carbineers provided supporting fire for the Transvaal Scottish, who still occupied a rather precarious position. Realising that the Transvaal Scottish needed to get a move on, the OC, Lt Col Scrubbs Hartshorn, committed his reserve, ordered his men to fix bayonets and stormed the hill. The general advance managed to dislodge the last Italian defenders. The South African infantrymen, however, could not follow up over the broken terrain due to the onset of combat fatigue and physical exhaustion.

Following the success at Combolcia Pass, Pienaar ordered a general advance on Combolcia once the remaining roadblocks had been cleared. On 25 April, the South African infantry secured some of the terrain features that commanded the approaches to Combolcia itself. Unknown to the South Africans, however, most of the Italian forces had retreated towards Dessie. After spending another cold, wet night at high altitude, the South Africans occupied Combolcia unopposed on the morning of 26 April and immediately resumed the advance on Dessie. Although they encountered further roadblocks and a demolished bridge, and also accurate Italian artillery fire from strong defensive positions, 1 SA Inf Bde successfully occupied Dessie later that day.

After consolidating their immediate positions, Pienaar and his staff took stock of their first offensive operation conducted in mountainous terrain. Casualties had been comparatively low: eight killed, with a further 12 wounded and a staggering 114 reporting sick or injured. The Italian defenders, in contrast, had lost nearly 400 men killed and 1 200 taken prisoner. It was agreed that the light casualties sustained were largely attributable to the tenacity and determination of the infantry and artillery, combined with the excellent leadership and decentralised command demonstrated by several sub-unit commanders, as well as the great initiative and courage displayed by the rank and file.

Pienaar particularly noticed that operating in a motorised column had a marked effect on the speed and fitness of his infantry. Tasks that would have been carried out with comparatively little distress by his troops a year earlier now proved to be extremely exhausting, affecting the speed of operations. In future, he argued, opportunities for combined training on foot at regular and frequent intervals were needed.

The South African success at the Battle of Combolcia and the occupation of Dessie were heralded by Gen Cunningham as 'a considerable victory'. Outnumbered in both men and guns, unaccustomed to the exigencies of mountain warfare and facing Italian troops who occupied well-prepared defensive positions at high altitude, 1 SA Inf Bde achieved the remarkable while sustaining notably few losses. The remaining obstacle was the strong Italian defensive position in the mountainous stronghold of Amba Alagi, which, at more than 3 000 m above sea level, seemed almost impregnable.

The Battle of Amba Alagi

At the end of April, 1 SA Inf Bde left Dessie and travelled north towards Amba Alagi to join the final assault on the Italian mountain stronghold. The South Africans would be supporting the attack of 5 Ind Div, with 4 May tentatively fixed as the starting date of operations. Dislodging the Duke of Aosta and the remainder of his forces from Amba Alagi would be no easy matter, as the nature and extent of the natural defensive positions were formidable.

On 11 May, 1 SA Inf Bde reached the vicinity of Amba Alagi. Pienaar and his staff immediately met with Maj Gen Mosley Mayne, the commander of 5 Ind Div, under whose control they now resorted. During a preliminary forward reconnaissance, Mayne pointed out to Pienaar and his staff the features that dominated the Italian defensive positions. These were centred on the imposing peak of Amba Alagi (3 400 m). Around Amba Alagi was the imposing Fort Toselli, atop the Toselli Pass. Further to the right was Mount Corarsi, which commanded the approaches to the pass and the fort. The right flank of Mount Corarsi was secured by two adjacent peaks, christened the Twin Pyramids. The right and left flanks of the Amba Alagi complex were dominated by high ground and mountain passes, which elements of 5 Ind Div had already successfully occupied, hemming in the Italian defenders from three sides. Despite some initial tactical successes by 5 Ind Div, the Italian troops were fighting well and conducting a spirited defence.

Mayne planned a complete encirclement of the Italian positions by employing the South African troops to advance from the south and occupy Mount Corarsi. The intended move would then allow intercommunication to be established with the 9th Indian Infantry Brigade (9 Ind Bde) to the right of the Twin Pyramids and also with the 29th Indian Infantry Brigade on Centre Hill, on the right flank of the Italian positions. Mayne proposed a night attack on Mount Corarsi, but Pienaar strongly opposed such an undertaking. He argued that an arduous approach march at night, over unfamiliar terrain, would be treacherous and remove the element of surprise. Instead, he insisted on launching a daytime attack on 15 May.

Following the meeting with Mayne, Pienaar positioned his troops for the upcoming offensive operations. He deployed the Carbineers to Khaki Hill while forward reconnaissance parties established the best possible positions for the artillery. The Transvaal Scottish, earmarked to lead the assault on Mount Corarsi, also started preparations to move forward the following night. Once the South Africans occupied their advance positions on 12 May, they came under heavy Italian fire from the Amba Alagi complex. They had to limit their movements during daylight hours since their positions had been fixed by the Italian gunners. Pienaar's headquarters was connected to the Indian brigades on their flanks via telephone line, which improved communication and cooperation. In the late afternoon Pienaar issued final orders to the infantry commanders for the combat operations. With dusk settling in, the area around Amba Alagi became engulfed in heavy mist, which, along with howling winds and intermittent rain, made for another uncomfortable, cold night.

On 13 May, the Transvaal Scottish advanced towards the first of their objectives along narrow, treacherous mountain paths. Initially, the South African troops carried their own support weapons, first-line ammunition, water and food. As their lines of communication became stretched, though, arrangements were made for parties of Abyssinian patriots to ferry combat supplies to them. Without pack animals, supplies had to be

The Battle of Amba Alagi, 1941

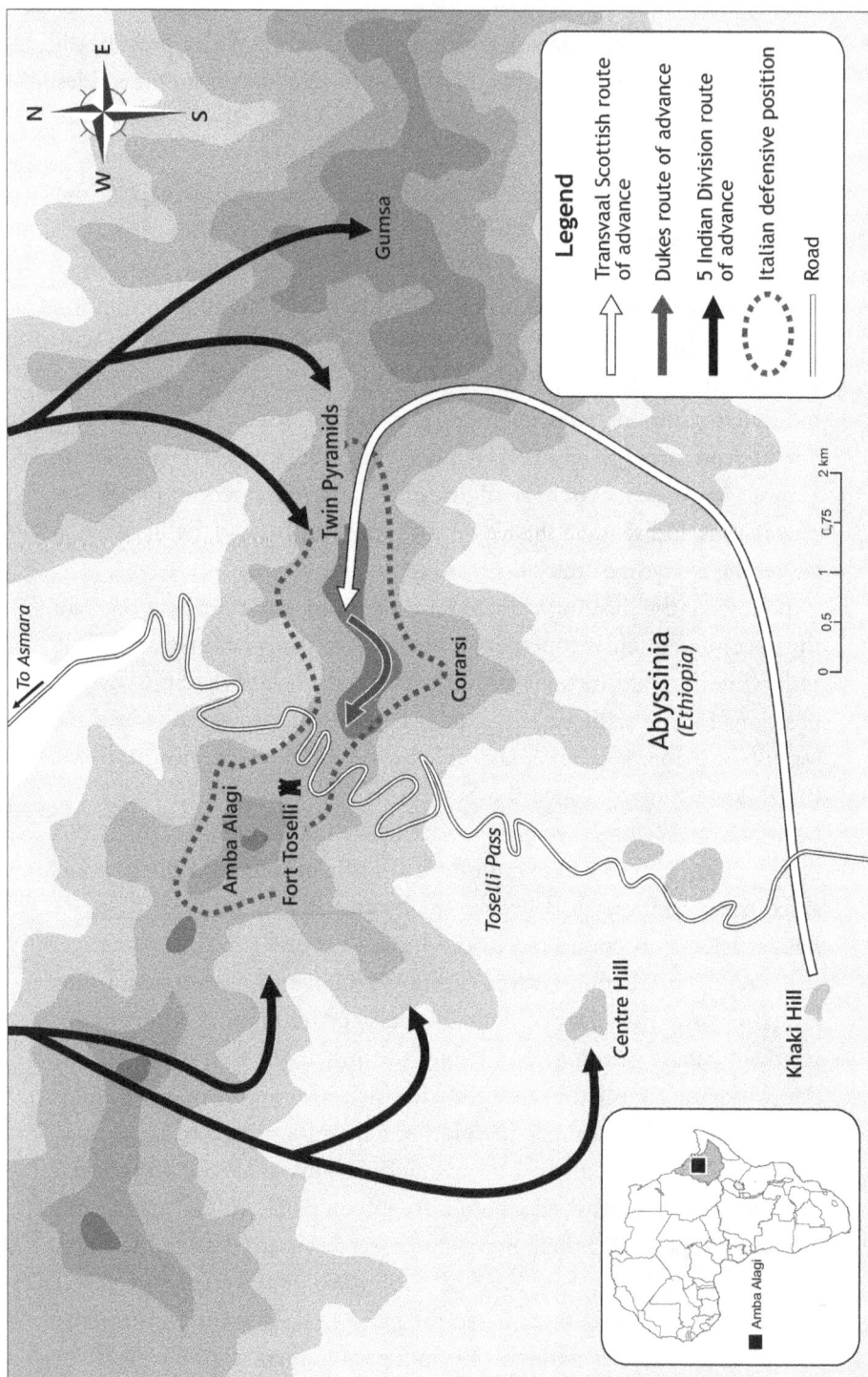

Legend

Transvaal Scottish route of advance

Dukes route of advance

5 Indian Division route of advance

Italian defensive position

Road

Gumsa

Twin Pyramids

Corarsi

To Asmara

Amba Alagi

Fort Toselli

Toselli Pass

Centre Hill

Khaki Hill

Abyssinia
(Ethiopia)

0   0.5   1   0.75   2 km

Amba Alagi

moved forward and upward on foot. Although coming under sustained machine-gun and artillery fire throughout their advance, the Transvaal Scottish secured their allotted objectives by nightfall with support from their artillery. After consolidating and fortifying their immediate position, they were resupplied and reinforced for another cold and wet night at high altitude.

The next morning, the men of the Transvaal Scottish took stock of their immediate surroundings. From their overnight position, they faced an exposed route of advance towards Wade's Post, from where they would have to cross an open valley to Mount Corarsi. After occupying Wade's Post, the Transvaal Scottish could start engaging the Italian defences on Mount Corarsi. During the previous night, the Garhwal Rifles of 9 Ind Bde had occupied the adjacent Twin Pyramids, placing further pressure on the Italians. The newly won positions allowed heavy and accurate artillery fire to be called in on Mount Corarsi as part of an integrated, divisionally coordinated fire plan that helped to prepare the way for the final assault on Amba Alagi.

Throughout the afternoon, the lead elements of the Transvaal Scottish continuously probed the Italian defences near the summit of Mount Corarsi. Accurate artillery, mortar and machine-gun fire further helped to dislodge the Italian defenders from their strong defensive positions. By nightfall, the South African infantrymen had advanced to within 200 m of the summit and started consolidating their high-altitude defensive positions after a haphazard Italian counterattack was thwarted. During the night the remaining Italian defenders retreated towards Fort Toselli and the Amba Alagi complex.

The occupation of Mount Corarsi on 15 May ensured the complete envelopment of Amba Alagi. Preparations were now made for the final assault on Fort Toselli and Amba Alagi. The Dukes relieved the Transvaal Scottish and began their advance across an intervening valley towards Fort Toselli. Elements of 9 Ind Bde also worked their way around the Italian flanks. Notwithstanding strong support fire from the South African gunners, the Italian defenders offered staunch opposition in the form of heavy mortar, machine-gun and artillery fire.

During the morning of 16 May, the forward elements of the Dukes, who were resupplied throughout the night, continued to probe the

125

Italian defensive line. The Italians, aware of the encroaching threat, subjected the South African infantry to perhaps the heaviest artillery bombardment experienced by 1 SA Inf Bde to date. Nevertheless, the men of the Dukes clung to their forward positions and effectively prevented Italian troops from reoccupying Mount Corarsi.

In the meantime, Italian envoys met with Mayne to request a brief armistice to evacuate their wounded and be resupplied with water. Mayne, however, was only willing to discuss surrender terms. After the Italians agreed to Mayne's proposal, a general armistice was issued that extended until noon the next day. During 17 May, staff officers of 5 Ind Div reached Amba Alagi to start negotiations for an honourable Italian surrender. The Duke of Aosta, his defensive positions at Amba Alagi encircled and on the verge of collapse, agreed to the terms of surrender. On the afternoon of 18 May the South Africans were informed that the Italians had surrendered.

Once combat operations around Amba Alagi ceased, Pienaar and his staff once more took stock. Like Combolcia, the operations around Amba Alagi had been predominantly an infantry and artillery affair. Moreover, when compared to Combolcia, the casualties sustained were considerably lower, despite more difficult terrain and more resolute defenders.

Pienaar and his staff were particularly impressed by the infantrymen of the Garhwal Rifles – regarded as specialists in mountain warfare. As a matter of long-range policy, Pienaar suggested that it would be beneficial to attach South African officers and men to units of the Indian Army serving in the North-West Frontier region in India. This would allow the South Africans to gain practical experience of mountain warfare, since the UDF offered no specialised mountain warfare courses and had no dedicated mountain warfare capability of its own.

After the fall of Amba Alagi, Defence Headquarters in Pretoria decided to withdraw 1 SA Inf Bde from the East African theatre of operations. Following a short period of respite, Pienaar and his men departed for the Middle East on 12 June to join the remainder of 1 SA Div. During their deployment to East Africa, Pienaar and his brigade had covered nearly 4 000 km, from El Wak to Amba Alagi, without suffering any serious reverses.

*A group of Italian POWs photographed after the capitulation
of the Duke of Aosta at Amba Alagi*

*South African troops
occupying high-altitude
forward positions during
the attack on the Italian
positions at Amba Alagi*

The initial South African deployment to the East African theatre was characterised by highly mobile combined-arms operations on favourable terrain. The terrain in northern Kenya, southern Ethiopia and Somalia allowed for the varied employment of South African armour and motorised infantry. This allowed South African commanders to effect envelopments through wide flanking movements and to gain both tactical and operational surprise. As the campaign progressed into the mountains of northern Ethiopia, South African operational deployment underwent a drastic change. After the occupation of Addis Ababa, the open flanks so conducive to mobile warfare completely disappeared. The highly mobile phase of the southern advance was thus replaced by a tedious, and at times static, infantry slog through the mountains.

The penultimate battles in the East African theatre were fought in the mountains of northern Ethiopia. For the South Africans in particular, the battles of Combolcia and Amba Alagi took place in trying mountainous terrain and under adverse weather conditions. Without specialised troops, training and equipment, and in the absence of actual experience, institutional expertise and an accompanying doctrine, the UDF had to adapt quickly to the demands of mountain warfare. The battles of Combolcia and Amba Alagi showed that combat operations at high altitude were extremely taxing on men and equipment – reflected in the higher number of casualties among the infantry. The South Africans also realised that artillery played an indispensable role during combat operations at high altitude, despite the difficulties of deploying the guns. And, regardless of their well-sited defensive positions, the Italian defence of the Dessie–Amba Alagi sector had been negligible, to say the least.

The physical environment proved to be the single biggest challenge faced by the South Africans at Combolcia and Amba Alagi. The rugged terrain highlighted the fact that, militarily speaking, some features mattered more than others. The UDF realised that understanding and manipulating the operating environment to their advantage during combat operations at high altitude was crucial to success. The challenges experienced by 1 SA Inf Bde, regarding manoeuvre, supply, equipment and communication with forward operating forces, to some degree overshadowed actual combat operations. Nevertheless, reflecting on overall battlefield performance and combat experience enabled the

South Africans to innovate and adapt to the challenges posed by mountain warfare.

The South African experience of mobile and mountain warfare in East Africa was, however, something of an anomaly. Their next deployment, to the Western Desert, brought them up against a far more resolute enemy and an even more trying military operating environment. The defeat of 5 SA Inf Bde at Sidi Rezegh in November 1941 serves as a stark reminder of the adversity in facing a more resolute enemy and an even more trying military operating environment.

The Battle of Sidi Rezegh, 1941

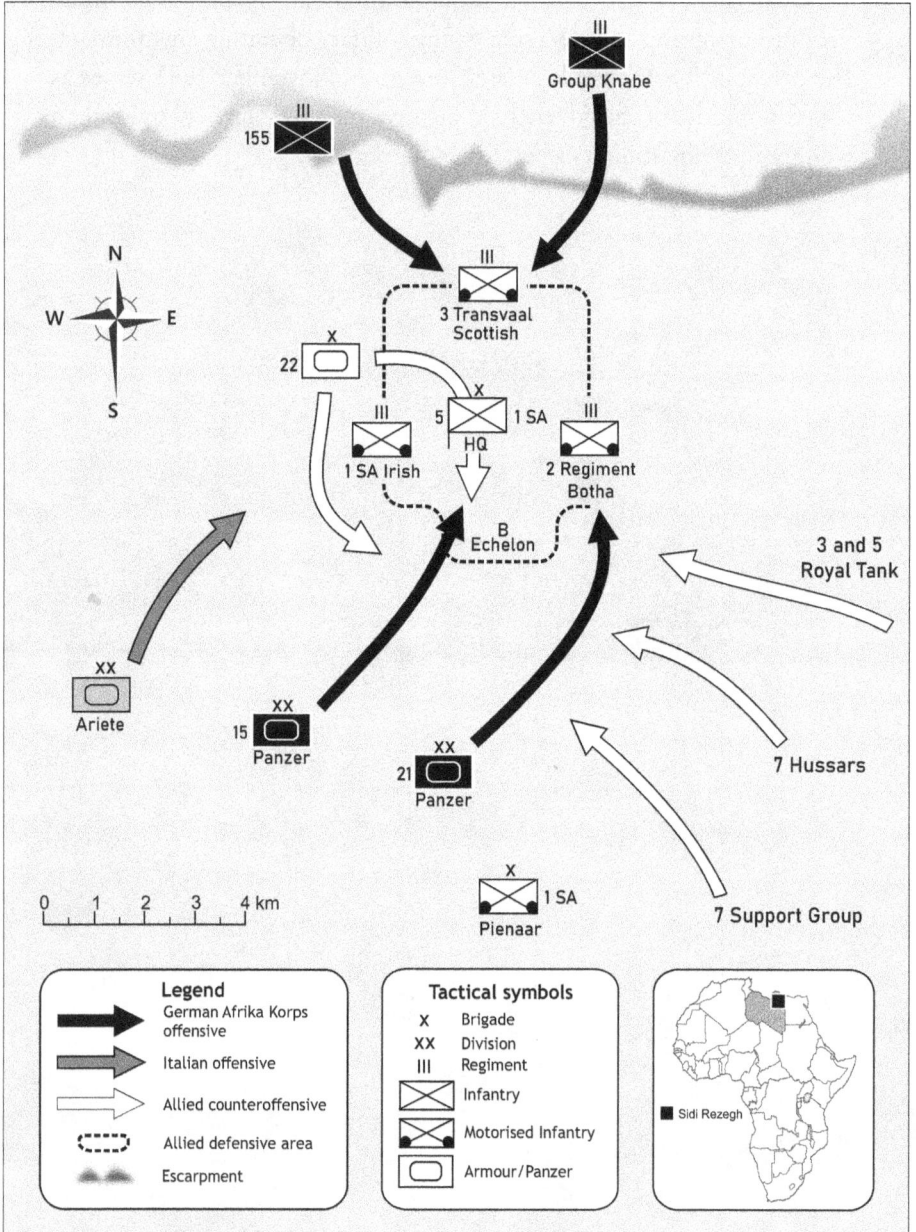

III
Group Knabe

III
155

N
W — E
S

III
3 Transvaal
Scottish

X
22

X
5   1 SA
HQ

III
1 SA Irish

III
2 Regiment
Botha

B
Echelon

3 and 5
Royal Tank

XX
Ariete

XX
15
Panzer

XX
21
Panzer

7 Hussars

0   1   2   3   4 km

X
1 SA
Pienaar

7 Support Group

Legend
German Afrika Korps
offensive
Italian offensive
Allied counteroffensive
Allied defensive area
Escarpment

Tactical symbols
X   Brigade
XX   Division
III   Regiment
      Infantry
      Motorised Infantry
      Armour / Panzer

Sidi Rezegh

130

10

SIDI REZEGH, 1941

Following the successful campaign to oust the Italians from East Africa, the UDF began to redeploy to North Africa at the end of May 1941. Flushed with victory, they had little inkling of the disaster that awaited them at the hands of Lt Gen Erwin Rommel, the 'Desert Fox', and his formidable Deutsches Afrika Korps (hereafter Afrika Korps), which had been sent to North Africa in early 1941 to bolster the Italian army in Libya. The Italians had suffered a series of humiliating defeats at the hands of the numerically inferior British and were in danger of being completely ousted from North Africa, and Hitler felt compelled to come to the aid of Mussolini. The South African disaster at Sidi Rezegh formed part of the larger and ambitious Operation Crusader. It would amount to the single most expensive military operation ever undertaken by South Africans to date. Approximately 3 800 men were killed, wounded or taken prisoner in the battle, surpassing the calamity of Delville Wood in 1916.

Operation Crusader was born of the necessity to relieve the Libyan coastal city of Tobruk, which had been besieged by Axis forces since 11 April 1941. The relief of Tobruk would allow airfields to be established to cover the passage of convoys between Alexandria and Malta. The main objective, and the first phase of the operation, was to lure the German and Italian armoured forces to Gabr Saleh, a central position, for a pitched battle with the British armoured divisions, which, owing to their superior numbers and concentration, would defeat the Axis tanks in detail.

The second phase of the operation, once the Axis armour was destroyed, involved South African and New Zealand infantry linking up with the garrison of Tobruk, who on a given signal would break out of the fortress to meet the relieving troops. The initial objective for the 5th South African Brigade was to hold the extreme left wing of the British XXX Corps, part of the Eighth Army, and protect the western and southwestern flanks of the 7th Armoured Division.

The strategic plan seemed sound, given the overall superiority the British enjoyed in manpower and materiel. At the outset of Crusader, the British significantly outnumbered the Axis in the crucial area of tank numbers – by close to a 2:1 ratio. The British also had the luxury of greater tank reserves. But it was at the operational level that Crusader contained the seeds of the destruction of 5th South African Brigade. The whole operation, in deference to British doctrine, was pinned on the destruction of the enemy tank forces, relegating the infantry to a secondary role vulnerable to attacks by Axis armour. The lack of a combined-arms doctrine meant that British armoured formations often lacked an infantry and artillery component. On the other hand, precious armour resources were often assigned to ensure the safety of, and on occasion to rescue, vulnerable infantry brigades. A further flaw in the operational plan was the choice of Gabr Saleh – a point on the map of no real consequence – to lure the German armour into a destructive tank battle on British terms. Had the British chosen a more strategic objective, such as Sidi Rezegh or even Tobruk, and seized the initiative, it would have forced Rommel to take decisive action.

The first formations of South Africans arrived in Egypt on 4 May 1941, taking over the fortress of Mersa Matruh and eventually manning it with 5th Brigade, which arrived on 14 June, followed by 2nd Brigade on 30 June. Both had seen active service in East Africa. The 1st South African Infantry Division (1 SA Div) busied themselves with strengthening the Mersa Matruh fortifications while acclimatising themselves to the harsh desert conditions and getting used to the different military atmosphere under British command – quite different from the campaign in East Africa, where the South Africans had enjoyed considerable autonomy. In fact, more time was spent on the defences of Matruh than on essential desert training.

The role of the South Africans in Crusader was explained to the divisional commander, Maj Gen George Brink, at a conference held on

6 October. Brink was concerned that his division would field only two brigades instead of the three called for in the order of battle. The lack of a third brigade would limit his division's full fighting and defensive power. On 2 November Brink was still not in possession of his transport, despite assurances from headquarters in Cairo that he would receive it by the end of October. Brink placed his position in writing, stating that due to the delays in receiving his transport, he was unable to undertake the required desert training and would therefore not be ready for any deployment until 21 November. The commander of the Eighth Army, Lt Gen Alan Cunningham, threatened to reassign the South Africans to a semi-defensive role, forcing Brink to relent and move the date back to 18 November.

The battle begins, 18 and 19 November

The British achieved complete surprise, leaving the Germans unaware of the developing British threat at Gabr Saleh. The failure to entice the German armoured forces indicated that the choice of Gabr Saleh was fallacious. The German inaction forced the British to change the plan and aim for Sidi Rezegh, thus threatening the opening of a corridor to Tobruk. This they would have to accomplish alone as Lt Gen William 'Strafer' Gott, commander of 7th Armoured Division, comprising the 4th, 7th and 22nd armoured brigades with support troops, decided that the Italian 132nd Armoured Division (Ariete) at Bir El Gubi must be dislodged by the 22nd Brigade. The 4th Armoured Brigade was left with the task of guarding the flank of XIII Corps. At a stroke, the British armoured forces were split into three.

By evening, the 1st South African Brigade had advanced 144 km, covering the west flank of XXX Corps, reaching its objective at El Cuasc, with 5th Brigade just 32 km to the south. Their orders for the next day entailed the occupation of Bir El Gubi by 1st Brigade and Gueret Hamza, 16 km to the south, by 5th Brigade. The task of dislodging the Ariete Division, based at Bir El Gubi, was left to 22nd Armoured Brigade.

At noon on the second day, Brink received orders to move 1st Brigade to Gueret Hamza and 5th Brigade to El Cuasc, and to await news and developments of the armoured attack on the Ariete Division at Bir El

Gubi. At 16:00, Brink received orders from XXX Corps to occupy Bir El Gubi by 18:00. At 17:15, he received an immediate halt order as the position at Bir El Gubi was now unknown, signalling that the British armoured attack might not have been successful (in fact, the Italians still held the position in strength). Brink was now given the task of occupying Bir El Gubi with an infantry brigade where a British armoured brigade had failed.

Earlier that day, 7th Armoured Brigade had seized the important airfield at Sidi Rezegh and the British opted for a much bolder plan of shifting the emphasis and concentration of forces there. Concentrating the armoured forces proved to be a near impossible task as 22nd Armoured Brigade had been defeated by the Italians with great loss and 4th Armoured Brigade had the dual purpose of guarding 2nd New Zealand Infantry Division and providing a component of the concentrated armour at Gabr Saleh. The new concentration point of Sidi Rezegh increased the distance between the brigades, which countered the intention to consolidate all available armour against a German attack.

The British arrival at Sidi Rezegh forced Rommel to reconsider their true intentions and he authorised an attack, to be launched by Kampfgruppe Stephan, a hastily formed all-arms battle group, on 4th Armoured Brigade near Gabr Saleh. In what was the first large-scale clash of armour in desert warfare, the two sides crashed into each other in an increasingly confusing battle. The battle ended at dusk with the British forces, unsupported by artillery, unable to harass the Germans, who were resupplying on the battlefield behind a screen of antitank fire.

Rommel realises that Crusader is not a diversion

Rommel was now convinced of the British intentions, and he realised that Crusader was more than a mere diversion to distract him from his plan to attack and capture besieged Tobruk. He ordered Gen Ludwig Crüwell to seek and destroy the British armour and concentrate his two tank divisions – 15th Panzer and 21st Panzer – on Gabr Saleh and attack the British 4th Armoured Brigade using overwhelming force. Fortunately for the British, the German plan was revealed through intelligence intercepts. This prompted Lt Gen Charles Willoughby Norrie to order 22nd Armoured Brigade to disengage with Ariete and move across from

Bir El Gubi to Gabr Saleh to support 4th Armoured Brigade. When the clash occurred at 16:30 on 20 November, it took place between 4th Armoured Brigade and 15th Panzer Division, as 22nd Armoured Brigade and 21st Panzer Division had not yet arrived on the battlefield. The British, who had assumed a strong defensive position, were steadily forced backwards, once again leaving control of the battlefield to the Germans. This enabled the Germans to recover and repair their damaged vehicles, while the British tanks damaged in the clash were permanently lost.

That morning the South Africans received orders to move their 1st Brigade up to Bir El Gubi. They were to either capture the point if it was not too heavily defended or mask it if it was felt that an attack would draw unnecessary casualties. The British obviously felt that 22nd Armoured Brigade had dealt the Ariete Division a sharp blow and that the South Africans would be able to dislodge the supposedly weakened Italians from Bir El Gubi with ease. The 5th Brigade was to move up to the vicinity of Sidi Rezegh in support of 7th Armoured Brigade and to meet the sortie that was being sent from Tobruk. The South Africans were to provide 7th Armoured Brigade with valuable infantry support by seizing and holding the raised rim of the escarpment to the north, allowing observation as far as El Duda.

As described above, 22nd Armoured Brigade had been rushed to Gabr Saleh to bolster 4th Armoured Brigade for the much-anticipated tank clash. This exposed the South African infantry to the Italian armoured formation at Bir El Gubi, and they were decidedly edgy at the prospect of being pitted against a tank formation, albeit an Italian one. Brigadier Dan Pienaar, in command of 1st Brigade, was hesitant and lacked precise information as to the strength and disposition of the Ariete Division. At 09:00, while advancing cautiously, the lead elements of 1st Brigade came under Italian artillery fire. The South Africans halted and began an artillery duel with the Italians that lasted the whole day. The South African 5th Brigade also advanced to Sidi Rezegh, cautiously halting at night and thus delaying their arrival at the objective. The South Africans' inability or unwillingness to move at night put them at a severe disadvantage and cost them dearly when the two brigades were unable to combine to offer a common defence. Pienaar felt that an infantry attack on the Ariete Division at Bir El Gubi would be a useless waste of lives. Brink fully concurred with Pienaar and instructed him to take up defensive positions, effectively masking Ariete.

21 November

During the evening of 20–21 November, Rommel realised that the British forces gathering at Sidi Rezegh were poised to relieve Tobruk. As a result, he encouraged Crüwell to concentrate the Afrika Korps in the vicinity of Sidi Rezegh and neutralise the threat. At dawn the British 70th Infantry Division in Tobruk launched an attack towards Sidi Rezegh, a mere 18 km away, and after some hard fighting against resilient Italians and the Germans from the 90th Light Division it managed to penetrate to within 6 km of El Duda. The 70th Division lost 60 of their complement of 109 tanks.

The southern pincer was to be formed by 7th Armoured Brigade, but instead of launching an attack to meet the forces breaking out of Tobruk, it found itself fighting for its life. Half an hour before the attack was to be launched, news came of the arrival of both German panzer divisions. The Germans crashed into the British armour at Sidi Rezegh and all but annihilated 7th Armoured Brigade, reducing it to 28 tanks out of an original strength of 141. In four days of intense fighting, the Eighth Army had lost some 530 tanks, while the enemy had lost about 100.

The 1st South African Brigade maintained their screening duties of Ariete in the Bir El Gubi area on 21 November, with the artillery duel continuing throughout the day. The 5th Brigade had reached a point 22 km south of Sidi Rezegh the previous day before stopping as night approached. A dispatch written by the British commander-in-chief, Field Marshal (Sir) Claude Auchinleck, although carefully worded, throws some light on the excruciating slowness of the South African efforts to close up on Sidi Rezegh. It basically boiled down to inexperience and the presence of the Italians, who harassed 5th Brigade with sporadic attacks during the day. Brink had instructed Brig Frank Armstrong to leave all his non-essential 'B' echelon vehicles behind in the staging area before departing for Sidi Rezegh. However, contrary to Brink's instruction, Armstrong's brigade was accompanied by its entire 'B' echelon.

British decision-making throughout Crusader would be adversely affected by the vast overestimation of the damage they had inflicted on

South African troops before the Battle of Sidi Rezegh, 1941

Destroyed German tanks on the Sidi Rezegh battlefield

German armour. British intentions to destroy the Axis armour in detail had not materialised and their overwhelming superiority in tanks was rapidly diminishing through the failure to concentrate their armour assets against the Axis.

22 November

Dawn saw the tactical withdrawal of the two victorious panzer divisions, and the resultant lull afforded by the German withdrawal from the battlefield encouraged Gott to order 1st South African Brigade to move up to Sidi Rezegh. In response, Brink ordered Pienaar to move up to Sidi Rezegh as the 22nd Guards Brigade would be taking over the masking duties of Ariete from 1st Brigade. Pienaar, reluctant to move until he had been fully relieved by the Guards, procrastinated for the entire day. The continued presence of Ariete on the South African flank invoked hesitancy in Armstrong, and especially in Pienaar, who continued to cast a wary eye towards Ariete.

The 5th Brigade, although only a few kilometres from the epic tank battles taking place, manoeuvred up to the edge of the southern escarpment, where Gott ordered them to attack point 178 and occupy the positions held there by the German 155th Infantry Regiment. However, the lack of effective reconnaissance ensured that the artillery was not able to engage the enemy, as targets had not been identified, and the South African attack was repulsed with casualties. Pienaar started to move only at 17:30 despite being asked to do so many hours before. His hesitancy and obduracy led some critics to believe that Pienaar, out of excessive caution, had abandoned 5th Brigade to its fate. In the interim, the German panzer divisions were able to capture the British positions around Sidi Rezegh in a bold armoured attack later in the day. The British now had little prospect of forcing a corridor to Tobruk as they had lost their numerical advantage in tanks and were now in fact outnumbered by the Axis forces, which had recaptured the airfield at Sidi Rezegh. The day's events had almost sealed the fate of the 5th Brigade. It was left isolated by the tardiness of its sister unit, 1st Brigade, which was languishing kilometres to the south. The 5th Brigade was now effectively bereft of tank support because of the near destruction of British armour and the inability to coordinate a defence with the remaining tanks in the vicinity.

The annihilation of 5th Brigade, 23 November

Rommel now sought to eliminate the 7th Armoured Division and 1 SA Div by concentrating most of his tank assets in a final assault. Norrie, faced with an increasingly bleak situation, intended to build a strong infantry position around 5th Brigade and use the remaining British armour to hold off attacks by the 'depleted' enemy armour. Brink had little sense of foreboding and incorrectly evaluated that the 'situation was in hand', relying on the false premise that the British retained their superiority in tank numbers and on the expected arrival of the New Zealand division, which would add its 'I' tanks (infantry tanks) to the armoured strength of the British forces south of Sidi Rezegh.

The 5th Brigade occupied a position some 3 km short of point 178, arranged in a three-square-kilometre defensive box. The southern portion of the box consisted mainly of the 'B' echelon elements. The 22nd Armoured Brigade was deployed 1.6 km to the west of 5th Brigade. To the east lay the Support Group and a remnant of 7th Armoured Brigade, both of which had borne the brunt of the German attack on the Sidi Rezegh airfield the previous day. The largely intact 4th Armoured Brigade would play no role on the day, having been incapacitated by the capture of its headquarters the previous day. The British dispositions around Sidi Rezegh were not concentrated and formed three distinct formations, a situation not conducive to meeting the impending Axis onslaught. Furthermore, there was no means of direct communication between Armstrong's headquarters and British forces to the east and west of the South African laager. The South Africans' inability to communicate effectively with other units in proximity, including the armoured formations, was also a severe disadvantage in coordinating a common defence. The 5th Brigade failed to coordinate its defences effectively with the units that had deployed in proximity on 23 November.

Rommel intended to crush the British in an overwhelming attack and sent 15th Panzer Division with the tank regiment of 21st Panzer Division around the eastern flank of 5th Brigade to link up with the Ariete Division. They would then launch an attack northward to Sidi Rezegh. The panzer divisions in the south would be the hammer that drove towards the anvil – the German infantry manning the escarpment in front of the South Africans. The Germans had no idea that their

139

drive south would place them between 5th Brigade and 1st Brigade as their intention was to be south of the entire XXX Corps.

Pienaar and his 1st Brigade had declined to undertake a night march and close the southern flank of 5th Brigade, leaving it vulnerable and undefended, with the entire 'B' echelon exposed. This meant that an opportunity was lost to combine the strength of the South African brigades under cover of darkness. All chances of linking up began to disappear at daybreak as the Axis armour gathered in the south and effectively drove a wedge between the two brigades. The growing armoured threat directly in his path to the north forced Pienaar to abandon all hope of joining forces with 5th Brigade. By 14:30 the Germans had completed their assembly and reorientation to face north, together with Ariete, and were now disposed facing the weak southern flank of 5th Brigade. Fortunately, owing to the timely intervention of Gen Gott, the southern sector now contained 50 per cent of the brigade's available artillery to meet the German attack.

The Axis, having assembled all their armoured forces, began their attack at 16:00. The Germans faced an extremely deep position, and under normal circumstances would have had to deploy in depth rather than the 16 km breadth that their three armoured formations now found themselves in. Crüwell's decision to leave half his infantry and artillery to man the northern escarpment meant that the remaining infantry and artillery component of the panzer divisions were covering double the normal frontage. The effect was that once the attack got under way, only the central portion managed to engage 5th Brigade solidly, while the two wings, Ariete on the left and 5th Panzer Regiment and 200th Infantry Regiment on the right, brushed past 5th Brigade's flanks. The Germans had failed to concentrate their forces effectively, and this would cost them dearly.

In what was one of the largest tank attacks of the desert war, the Germans charged at the South Africans with 110 tanks of 8th Panzer Regiment, followed closely by two infantry battalions of the 115th Infantry Regiment, who were carried forward in their vulnerable lorries. They were met with a hail of fire from the South African gunners lurking among the lorries of the 'B' echelon. The German infantry following the tanks tried to stay in their vehicles for as long as possible but were met with withering fire that claimed many of them. The South Africans continued to fight in small pockets and opposed the German infantry vigorously. Assistance for the South Africans came in the form of a counterattack by the remnants of 22nd Armoured Brigade. The South Africans, although exacting a fearsome toll on the advancing Germans, were steadily overrun. Armstrong and his headquarters were taken prisoner. The 5th Brigade was annihilated, suffering 224 killed, 379 wounded and approximately 2 800 captured. The Germans lost 72 out of 162 tanks deployed in the attack and incurred severe casualties among commissioned and non-commissioned officers. The 15th Panzer Division lost both its battalion commanders, five of its six company commanders and most of its troop carriers. By all accounts, the South Africans fought bravely, inflicting significant losses in the face of overwhelming German superiority.

There is no single reason why 5th Brigade was shattered at Sidi Rezegh on 23 November 1941 but rather a series of factors. Poor preparation by the South Africans, coupled with an inferior battle doctrine and poor execution of an over-complicated plan, conspired to tip the balance against the brigade's survival. Nevertheless, the South Africans managed to inflict significant losses on the German armoured formations before their destruction, a fact underplayed or ignored in most of the secondary sources on the subject.

The British and South Africans succumbed to the superior battle tactics of the Germans. The British Army failed to adopt a combined-arms approach and relied on their tanks to force the issue, largely disregarding the other supporting arms. The British force structure, based on brigades rather than divisions, made it difficult to concentrate efforts at the *schwerpunkt* (point of main effort) and led to brigades often being committed piecemeal to the battle. This doctrine was responsible for the greater part of the British armour being destroyed for little gain. Once British armour strength was dissipated, it left the South African infantry brigades exposed and vulnerable to attack by the combined Axis forces.

The South Africans, too, must share responsibility for the tragic demise of 5th Brigade. The veterans of the East African campaign were poorly trained in desert warfare and reluctant to conduct night manoeuvres, which is an essential part of confronting a well-trained and highly motivated enemy. They were further hamstrung by fielding only two brigades instead of the normal three for a division. Brink had had to choose between withdrawing his poorly trained forces from Operation Crusader or risking them to maintain the good name of South Africa. He chose the latter, and his decision to commit an undertrained and understrength division into the teeth of battle was questionable at best and reckless at worst. Once the South Africans were committed to Crusader, they behaved tentatively throughout the operation. Pienaar's obstinate refusal to close up 1st Brigade with 5th Brigade severely weakened the fighting power of the South African division at the critical moment.

The South Africans adopted a static defensive posture that is often fatal in mobile warfare. They would have fared better if they had used their mobility to evade the German attack instead of meeting it head-on. When the Germans launched the final attack on the South African positions, it can be argued that more could have been done on the defences and that Armstrong should have taken more heed of the reconnaissance reporting the imminent German attack and its direction. As it turns out, the South Africans did indeed fortify their southern flank with half the artillery at their disposal and in so doing inflicted grievous damage on the Germans. The South Africans would again find themselves defending a static position a few months later at Tobruk. Their sacrifice of mobility for the sake of defending a fixed point on the map would cost them even more dearly than at Sidi Rezegh and mark one of South Africa's worst military defeats.

11

TOBRUK, 1942

On 26 May 1942, after four months of respite and with his resources replenished, Lt Gen Erwin Rommel unleashed the Afrika Korps on the British Eighth Army. The British, aware that the German offensive was imminent, decided to assume the defensive as they were confident behind their extensive fortifications and all-around dispositions. Rommel launched a diversionary attack on the northern section of the Gazala line, to the west of Tobruk, while sending the bulk of his mobile forces around the southernmost point of the Eighth Army line at Bir Hacheim, an oasis held by Free French troops.

Rommel's thrust behind the defences of the Eighth Army placed him in a position that became known infamously as the Cauldron. There Rommel's forces, after having stalled due to British defences and poor logistics, regrouped and formed a defensive position isolated behind the British lines. Strenuous efforts by the Eighth Army to destroy or dislodge this incursion met with high casualties and little success as the British, once again, failed to concentrate their superior forces and committed their armour brigades in a piecemeal fashion. These poorly coordinated and un-combined attacks were devoured by the concentrated Axis forces skilfully placed behind the British minefields and protected by their lethal antitank artillery. On 1 June 1942, Rommel eliminated the British 150th Brigade's position, thus creating a supply route through the minefields and effectively ending his encirclement by the Eighth Army. On 3 June, and with the supply route to his armoured force now secure, Rommel launched an offensive on Bir Hacheim and, in a hard-fought battle, overran the garrison on 10 June.

The Battle of Tobruk, 1942

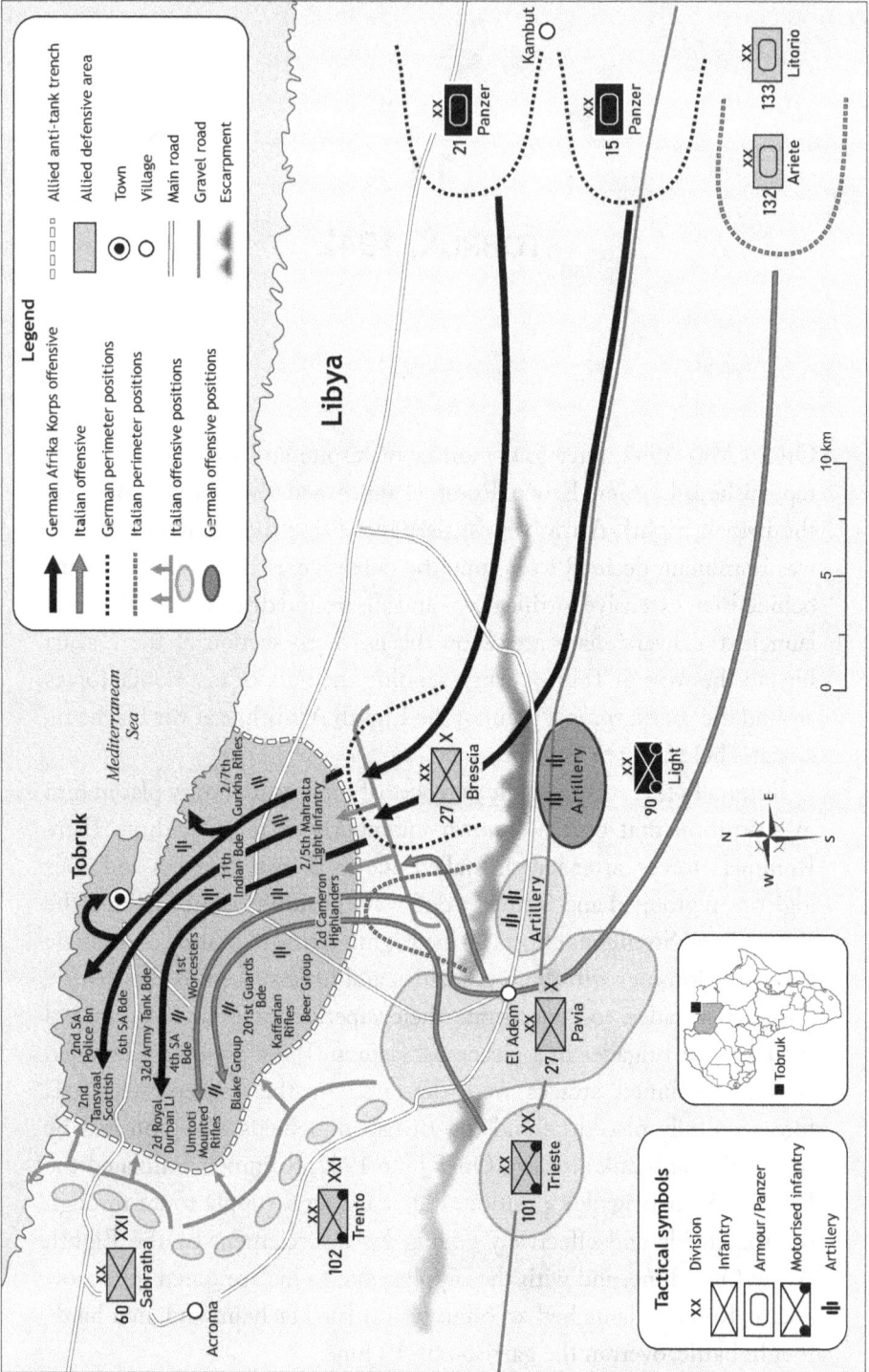

Tobruk

Legend

German Afrika Korps offensive
Italian offensive
German perimeter positions
Italian perimeter positions
Italian offensive positions
German offensive positions

Allied anti-tank trench
Allied defensive area
Town
Village
Main road
Gravel road
Escarpment

Libya

Mediterranean Sea

Tobruk

Kambut

XX 21 Panzer
XX 15 Panzer

XX 132 Ariete
XX 133 Litorio

2/7th Gurkha Rifles
11th Indian Bde
2/5th Mahratta Light Infantry
2d Cameron Highlanders

XX 27 Brescia
Artillery
XX 90 Light

2d SA Police Bn
6th SA Bde
32d Army Tank Bde
1st Worcesters
4th SA Bde
2d Royal Durban LI
Umvoti Mounted Rifles
201st Guards Bde
Blake Group
Kaffrarian Rifles
Beer Group

2d Transvaal Scottish

El Adem
X 27 Pavia

XX 101 XX Trieste

XXI 102 Trento

XX 60 XXI Sabratha

Acroma

N E S W

0 5 10 km

Tactical symbols

XX	Division
	Infantry
	Armour / Panzer
	Motorised infantry
	Artillery

144

The Eighth Army resistance at Bir Hacheim was conducted by the 1st Free French Brigade, commanded by Général de brigade Marie-Pierre Kœnig. He and his troops had the luxury of three months to prepare for the coming battle, which they used for digging trenches, setting up machine-gun nests and planting land mines around the fortress. The brigade was able to conduct a successful evacuation from a hopeless situation on 10 June after withstanding heavy attacks by the Afrika Korps over a period of 15 days. It is interesting to contrast this tenacious performance with the unsuccessful defence of Tobruk some 11 days later.

Following another major defeat of British armour, at Knightsbridge on 12 June, the Eighth Army began an eastward retreat to the Egyptian border, effectively abandoning the Gazala line and leaving Tobruk to be surrounded again by Axis forces on 17 June. The besieged garrison of Tobruk included the 2nd South African Division, among other Commonwealth elements, and was commanded by a South African, Maj Gen Hendrik Klopper. Klopper found himself in the unenviable position of having to defend Tobruk against a foe flushed with victory and high morale and led by a wily and capable commander. The fact that holding on to Tobruk was a last-minute decision, reversing a firm resolution not to defend it in the event of possible isolation, exacerbated what was becoming a rapidly confused situation.

Adding to the thickening fog of war enveloping the Allies was one of the most astounding feints in military history, when Rommel bypassed Tobruk to fool the defenders that they were to be left for later treatment. He executed the classic manoeuvre that Liddell Hart termed the 'indirect approach'. On 20 June, Rommel swung his entire force around to attack the startled defenders of Tobruk, mounting a concentrated attack supported by every available air asset on the southeastern perimeter of the fortress. The defenders, transfixed and having no answer to the sheer audacity of the offensive, put up little resistance, and on 21 June a triumphant Rommel received the surrender of Tobruk and its garrison of 34 000, yielding a colossal haul of booty in the form of fuel, rations and transport fundamental to sustaining the Afrika Korps in the weeks to come.

Tobruk is not to be invested again!

The fact that Tobruk was invested on 18 June was not entirely on account of the reversals suffered by the Eighth Army. There is no doubt that Tobruk could have been successfully evacuated before being encircled, had the British chosen this course of action. The decision to hold Tobruk was in fact made at the eleventh hour and went against the British policy of not allowing Tobruk to be invested for a second time. The withdrawal to the Egyptian border ordered by Gen Neil Ritchie was not some spur-of-the-moment improvisation in the face of a relentless enemy but was in line with an operational order to XIII Corps, dated 10 May, clearly stating that should the defence of the Gazala line become untenable, then the facilities at Tobruk were to be demolished and abandoned and the entire corps withdrawn to the Egyptian frontier.

When the Gazala line indeed became untenable, after the costly battles of 13 June, Field Marshal (Sir) Claude Auchinleck, Commander-in-Chief Middle East Command, intervened and proposed that the withdrawal of Eighth Army would be to the line Acroma–El Adem and southwards. This was a clear change of plan and not in accordance with Operation Freeborn, which involved the abandonment of Tobruk should the situation become untenable. Therefore, there existed, at the time of withdrawing the 1st South African Division and the 50th (Northumbrian) Division, an unfortunate difference of understanding between Auchinleck and Ritchie. Auchinleck believed that the line Acroma–El Adem–Bir Gubi would be defended, with the two retreating divisions taking up positions on that line, while Ritchie, clearly following the directives of Operation Freeborn, ordered the two divisions to the Egyptian frontier. Ritchie failed to inform Auchinleck of his true intentions, and it is clear that he planned to withdraw to the Egyptian frontier whether Tobruk was to be held in isolation or abandoned. Auchinleck now envisaged that Tobruk would be held as part of a defensive line manned by relatively unscathed troops. He was not aware that what remained was a thin veneer, the relatively unscathed divisions having withdrawn to the Egyptian frontier.

On 14 June, the 1st South African and 50th divisions successfully withdrew from the Gazala line and made for the Egyptian border, contrary to what Auchinleck had planned. The 1st South African Division, under

Maj Gen Dan Pienaar, retreated through Tobruk. It is impossible to imagine that Klopper had any illusion that Pienaar's division would play a part in a defensive line at Tobruk. The 50th Division had to fight its way through Italian forces and make a wide detour through the desert behind enemy lines as far south as Bir Hacheim, reaching the Egyptian frontier virtually intact. The two divisions, by not taking up defensive positions on the Acroma–El Adem–Bir Gubi line, were in effect allowing for the isolation and investment of Tobruk. The force that was now expected to hold the rampant Afrika Korps at bay consisted of the remnants of infantry brigades and a much-weakened 4th Armoured Brigade, recently mauled in the battles of the Cauldron.

On 15 June, the panzer divisions were ordered forward to attack Belhamed and El Adem, positions effectively screening the vulnerable southeast corner of the Tobruk perimeter. The initial German attacks were repulsed, but Rommel, not to be denied, forced the defenders of El Adem to abandon their position on 16–17 June, finally exposing the cornerstone of the outward defences of Tobruk. Klopper, inexplicably, was not informed of the abandonment of El Adem and became aware of the grave situation only when reconnaissance units of the Umvoti Mounted Rifles discovered it to be in enemy hands on 17 June. Simultaneously, the British forward airstrips were captured, severely hampering future air support for the Tobruk garrison. Rommel was able to report triumphantly to Berlin on 18 June that he had surrounded the port of Tobruk and that the nearest enemy force of any consequence, besides those invested in Tobruk, were 64 km away on the Egyptian frontier.

Tobruk besieged

Historians generally agree that the defences of Tobruk in June 1942 were in a poor state compared to the first siege, in 1941, when the garrison, under Lt Gen LJ Morshead, withstood two serious attacks and many minor ones in a brilliantly coordinated defence. But the defenders of Tobruk in 1941 had not faced such a concentrated and powerful attack as that delivered by Rommel on 20 June 1942. The Tobruk fortress comprised a double line of prepared strongpoints, consisting of concrete dugouts and wire defences, along a 53 km perimeter that was enclosed by a double line of wire, an antitank ditch and a perimeter

147

minefield. The inner defences, much strengthened by Morshead, consisted of strongpoints at strategic positions and internal minefields coordinated into an internal line of defence known as the 'blue line'.

The South African official history describes the deterioration in the Tobruk defences, claiming that the long-neglected antitank ditch had begun to silt up, having been filled in to facilitate an evacuation. There appeared to be, according to the official history, little knowledge of the composition or layout of the minefields in the southeastern corner of the fortress, which had been laid by successive defenders, of varying nationalities, over the previous two years. The most vulnerable sector of the fortress remained the southeast, where large quantities of mines had supposedly been lifted 'and were never replaced' during the Crusader operations in November 1941 – once again to facilitate a planned breakout. More than a few sources mention that the perimeter defences had been denuded of wire and mines to strengthen the Gazala positions. What remained was poorly maintained due to the general understanding that in the event of the Gazala line not being held, Tobruk would be evacuated.

However, this dismal picture of neglect flies in the face of evidence presented at the subsequent court of inquiry. Brigadier C de L Gaussen, the Chief Engineer XIII Corps, stated that 'it was not the policy to touch any of the perimeter defences at all' and that very little dismantling was undertaken. Brigadier FH Kisch, the Chief Engineer Eighth Army, giving evidence at the same inquiry, felt that the defences of Tobruk had deteriorated and that extensive use had been made of mines and wire for the Gazala defences. However, Kisch reported discussions with the Chief Engineer 2nd South African Infantry Division, Colonel Henderson, who felt that he had made good any deficiencies in the defences by laying new mines to close the gaps. Klopper himself stated that whole minefields had indeed been lifted for use at Gazala and Knightsbridge but that they had been replaced. He denied that the minefields were in a poor condition at the onset of the siege.

Despite the relative inexperience of the leader group commanding 2nd South African Infantry Division and the inexperience of the division itself, the morale of the commander at Tobruk seems to have been high. Klopper clearly stated his confidence and described a 'general feeling of optimism' in Tobruk in a letter to Maj Gen Frank Theron, the General Officer Administration of South African forces in the Middle East, dated 16 June. It must be noted that at the time of writing the letter, Klopper believed that Tobruk was part of a defensive line and would not be left isolated, having been assured by the Eighth Army that El Adem and Belhamed, both key to the Tobruk defences on the southeastern front, would be held. This general feeling of optimism was again confirmed in a meeting held in Tobruk on 16 June attended by Ritchie, Lt Gen William 'Strafer' Gott and Klopper, where the South African agreed that he was able to hold the fortress for at least 90 days. Whether the same confidence permeated down to the lower command structures is less certain, keeping in mind the recent series of reversals suffered by the Eighth Army. A good proportion of the garrison consisted of disparate units, some of them mauled by the Afrika Korps during the Cauldron battles, others being stragglers from units retreating to the Egyptian frontier. The point is made that Klopper was an unknown quantity to most of those in Tobruk, including his own South African troops, and that this fact, combined with the inevitable confusion due to a rapidly developing situation, was not conducive to a state of high morale.

The South African contingent at Tobruk consisted of two infantry brigades, the 4th and 6th, together with a battalion from the 1st South African Division left behind by Pienaar as he retreated through Tobruk some days earlier. The South Africans manned the perimeter defences from the coast to the southwest corner of the fortress. The vulnerable southeast corner of the remaining 21 km perimeter was manned by the 11th Indian Brigade, under the command of the experienced Brig A Anderson, and a composite South African battalion called the Beer Group.

The mobile element of the defences consisted of the 32nd Army Tank Brigade under the command of the able Brig AC Willison. The brigade had seen extensive action and suffered hard blows in the Gazala battles. There was also the 201st Guards Motor Brigade, under the newly appointed Brig HF Johnson, which was in fact a hastily put-together composite unit. The mobile forces possessed 54 operational 'I' tanks and a number of the new and highly effective six-pounder antitank guns. The mobile forces took up positions in the Fort Pilistrano area, which was almost in the centre of the Tobruk fortress. The important crossroads of Kings Cross was devoid of units manning permanent positions, and in fact the only force covering this area was an artillery regiment and the reaction force of the 201st Guards Battalion.

The South African official history describes the field artillery as being formidable in quantity and well provided with ammunition. However, it was scattered among the entire defence and not homogeneous in organisation or structure. The artillery was uncoordinated and unable to bring down concentrated 'fire on any spot within the perimeter … at a moment's notice', as had been the case under Morshead in 1941. The artillery fire plans were inferior, as were the communication systems. Together with a poor chain of command, it all amounted to negating the garrison's ability to deter Axis penetration of the perimeter defences.

The antitank defences of Tobruk, consisting of 69 guns, were similarly dispersed among the various battalions, with little coordination or concentration. The anti-aircraft defences had 18 3.7-inch guns, roughly equivalent to the deadly German 88 mm, and they were authorised to use these in an antitank role if necessary.

The court of inquiry later found that the defenders of Tobruk in June 1942 enjoyed a significant superiority in nearly every area when compared to the previous garrison. Klopper fielded a far superior armoured component, having access to heavy infantry tanks rather than the obsolete lighter cruiser tanks, and having a good number of armoured cars at his disposal. In the all-important area of antitank weaponry, Klopper enjoyed significant advantages over his predecessor. He deployed more antitank guns, including 23 six-pounders, which, if deployed correctly, had the potential to wreak havoc on enemy armour. Regarding artillery and anti-aircraft artillery, Klopper was well supplied and there was an ample supply of ammunition for all weapons, which is not surprising, given that Tobruk was a designated supply base for the Gazala positions. Three companies of the Royal Army Service Corps were stationed in the fortress to provide transport should the garrison have to withdraw.

The organisation of the defence and counterattack force

Early indicators of a dysfunctional command structure in Tobruk were reported by Lt Col M Gooler, the official United States Military

Observer. Gooler noted a decided lack of cooperation between Klopper, his chief of staff and the heads of the various staff sections, in particular Operations and Intelligence. On 15 June at 14:00, Klopper called a meeting of his brigade commanders and explained that Tobruk was to be held for a minimum of three months. Apparently, no tactical questions were discussed at this conference, which is surprising, given the gravity of the situation and the altered role that the garrison was now expected to perform.

It was only after the meeting that Willison, a veteran of the previous siege, approached Klopper and expressed his concern about the dispositions of the forces defending Tobruk. Willison requested that all armoured cars and tanks be placed under his command, and that he be given the responsibility for any enemy attacks in the coastal area. This would free up all the brigades to man the perimeter, as had been the case in the previous siege. Willison also suggested that the gun emplacements occupy a central and concentrated position on the Pilastrino Ridge. Klopper, while politely listening to Willison's views, made little effort to define or clarify his role or his command. An administrative conference held the same day confirmed that the supply situation appeared to be adequate. However, according to the official history, there appeared to be an alarming shortage of medium ammunition, at only 450 rounds per gun. Klopper himself, in an interview after the war, confirmed the shortage of artillery ammunition, saying it was far below requirements and that on 20 June there were E Boats bringing in additional artillery ammunition.

On 16 June, Klopper assured Ritchie and Gott that he could hold the fort for three months. On the same day, Klopper agreed to a provisional plan drawn up by Johnson to coordinate the artillery, armoured force and infantry as a reaction and counterattack force by means of a combined battle headquarters. Unfortunately, at his own conference to implement the plans, it appears that neither the commander nor the representative of the Army Tank Brigade nor the commander of the Royal Artillery bothered to attend.

The next day, 17 June, was spent attending to the physical defences of the fortress: digging, wiring, minelaying and reconnoitring in certain areas. Any attempt at the vital task of coordinating the reserves to form a combined-arms counterattack force would have to wait for the next day, when Klopper held yet another conference. There it was decided that the 32nd Army Tank Brigade and the 201st Guards Battalion would form the reserve of the garrison. Klopper conceded to send the artillery commander, Col Richards, to see Willison about artillery support. This was very different from the first siege, when the counterattack force, consisting of all the armoured vehicles, a full infantry brigade and a regiment of guns together with a troop of antitank guns, was placed under the command of Willison. Therefore, rather than create a reserve of combined arms under one commander, Klopper had opted for Johnson's proposal rather to establish a combined battle headquarters when the need arose. It is patently obvious that Klopper and his staff neither produced a detailed counterattack plan nor organised the defences on a dynamic basis, which resulted in a static defence spread evenly along the perimeter. The arrangements to organise the artillery, infantry and armour reserve into a combined dynamic counterattack force were inadequate at best and led to the piecemeal and uncoordinated application of reserves to the breach.

The attack

When it became apparent that the noose was steadily tightening around Tobruk on 18 and 19 June, Johnson proposed to counter the enemy threat forming in the El Adem area by launching a bold pre-emptive counterattack. This was soon reconsidered and then reformulated as a concentrated artillery barrage, designed to disperse the enemy gathering in the area. This shoot has been singled out by the official South African history as the reason for the ammunition rationing, as the artillery exceeded its daily allowance and had difficulty securing more ammunition. However, the artillery barrage seemed to have little effect on the Afrika Korps, who were now preparing to launch a massive offensive against Tobruk.

It is debatable whether the offensive launched by the Germans on the morning of 20 June came as a surprise to the Eighth Army or indeed to the garrison. What is certain, though, is that the German manoeuvre of bypassing the garrison in an eastward drive to the Egyptian border and then leaving a screening force to deal with the Eighth Army while

*South African troops shoring up the Tobruk defences
with barbed wire*

*Field Marshal Jan Smuts with
then Brigadier General Hendrik Klopper prior to Tobruk*

turning 180 degrees to drive westwards on Tobruk, was a remarkable achievement. The fact that this movement took place at night, on 19–20 June, and required a massive effort of coordination to ensure the assault troops and artillery were ready in their exact jumping-off points before the assault, shows how far ahead the Germans were at this stage in the art of mobile warfare. Rommel's complicated attempt at subterfuge seems not to have fooled Ritchie, who communicated to Auchinleck on the night of 19 June that he believed that the Germans were going to attack Tobruk rather than the frontier. The 11th Indian Brigade, manning the exact sector that was to be attacked, realised, after sending out patrols, that an attack was imminent.

As dawn broke, the German forces preparing to attack came into full view of the garrison. A South African battery commenced fire on the German concentration and the Germans replied in kind with artillery and air attacks, mainly concentrated on strongpoint 63. Eyewitness accounts, including that of Rommel, describe how effective this massive air and artillery assault was on the defences and the morale of the defenders. When the preparatory bombardment lifted, the infantry assault troops moved up to the defences through lanes cleared in the minefields the night before. It took two hours to drive a wedge into the defences, and by 08:00 the antitank ditch had been bridged, making it possible for the German armour to be released and to penetrate the heart of the garrison. The Germans were surprised at how weak the initial resistance was in the zone of attack, with perimeter strongpoints R58 to R69 falling into German hands in quick succession. The poor defensive efforts cannot be put down to the element of surprise, as Anderson's 11th Indian Brigade had anticipated the German attack, and he promptly threw his reserve company and platoon into the fray.

Meanwhile, Johnson of the 201st Guards Mobile Brigade had not been idle, and he now attempted to set up a combined headquarters at Kings Cross in accordance with the arrangements agreed to for a counterattack. At this crucial moment, while Johnson was setting up headquarters and appropriate communications, Willison declined to leave his headquarters. Klopper intervened and issued orders for Willison to take command of a combined force and launch a counterattack in cooperation with the 11th Indian Brigade. Anderson sent a liaison officer to the combined headquarters at Kings Cross at 07:00 in anticipation of the arrival of Willison and the 32nd Army Tank Brigade. At 07:45 the Royal Artillery's 25th Field Regiment opened fire, having held out so as not to disclose their positions and compromise their antitank role. Speed was of the essence at this point, as the tanks needed to be thrown into the fray before the Germans had a chance to set up their antitank defences. The crucial objective should have been to seal off the attack and immediately throw the German offensive back to its start line.

Willison ordered Lt Col B Reeves of the 4th Royal Tank Regiment, as the armoured unit closest to the action, to send his tanks against the German penetration at 08:00. In an inexplicable display of sluggishness, the regiment's two squadrons of tanks arrived at Kings Cross only at 09:30. An opportunity to marry up with the infantry component of the counterattack force was lost when Reeves, on receiving a party of officers from the Coldstream Guards, denied all knowledge of, or responsibility for, cooperation with any infantry force. The Guards received no instructions from headquarters and as a result stayed put while the group of liaison officers made their way to Kings Cross and languished there. At the insistence of Anderson, who was growing more desperate as the situation deteriorated, the Coldstream Guards were ordered forward to Kings Cross to join their officers at 10:00. On their arrival they remained there, never forming part of an essential combined-arms counterattack reserve. They failed to leave the Kings Cross area and counterattack at the insistence of Johnson, who would only commit them to exploiting the successes gained or making good any ground recovered by the tanks. The failure of the tanks in this impossible endeavour ensured that the infantry never ventured forth.

Two-and-a-half hours had elapsed since the order had been given to Willison to send his tanks into the fray. To add to the general slowness of the operation thus far, Reeves proceeded to commit his tanks to the battle without bothering to liaise either with the headquarters of 11th Indian Brigade or with combined headquarters. The artillery also failed to come in at the crucial early stage of the attack; the Afrika Korps reported that the fire of the Allied artillery increased noticeably only after 08:50, and up to then it had been essentially weak and ineffective.

The picture on the German side looked decidedly different. The penetrating forces were led by Rommel himself, with Gen Walther Nehring not far behind in the advance headquarters of the 15th Panzer Division. The Germans overran the headquarters of the 5th Mahratta Light Infantry and eliminated a troop of South African artillery at 10:00. At the same time, the 4th Royal Tank Regiment made slow progress along the Bardia road to arrive in the inner minefield gap. The 7th Royal Tank Regiment was ordered to form up west of Kings Cross and their commander, Lt Col Foote, after conferring with Reeves, deployed to the right of the 4th Royal Tank Regiment at L Gap, thus forming a defensive line behind the inner minefield. It was there that the two tank regiments, unsupported by infantry and antitank weapons, began to take steady losses. With the greater part of their strength destroyed for little profit, the survivors withdrew to Kings Cross. Their commander, Reeves, bumped into the immobile Coldstream Guards at 13:00 and reported that his command had been all but destroyed and only six tanks remained.

Information was slow to reach Fortress Command, who remained dependent on 11th Indian Brigade for all their information. The latter were dependent on the Mahrattas for understanding the extent of the perimeter breach. Unfortunately, 11th Indian Brigade were struggling to gain a clear picture of what was happening on the ground, as the initial German bombardment had wrecked communications in the sector. After the Mahrattas destroyed their wireless sets at 10:00 as their headquarters was overrun, the sole remaining source of inform-ation was the forward observation officer of the 2nd South African Field Battery. The intermittent communication system lagged substantially behind the events developing rapidly at the front, leaving the garrison headquarters with a false sense of security. As far as Fortress Command was concerned, the counterattack had been ordered in good time and the Indian brigade had reported that the situation was in hand. Further-more, Willison's non-communication was taken as an indicator that all was well. At 11:00, in a reversal of mood and now clearly perplexed, Klopper complained that he 'was completely in the dark' as to what the situation was and he proposed that he proceed personally to Kings Cross to assess the situation for himself. Unfortunately, he allowed himself to be dissuaded by some members of the leader group, including his chief of staff, Lt Col Kriek, who advised him that his place was at headquarters. At 13:00, as they were finishing lunch, their complacency was shattered as news of the impending disaster reached the divisional headquarters. Willison reported the destruction of 4th Royal Tank Regiment to Klopper and at 14:40 reports came in that the enemy had penetrated the inner minefield. At 15:25 it was reported that 60 enemy tanks had penetrated the inner defences and were approaching Kings Cross, which had now become effectively indefensible. Somewhere between 15:00 and 16:00, Willison reported the destruction of the 7th and 4th Royal Tank Regiments, signalling the demise of the entire armoured reserve force. The Germans, after a lightning assault, were in possession of Kings Cross, defeating the British armour and overrunning the 11th Indian Brigade and the 25th Field Regiment. Rommel was now able to deliver the final blow.

Klopper, learning of the proximity of the German offensive to Kings Cross and seemingly spurred on by the destruction of the greater part of his reserve force, did not remain idle. He set about organising a new defensive line to protect the crossroads at Pilastrino, which ran roughly along the El Adem road. A company each was ordered to detach from the 4th and 6th South African Brigades to form a counterattack force near the new line.

When Kings Cross fell to the Germans the defences of the Tobruk fortress became fragmented and uncoordinated, with units fighting where they stood, constituting individual actions, uncoordinated and without central direction from Fortress Headquarters. It was a simple matter for the Germans to proceed from Kings Cross virtually unopposed and enter the harbour of Tobruk at nightfall. Fortress Headquarters in the meantime destroyed wireless sets and moved office to the headquarters of the 6th South African Brigade. A pall of smoke rose into the sky from Tobruk harbour, signalling the partial and unofficial demolition of supplies and vehicles. The capture of Tobruk had been achieved with such speed that no official orders had been given for the destruction of supplies to prevent them falling into German hands.

By nightfall the German forces were in possession of Tobruk and a considerable salient in the eastern half of the fortress. The two South African brigades remained unscathed and unaffected by the day's events.

Klopper was able to re-establish contact with the Eighth Army at 20:00; he reported the desperate plight of his forces and requested permission to break out that night. He sought clarity whether the promised relieving force was about to counterattack the enemy. Brigadier Whiteley, standing in for Ritchie, who was away with XXX Corps, gave permission for a breakout, signalling, 'Come out tomorrow night preferably if not tonight.' He repeated at the end of his transmission: 'Tomorrow night preferred.' Klopper was dissatisfied with the inconclusive conversation with Whiteley and requested his signaller to maintain contact with Eighth Army and to try to locate Ritchie.

After a series of informal discussions between Klopper and several battalion commanders, Klopper issued a warning order for a breakout at 22:00. An opposing plan, mainly propagated by Brig Hayton and the leader group of the 4th South African Brigade, and seemingly motivated by the fact that the brigade had lost most of its transport, which precluded a breakout, suggested forming a redoubt in the southwest corner of the fortress. Klopper – seemingly swayed by the promise of a relieving force, and unable to get hold of Ritchie, together with what seemed to be a request by Whiteley to hold on for one more day – countermanded the breakout order. Instead, preparations began for a last stand based on the 4th Brigade proposal. In the meantime, Ritchie, who had returned to his headquarters at 03:30, signalled detailed instructions approving a breakout.

In a curious twist, Hayton returned to his headquarters at 03:30 and met with Lt Col Blake of the Blake group – elements of Pienaar's 1st Division left behind in Tobruk – who vigorously denounced the absurdity of Hayton's proposed defensive plan. Hayton then telephoned Klopper to tell him that his battalion commanders did not wish to fight. Klopper insisted that this change of heart would put him in 'a hell of a jam' and convinced the commanders once again to resist. However, soon after speaking to Hayton again, Klopper had yet another change of heart, believing that little advantage would be gained from a last stand, and that casualties would inevitably be high.

At 06:30 on 22 June, Klopper, after famously signalling Ritchie that he was 'doing the worst', sent a parlementaire to the Germans to offer capitulation. An anxious Ritchie enquired whether the petrol and water installations had been destroyed. Klopper answered in the affirmative, which was true in the case of the current positions held, though not in the areas already under German control. At 07:45 the German officers tasked with receiving the surrender arrived at Klopper's headquarters and, with the last wireless set destroyed, 10 722 South Africans, together with the rest of the 33 000-strong garrison, marched into captivity. A great bounty fell into German hands, consisting of arms, ammunition, fuel, foodstuff, clothing and 30 undamaged tanks.

The fall of Tobruk is a tragic example of the consequences that can befall a military leader forced into a situation that is contrary to their doctrine and beyond their skills. Klopper was a victim of his own inexperience and was promoted to his level of incompetence. That he was forced to sacrifice his mobility in defending a fixed position can be firmly blamed on the British, who vacillated in the face of inexorable pressure from Rommel. However, Klopper had many opportunities, both before and after he was surrounded, to grasp the initiative, restore mobility to the forces under his command and break out of the Axis encirclement.

Manoeuvre warfare demands a high degree of initiative throughout the command structure; unfortunately, the South Africans under Klopper proved unequal to the task. The fall of Tobruk and the surrender of the 2nd South African Infantry Division left an indelible stamp on the morale and standing of the UDF that would accompany them on their deployment to Italy. They found solace to some extent in their transformation into an armoured division. However, in terms of armoured warfare, the baptism of fire would occur at the Battle of Celleno in June 1944. That encounter directly tested the training, organisation and employment of the newly formed 6th South African Armoured Division.

The Battle of Celleno, 1944

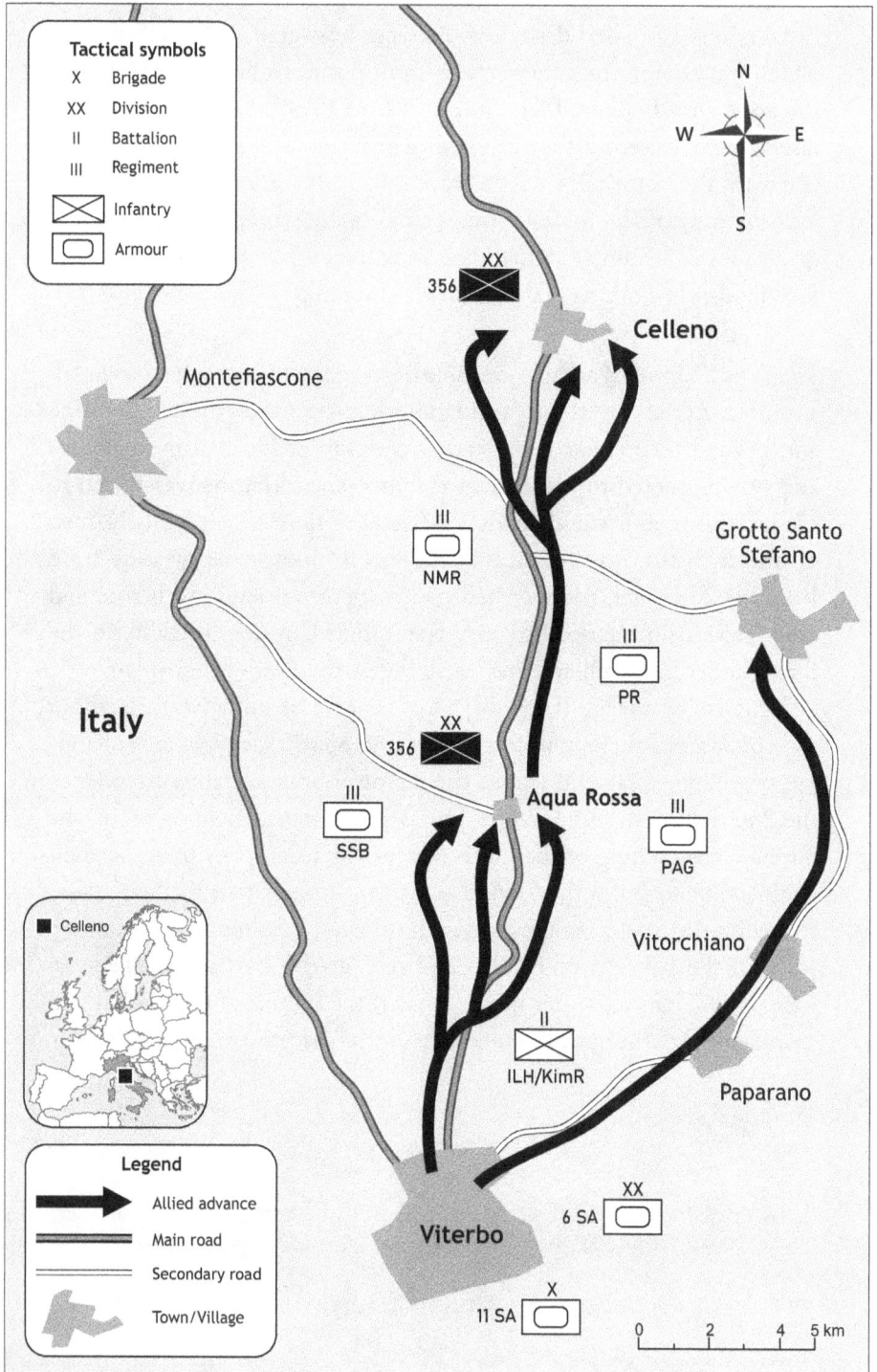

Tactical symbols

X	Brigade
XX	Division
II	Battalion
III	Regiment
[Infantry symbol]	Infantry
[Armour symbol]	Armour

356 XX

Celleno

Montefiascone

III NMR

Grotto Santo Stefano

III PR

Italy

356 XX

Aqua Rossa

III SSB

III PAG

Celleno

Vitorchiano

II ILH/KimR

Paparano

Legend

[arrow]	Allied advance
[double line]	Main road
[thin line]	Secondary road
[shape]	Town/Village

Viterbo

6 SA XX

11 SA X

0 2 4 5 km

160

12

CELLENO, 1944

In January 1944, the 6th South African Armoured Division (6 SA Armd Div) moved into a transit camp at Helwan, in Egypt, awaiting deployment to the Italian theatre of operations. At this stage, the Allied armies in Italy already numbered some 20 divisions and the British Eighth Army in particular, which was quite cosmopolitan in its make-up, did not want to add 6 SA Armd Div to its ranks. Moreover, the Allied armies in Italy already had enough armoured divisions at their disposal and it was felt that the South Africans should rather be sent to Palestine as garrison troops. Even among the headquarters staff, doubts still existed as to the suitability of the South African armoured division for operational duty in Italy.

The newly formed 6 SA Armd Div had arrived in Egypt in May 1943. There, the members of the division embarked on three training phases. During the basic phase, the emphasis was placed on armour training – gunnery, driving and maintenance, and the different functions of crew and troop commanders. Specialist training was first presented at an individual level, followed by general training to integrate the individual into the tank crew/fighting vehicles. During the unit phase, training was at the troop/platoon level up to regimental level. The third and final phase of training was spent on honing the skills of combined-arms warfare. Formation training focused primarily on putting the brigades through their paces under the leadership of the divisional and brigade commanders. This phase was immensely valuable to the divisional commander, Maj Gen Evered Poole and his divisional staff, allowing them to test their skills in applying the theory of combined-arms warfare. It was envisaged that the training period would last roughly eight months, making 6 SA Armd Div operationally deployable by the end of December.

The successful occupation of Sicily in August, coupled with the overthrow of Benito Mussolini in July that year, meant that the invasion of the Italian mainland became imminent. In September 1943, the British Eighth Army landed at Reggio di Calabria, while the US Fifth Army landed at Salerno. On his way back from the signing of the Italian armistice in September, Maj Gen Frank Theron, the GOC South African Administrative Headquarters in Egypt, paid a visit to Eighth Army headquarters in Sicily. There he was urged to reconsider the South African conversion to armour and whether the UDF troops would be better employed as an infantry complement. This was not the first time doubt had been cast on the formation of 6 SA Armd Div. Theron knew that neither Prime Minister Jan Smuts nor Lt Gen Pierre van Ryneveld, the Chief of the General Staff, would succumb to pressure from the Allied authorities – politically as well as practically – as an armoured division was less vulnerable and required fewer men than an infantry division.

However, the divisional training undertaken at El Khatatba, a base camp near Cairo, differed greatly from actual deployment in the Italian theatre of operations. Despite the emphasis on road movement, movement discipline, battle training and combined arms, desert training essentially left the South Africans unprepared for deployment to Italy, where the division would operate in close country. In fact, the desert expanses of North Africa were most appropriate for armoured warfare, whereas Italy was considered largely 'untankable'. The desert conditions also did not prepare the men for the adverse weather conditions and topographical obstacles they would experience in Italy.

In the latter half of September 1943, and following the outcome of the Quadrant Conference held in Quebec City, Poole and his staff felt almost certain that they would see action on the Italian mainland within the next year. While their future deployment was still uncertain, the ranks of 6 SA Armd Div gradually swelled during October despite severe manpower limitations within the Union. This was largely the result of a UDF policy directive in terms of which understrength units would be amalgamated to bring them up to battle strength. The ranks of the division were further bolstered by the arrival of Rhodesian soldiers, which added a complement of artillery and armour. Thus, by the end of 1943, 6 SA Armd Div started to resemble an operational armoured formation in both manpower and equipment.

When Van Ryneveld visited London in November 1943, the establishment and suitability of 6 SA Armd Div was once more brought into question. The argument centred on the fact that the British Army had more armoured divisions than were required operationally. The Director of Military Training at the War Office, Maj Gen John Whittaker, argued that some of the British armoured divisions were being reorganised into infantry equivalents and asked whether it would still be feasible and cost-effective to establish a South African armoured division. The matter was left unresolved, and for the time being 6 SA Armd Div remained in Egypt and continued with its desert training. In fact, as far as Van Ryneveld was concerned, Smuts's steadfast resolve was that a part of South Africa's forces must convert to armour. Moreover, it was easier for the UDF to provide personnel for an armoured division, as it required far less manpower than a conventional infantry division. Given the limited South African manpower by late 1943, this was the right course of action to follow.

By December, the division's training cycle in the desert was nearing completion. Despite all the criticism, and the doubts from within the division, South Africa had much to be proud of. It was the first South African division to convert successfully to armour and no division in the UDF had undergone such intensive training prior to deployment. Moreover, the officers and men had operational experience dating back to the campaigns in East Africa, North Africa and Madagascar. During March 1944 the decision was taken to deploy 6 SA Armd Div to Italy to assume offensive operations under the British Eighth Army. The move to the Italian theatre surprised everyone.

The Battle of Celleno

Towards the end of March, transit arrangements for 6 SA Armd Div started to fall into place. By 16 April most of the division had embarked for Italy, with units starting to arrive on the mainland from 20 April onwards. The South African division quickly organised itself for battle and a decision was taken to send the 12th South African Motorised

Brigade (12 SA Mot Bde) into the line near the town of Cassino to relieve the 11th Canadian Infantry Brigade. Falling under the command of the 2nd New Zealand Division for this operation, the South African infantrymen received their baptism of fire while deployed in a largely static role. They were able to test their mettle during forward patrols that brought them into direct contact with their German foes; they also experienced heavy enemy shelling. The tactically defensive deployment of the 12 SA Mot Bde formed part of the larger Allied offensive on Cassino, which was aimed at opening the road to Rome. On 20 May, the South Africans withdrew from their positions after nearly two weeks in the line, having suffered their first operational casualties in the Italian theatre. On 27 May, and after the return of the 12 SA Mot Bde, Poole and his division continued their advance towards Rome under the direct command of I Canadian Corps.

On 6 June, and coinciding with the start of Operation Overlord in Normandy, the lead elements of 6 SA Armd Div passed through Rome. The pursuit northwards from Rome was entrusted to the US Fifth Army and the British Eighth Army. The South Africans then fell under the direct command of the XIII Corps of Eighth Army, which was to advance along the Tiber River. The two armoured divisions of Eighth Army, one South African and one British, would advance along Route 3 and Route 4 respectively. The final objective of 6 SA Armd Div was the liberation of Florence and the 11th South African Armoured Brigade (11 SA Armd Bde) was designated to act as the armoured spearhead of the division for the entire advance. Their advance to Florence, 290 km by road, would commence with an offensive along the Via Flaminia aimed at the German strongpoint of Narni.

The advance along the Via Flaminia was mostly unopposed on 6 June, with the South African lead elements penetrating up to 50 km north of Rome. The speed of 11 SA Armd Bde's advance was extraordinary, especially considering that the brigade comprised approximately 1 050 vehicles moving northwards in a single column. Some German resistance was met along the route, part of a broader pattern of delaying actions fought by German forces.

As 6 SA Armd Div neared Civita Castellana on 7 June, German resistance intensified. Intelligence reports indicated that the Germans were covering their withdrawal to the Gothic Line further north. The German withdrawal also coincided with planned demolitions of vital bridges over the Tiber River. Extensive demolitions by the Germans meant that 6 SA Armd Div would in turn have to shift its axis of advance. While the South African objective remained the capture of Narni, the new axis of advance centred on the road that passed through Civita Castellana, Fabrica di Roma, Vallerano and Orte to the main objective of Narni. During the advance through Civita Castellana, 11 SA Armd Bde operated as the vanguard of the division, while the motorised brigades brought up the rear.

On the morning of 8 June, Poole was informed that it would be impossible for his division to cross the Tiber River. Once again, the division's axis of advance had to be altered. The South Africans would now continue their vanguard duties west of the Tiber, having to capture Fabrica and Vallerano and then swing their axis of advance to the west to capture Canepina, Viterbo, Orvieto and eventually Florence.

The South Africans continued their advance on Vallerano, with the tanks of the Natal Mounted Rifles (NMR) and the Special Service Battalion (SSB) leading the advance, though 11 SA Armd Bde met stiff resistance as it neared Viterbo. The German 356th Infantry Division, essentially inexperienced and raw but bolstered by the 4th Parachute Division and crack elements of the 3rd Panzer Grenadier Division and the 362nd Infantry Division, opposed the South African advance. The stiffening of German resistance was unsurprising: elements of these formations included veteran troops who had seen action throughout the war.

By 9 June, the South African forces had captured Vallerano, Canepina and the all-important town of Viterbo. General Harold Alexander, the commander of 15th Army Group, which included Eighth Army and Fifth Army, confirmed that 6 SA Armd Div would remain the spearhead of the Allied advance on Florence. On 10 June the South Africans deployed their entire armoured brigade in the advance. This was the first, and last, opportunity of the entire Italian campaign for the entire 11 SA Armd Bde to be deployed in unison. In a daring move, Poole deployed his armoured brigade without the necessary support from the divisional artillery. Brigadier JPA Furstenburg, the commander of 11 SA

Armd Bde, realised that the 356th Infantry Division would withdraw northwards via Route 2, with its left flank along the road. Furstenburg's intention was therefore to attempt to turn the German left flank by ordering the SSB to advance on his right flank.

The advance on the German right flank started at first light on the morning of 10 June. The motorised infantry of the Imperial Light Horse/Kimberley Regiment (ILH/KimR) and the tanks of the SSB immediately moved forward to establish contact with the German defensive line north of the town of Aqua Rossa. The advance north was intended to secure the bridgehead around Aqua Rossa, but the initial South African advance was soon halted by heavy enemy mortar fire. The NMR, acting as the divisional armoured reconnaissance regiment, moved forward early in the morning to scout the enemy dispositions around Aqua Rossa. It immediately started to draw heavy enemy fire from the German antitank screen, losing two tanks early on. The SSB was ordered forward to come to the rescue of the NMR. But the tanks of the SSB had barely advanced a single kilometre along the road when they met determined resistance in the form of heavy machine-gun and antitank fire. Moreover, as soon as the SSB formed up for the attack, they also came under heavy enemy shellfire. Having committed to the attack without the necessary divisional artillery support, the lead elements of the brigade were now in a rather perilous position. The OC of the SSB, Lt-Col Papa Brits, then decided to advance against the enemy in a two-up formation, with his 'A' Squadron forming a fire support base on the high ground while the other two squadrons advanced further forward. Under covering fire from the SSB tanks, the NMR were able to extricate themselves from danger.

Under the cover of the firm base established by two troops of 'A' Squadron SSB, the rest of the squadron was ordered forward into hull-down positions. Brits's gamble paid off, for as soon as the tanks started to lay down suppressing fire, the enemy broke ranks. The left flank of the German defences almost immediately collapsed as the enemy infantry was routed. The two forward operating squadrons, acting in unison, were able to silence the enemy defensive screen through the superb marksmanship of the South African and Rhodesian gunners. The ILH/KimR accompanied the advance of the SSB, with some infantry

South African tanks advancing through the narrow, confined streets of Allerona

The 6 South African Armoured Division advancing north along the spine of Italy via the congested Route 6

South African tanks passing through Rome during the Allied pursuit northwards, June 1944

going into action on the back of the advancing tanks. Brits committed all his tanks into the action. Following rapid replenishment, the SSB were once again ready to move onto the offensive. While replenishment was under way, forward observation officers of the divisional artillery moved forward and linked up with the lead elements of the SSB. The ILH/KimR proceeded to secure the area, which was a patchwork of fields, hedges and farmhouses, from the remaining pockets of enemy resistance.

By midday, the divisional artillery started engaging the numerous enemy targets in and around Aqua Rossa and the town of Celleno. Within two hours, the divisional artillery had accounted for five 88 mm guns, 16 50 mm antitank guns, three machine guns, one Mark IV tank, four Mark III tanks and many infantry. Under cover of the artillery barrage, two companies of the ILH/KimR joined ranks with the SSB and advanced towards Celleno itself. Acting in the van, 'A' Company ILH/KimR cleared the slopes leading up to Celleno. Clearing the enemy's prepared defensive positions was possible only through close cooperation between the tanks of the SSB and the infantry of the ILH/KimR. The thickly wooded area concealed numerous machine-gun nests and Panzerfaust antitank guns. To silence the German guns effectively, a slow and dangerous process, the infantry dismounted from the tanks so that the momentum of the attack would not be lost. Brits realised that he had to keep his tanks moving forward towards the vicinity of Celleno, the approach to which was obstructed by a railway embankment running right across the South African axis of advance. The only way to negotiate the obstacle was via a small road that ran beneath the railway line. The German troops had prepared a series of defensive positions along this route, including antitank guns and infantry armed with Panzerfausts, Spandau machine guns and sniper rifles, which made the advance rather dangerous.

The tanks of 'C' Squadron SSB soon managed to break through this German defensive position, though. The tanks advanced further up the road and moved into hull-down positions on the high ground, acting as a direct fire support base for the advancing ILH/KimR infantry. The tanks, essentially acting as artillery, started to bring down accurate fire on Celleno itself. Under the cover of the fire from the tanks, the infantry were able to clear the area of the remnants of the 356th Infantry

Division. Enemy resistance continued, however, and 'A' Squadron SSB suffered further losses.

Offensive action by 'C' Squadron SSB allowed the ILH/KimR infantry to advance towards the village. 'B' Squadron SSB then turned their advance to the high ground immediately north of Celleno. Having managed to move one troop of 'B' Squadron SSB onto the high ground, Furstenburg ordered 'C' Squadron SSB into an area on the right of the village that had to be cleared. The ILH/KimR infantry moved further forward, along with 'A' Squadron SSB, and then successfully dealt with enemy resistance on the right of the village. The mopping-up operations of the ILH/KimR quickly developed into a full-scale attack on Celleno. The three squadrons of the SSB were now all moved onto high ground surrounding the village and from there the tanks provided ample direct fire support to the advancing infantry. The infantry quickly moved through the town, clearing the enemy resistance out house by house.

During the day's action in and around Celleno, the tanks of Prince Alfred's Guard (PAG) were ordered by Furstenburg to cover the SSB's right flank. Having moved out of Viterbo, the PAG tanks met strong enemy resistance as they neared Grotte Santo Stefano. Without adequate infantry support, the advance was halted early in the morning. The tanks of the Pretoria Regiment (PR), then operating under the command of the 24th Guards Brigade, was ordered to move forward at around dawn to provide 11 SA Armd Bde with fire support around Celleno–Grotte Santo Stefano. The tanks of the PR soon moved into turret-down positions and provided fire support to the main attack throughout the day.

The Battle of Celleno, fought over 12 hours, was effectively over by sunset, with 11 SA Armd Bde emerging the victors. The brigade took many prisoners and inflicted heavy casualties on the German 356th Infantry Division. On the evening of 10 June, Furstenburg ordered Brits to halt his advance. Enemy fire had died down and the tanks of the SSB had exhausted their first-line ammunition and petrol. The South Africans were thus ordered to hold the ground and the SSB tanks withdrew to an area three kilometres to the south of Celleno to rest and replenish. The 24th Guards Brigade would resume the advance northwards the next morning and continue the rout of the 356th Infantry Division.

The battle in retrospect

The Battle of Celleno was South Africa's first real operational victory in the Italian theatre. The 11 SA Armd Bde, having lost only 14 men killed and 38 wounded, had inflicted more than 200 casualties on the opposing German forces during the day's fighting. Just a year earlier, however, the division was still training in the desert expanses of El Khatatba. Under-equipped, understrength and unsure of their future in mid-1943, Poole and his men had turned themselves into a capable fighting force in less than a year.

The lessons learned by 6 SA Armd Div, and most notably 11 SA Armd Bde, during the Battle of Celleno are worth noting, since they had an immense effect on the remainder of the South African operations in Italy. At Celleno, Poole wanted to see how 11 SA Armd Bde would cope with their first armoured battle. He believed that his tactical headquarters should always be deployed as close as possible to the frontline. This gave him freedom of movement and the ability to keep up to date on developments. However, while the presence of a divisional commander at the frontline could be a burden to the brigade commanders, it could also boost the morale of the soldiers on the ground. In fact, Poole's course of action was not an anomaly: it proved to be a hallmark of the South African style of mission command, with its penchant for leading from the front, as practised by Smuts in German East Africa in 1916 (see Chapter 4) and by Col William Dixon at Bangui in 2013 (see Chapter 20).

Topographically, the Italian theatre was extremely challenging. The many rivers, steep mountain ridges and deep valleys made armoured warfare and the movement of armoured divisions exceptionally difficult. Adverse road and weather conditions also severely hampered the move-ment of men and equipment during operations. The divisional staff soon realised that there was a definite difference between physical and tactical mobility. The South Africans incrementally came to understand that, in modern combat, and particularly in the Italian context, their infantry complement was often more important than their tanks. The Battle of Celleno further reinforced this notion. Adverse weather could abruptly change the conditions on the ground, often rendering farm tracks impassable to the tanks of the brigade. Movements along the roads proved even more difficult for the divisional staff, and traffic jams often made it difficult for the formation to be in the right place at the right time. In fact, the advance northwards was extremely hard on the tanks of 11 SA Armd Bde, with at least one tank knocked out for every 16 km advanced.

The relationship between armour and infantry during offensive operations received specific attention. It was appreciated that only after the infantry and armour understood one another's roles completely could they cooperate successfully during operations. Hence, when armour was held up, the motorised infantry had to pass through their ranks and clear up the enemy obstacles or strongpoints for the advance to continue. When the South African armour encountered antitank weapons, the accompanying infantry had to move up immediately, fight through the obstacle and secure the ground. This allowed the armour to halt and tactically withdraw on immediate contact, offering the infantry the time and space needed to manoeuvre on the battlefield and engage the enemy. However, infantry and armour cooperation was predicated on good communication between the two arms, which in turn ensured unity of action and command and greatly facilitated the combined-arms approach as practised by 6 SA Armd Div.

After the attack on Celleno, 6 SA Armd Div continued their advance on Florence better honed for fighting in Italy. The changing nature of the military operating environment and the increasingly built-up urban terrain encountered meant that offensive operations were mainly led by the men of 12 SA Mot Bde. After all, the conventional wisdom was that Italy was 'untankable'. The South African infantry would consequently bear the brunt of the fighting towards Florence and up to the German surrender in 1945.

Celleno would, however, remain the only battle of the Italian campaign during which the entire 11 SA Armd Bde fought as a complete entity. Furthermore, Celleno would prove to be the division's only real armoured battle in the theatre, despite hardly engaging any tanks head-on. For the rest of the campaign, the armoured regiments often acted as independent entities on the battlefield. Later, with the advance into the Apennines, large-scale independent mobile operations by the armoured brigades became nearly impossible and the fighting, in essence, became an infantry affair. From then on, the South African tanks mainly provided direct or indirect fire in support of the advancing infantry during combat operations.

The Battle of Celleno, fought on 10 June 1944, was the first and only real tank battle fought by 11 SA Armd Bde during the Italian campaign. The brigade severely mauled the German 356th Infantry Division and emerged from the battle with flying colours. The South Africans, however, suffered 53 casualties on the day and lost several tanks. Nevertheless, the success of the armoured brigade increased confidence and boosted the entire division's morale. But the three armoured regiments and its motorised infantry battalion would never again be deployed in such a manner. During the remainder of the campaign, the infantry of 12 SA Mot Bde bore the brunt of the actual fighting, with small, independent armoured actions being fought by individual armoured regiments when needed.

After the success at Celleno, 6 SA Armd Div continued its advance northwards, capturing Orvieto in the coming days. However, the pace of the advance slowed as Poole and his division met increasingly stiff German resistance – most notably from the crack Hermann Göring Division. Despite suffering losses in men and equipment, South African operations had been largely successful to date. However, in the coming weeks, the South Africans would experience their first real taste of urban warfare since the 1922 Rand Revolt (see Chapter 6), during the Battle of Chiusi. Without specialised troops and training and lacking both actual wartime experience and institutional expertise in this regard, the South African infantrymen would have to adapt quickly to the demands of high-intensity combat operations in built-up terrain.

13

CHIUSI, 1944

Confident after their success at Celleno, the 6th South African Armoured Division (6 SA Armd Div) continued its advance northwards towards Florence via Route 71. The division, with the 12th South African Motorised Brigade operating in the van, captured Bagnoregio and Orvieto in quick succession. Although it was not appreciated at the time, the capture of Orvieto on 14 June indeed marked the end of the period of swift pursuit and the start of a series of positional battles.

From Rome to Orvieto the division had pursued an enemy who could not, and dared not, make a concerted stand. As the US Fifth Army and the British Eighth Army followed up their great victories at Anzio and Cassino, it seemed possible that considerable German forces could be cut off or overrun as they steadily fell back north on successive defensive lines. However, the German forces withdrew with great speed and considerable skill. Having extricated themselves from the Allied pincers, the Germans decided to fight a delaying action on the Trasimeno Line before falling back further north towards the Arno River and the Gothic Line.

On 15 June, elements of the Natal Mounted Rifles and the Witwatersrand Rifles Regiment/Regiment de la Rey (WR/DLR) encountered strong resistance at Allerona, and the advance of 6 SA Armd Div drastically slowed. The weather broke and heavy rainfall severely impeded the movement of the infantry, armoured fighting vehicles and accompanying artillery.

While the main German forces had successfully withdrawn to the Trasimeno Line, several detachments remained in the thickly wooded

The Battle of Chiusi, 1944

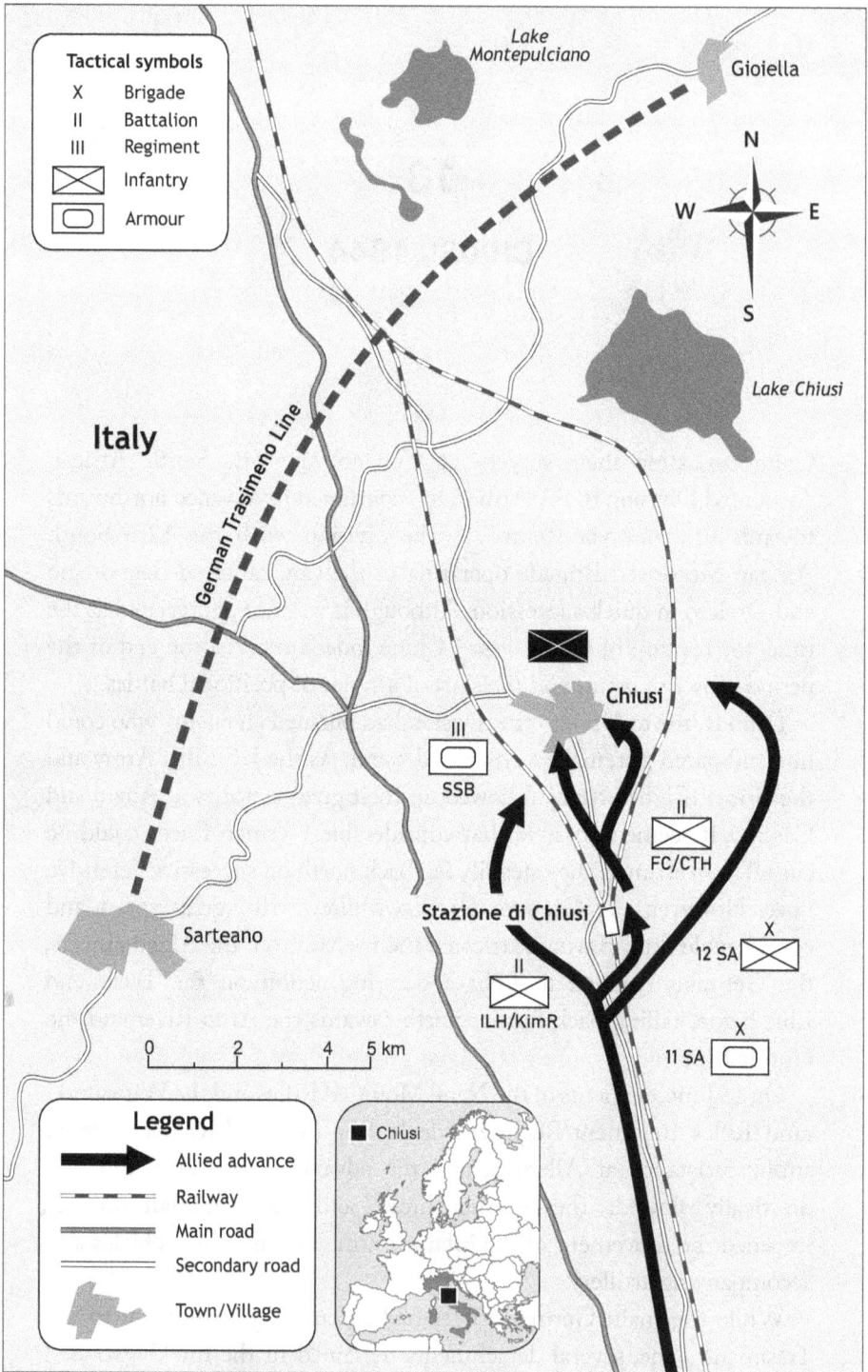

Tactical symbols

X	Brigade
II	Battalion
III	Regiment
⊠	Infantry
▭	Armour

Lake Montepulciano

Gioiella

N
W E
S

Lake Chiusi

Italy

German Trasimeno Line

Chiusi

III
SSB

II
FC/CTH

Stazione di Chiusi

Sarteano

II
ILH/KimR

X
12 SA

X
11 SA

0   2   4   5 km

Legend

➤	Allied advance
▬▬	Railway
▬▬	Main road
▬▬	Secondary road
	Town/Village

■ Chiusi

hills and hilltop towns with orders to delay the Allied advance. However, the Trasimeno Line was not continuous or even fortified. Instead, it was an area, stretching from Gioiella through Chiusi to Sarteano, in which the ground greatly favoured the defence and where for strategic reasons the Germans decided to resist. Even though inclement weather brought operations on the 6 SA Armd Div front to a halt, progress by French and British forces elsewhere on the front forced the Germans to pull out of Cetona and Città della Pieve.

On 19 June there was a break in the rainy weather and after the sun came out the roads began to dry. On the same day, Lt Gen Sidney Kirkman, commanding the British XIII Corps, ordered the northward advance to resume. The advance would follow the tarred Route 71 from the Lake Trasimene area through Chiusi to Florence on a two-divisional front, with the British 78th Infantry Division on the right and 6 SA Armd Div on the left. Major General Evered Poole and his division were specifically directed to advance through Chiusi to Sinalunga, and then in stages towards Florence. It is interesting to note that Kirkman's operational instructions included no reference to German forces delaying the advance of XIII Corps, nor was there a mention of the Trasimeno Line. In fact, it appeared as if Kirkman and his staff were more concerned with traffic control along Route 71 than with German defensive operations along their front. However, on 19 June, a South African intelligence summary mentioned the presence of the German 1st Parachute Division on the immediate front and anticipated they would offer at least 24 hours of determined resistance in the general area of Chiusi.

On 19 June, 6 SA Armd Div was located south of Città della Pieve in the Fabro area. The division was not yet in direct contact with the enemy, although elements of 12 SA Mot Bde patrols pushing beyond Cetona reported encountering light pockets of enemy resistance. After the 78th Infantry Division took Città della Pieve, it continued its advance along Route 71 towards Arezzo, which bypassed Chiusi, some 3 km to the east. XIII Corps had placed this route at the disposal of 6 SA Armd Div for the advance to Chiusi and it was Poole's overall intention to advance to the Trasimeno Line along two routes – the Red Route to Chiusi and the Green Route through Cetona and Sarteano.

Pensive thrusts

Since the Red Route passed through the proverbial central hinge of the Trasimeno Line barring the way northward, Poole and his staff first had to determine whether Chiusi was strongly held by German forces. Thus, during the evening of 19 June, a company of the Imperial Light Horse/Kimberley Regiment (ILH/KimR) from the 11th SA Armoured Brigade were ordered to advance and reconnoitre the Chiusi area. The commander of the ILH/KimR, Lt Col Robert Reeves-Moore, detailed 'A' Company for this task. They would be accompanied by engineers from 8 Field Squadron SAEC to investigate the road and bridges north of Città della Pieve.

At 21:15, Capt CE Hall, the second-in-command of 'A' Company, set off with the patrol towards Chiusi. Their advance north was delayed by several demolitions along the road, but they did not encounter any enemy resistance during the night. At daybreak on 20 June, Hall and two of his platoons moved forward on foot towards Stazione di Chiusi, a railway station and adjoining hamlet located nearly 2 km south of the actual town of Chiusi. Meeting nothing there, Hall and his infantrymen continued their advance along the road that climbs from the station to Chiusi itself. The small hilltop town, whose close-packed buildings extended along the crest of the hill, dominated the surrounding countryside and its narrow streets and numerous cellars made it an ideal defensive location. Most of Chiusi was then still enclosed by a medieval wall, although some houses lay outside on the surrounding hillside.

By 14:15 Hall and his men had reached the outskirts of Chiusi, encountering only two snipers and four deserters from the 3rd Panzer Grenadier Division and the 362nd Infantry Division. During interrogation, the deserters confirmed the presence of many tanks north of Chiusi the previous day and indicated that two companies of the renowned Hermann Göring Division were also present in the area. However, from Hall's vantage point, Chiusi itself appeared quiet. While there were no real indications of the presence of enemy forces, 'A' Company made no attempt to occupy Chiusi. Leaving a standing patrol on the outskirts of the town, Hall's raiding party withdrew back to Stazione di Chiusi and he reported their progress to Reeves-Moore, who passed the information up the chain of command.

From here on, however, reports on the situation itself became muddled, which would drastically affect Poole's operational intent. In late afternoon, Brig JPA Furstenburg incorrectly informed Poole that Chiusi was occupied by an ILH/KimR company and that the town itself was clear of enemy forces. Based on this information, Poole issued his intention for 21 June, ordering 11 SA Armd Bde to advance along the Red Route through Chiusi.

Shortly afterwards, 'B' Company ILH/KimR, under Maj AS Arlington, was sent forward to support Hall and his infantrymen at Stazione di Chiusi. During the evening, Arlington's company passed through Hall's position and advanced to the outskirts of Chiusi. It appears as if 'A' Company's standing patrol had at this stage withdrawn. Arlington halted his company some 550 m short of Chiusi and sent forward patrols. One of his patrols managed to reach the archway leading into the town and was challenged by a German sentry, who raised the alarm. Arlington's other patrols around the perimeter of the town began to draw enemy machine-gun fire. The patrols also reported hearing vehicle engines starting up in and around Chiusi. Arlington decided not to advance into Chiusi but rather to extend his patrols to the left and right of the town to reconnoitre and report on enemy movements. These patrols encountered increasing German resistance and soon suffered their first casualties. While it quickly became apparent that Chiusi was occupied in force, Reeves-Moore nevertheless ordered Arlington to probe further forward. However, with dawn approaching, Arlington realised that his men were in rather precarious positions overlooked from the town. At daybreak he pulled 'B' Company back to Stazione di Chiusi, suffering some further casualties.

On the morning of 21 June, the advance guard of 11 SA Armd Bde moved up Route 71. According to Poole's original operational intent, this force, under the command of Reeves-Moore, would pass through Chiusi after it had been taken by 12 SA Mot Bde. But as soon as the tanks of 'A' Squadron NMR reached the station area, they came under heavy enemy fire from small arms, artillery, mortars and antitank guns. From this encounter it appeared as if the force had indeed become involved in an initial frontal attack on Chiusi. Shortly before 08:00, 11 SA Armd Bde reported the presence of between 200 and 250 enemy troops in the town.

After arriving at the station area at midday, Reeves-Moore ordered flanking movements to the east and west of the town. However, the hilly terrain, heavy rainfall and determined enemy resistance severely impeded these movements. The tanks of 'A' Squadron NMR redeployed towards the east of Chiusi, but their advance was soon halted by drainage canals and demolitions. This force suffered some casualties during the day. Towards the west, 'A' and 'C' companies of the ILH/KimR were ordered to occupy high ground to the west of the town, while 'B' Company remained at the station. This force was soon engaged by German machine-gun, Nebelwerfer (multiple rocket launcher) and antitank fire, which led to further casualties. During the afternoon the Special Service Battalion was ordered to move up and secure high ground to the west of the town. Despite the bad terrain and incessant antitank fire, the tanks of the SSB's 'A' and 'B' squadrons occupied the high ground along the Sarteano and Cetona road and soon returned the enemy fire. Throughout the day the South African gunners also engaged German forces around Chiusi, despite accurate enemy counterbattery fire on their positions. As darkness crept in, there could have been no doubt in the minds of the South Africans that the Germans meant to offer staunch resistance in Chiusi.

It is uncertain when Poole decided to make a night attack on Chiusi. However, in the early evening Kirkman issued operational instructions for 22 June. It was clear that the German defence of the Trasimeno Line was not wavering. Kirkman's intent, however, was clear: XIII Corps would continue its advance on the Trasimeno Line on all fronts. Poole thus had no real alternative but to order an attack on Chiusi.

Poole's decision to attack Chiusi under cover of darkness, without conducting detailed reconnaissance or committing adequate forces was questionable. Logically, it made sense to order the ILH/KimR to carry out the attack. After all, they had been in close contact with the enemy throughout 21 June and had a good idea of the German defensive positions and the layout of the town. However, logic did not prevail. Instead, Furstenburg decided that the First City/Cape Town Highlanders (FC/CTH), under the command of Lt Col ON Flemmer, would carry out the night attack on Chiusi. The FC/CTH, less one company, had come under the command of 11 SA Armd Bde earlier that day and Flemmer was informed at mid-morning that his battalion might be employed in a left or right hook attack on Chiusi. He and his staff immediately went forward to study the terrain and identify possible debussing points. At noon the initial order was countermanded when Furstenburg indicated that FC/CTH would in all probability not be required to attack Chiusi.

However, at 16:00 Furstenburg backtracked and Flemmer was given his final orders to attack Chiusi on the night of 21–22 June. Flemmer maintained that he was given no accurate information about German dispositions and believed that Chiusi was not strongly held. While the information given to Flemmer was inadequate and misleading, there is no evidence that he attempted to obtain accurate information from Reeves-Moore. Furstenburg also made a grave mistake in selecting the FC/CTH for the attack, since an attack on a well-defended hilltop town such as Chiusi required careful planning and enough time to gauge, probe and pinpoint enemy positions.

Flemmer's first objective was to clear the town, after which his men would advance on and occupy the high ground some 700 m north of Chiusi. The divisional artillery would support the attack throughout and armoured support was promised by daybreak on 22 June. Flemmer planned for 'A' Company to lead the attack and clear Chiusi, while 'D' and 'B' companies would operate in close support and consolidate the flanks.

The unfortunate FC/CTH had to make a long approach march towards Chiusi, with their attack only scheduled to commence at 23:00. The troops debussed roughly 5 km from the predetermined start line, and the rifle companies had to struggle forward on foot over sodden, unfamiliar terrain and under heavy shellfire. The tired and weary troops of 'A' Company, under the command of Maj F Bartlett, reached the start line, north of the railway, only shortly before midnight and well behind schedule. They were aware that somewhere on their immediate front was a hilltop, and somewhere on that hilltop was their objective – an objective that none of them had seen before. The men were literally and figuratively in the dark.

The Battle of Chiusi

As soon as Bartlett and his men crossed the start line, the divisional artillery opened fire, which gave the men of the FC/CTH some moral support. However, the intense artillery barrage also removed the element of surprise, giving the German defenders in Chiusi ample warning that an attack was imminent.

While the initial advance towards Chiusi was slow owing to the difficult terrain encountered, 'A' Company nevertheless made good progress up the steep slopes lined with terraces and dotted with trees, hedges and booby traps. First contact with the enemy was made at about 01:00 on 22 June. Bartlett and his men immediately deployed, and a sharp exchange of fire took place. During the action, 'A' Company captured a prisoner who, upon questioning, indicated that Chiusi was strongly held by some 300 German infantrymen.

Bartlett's company continued their advance upwards through the terraces towards Chiusi. Lieutenant L Wylie's leading platoon was brought to a sudden halt when challenged by a German sentry. With their new positions betrayed, the German defenders fired flares that lit up the area and subjected the FC/CTH men to intense machine-gun and grenade fire from three sides. After the flares burned out and darkness returned, Lieutenant EP Hardy's platoon relieved Wylie's men and continued the advance towards the next terrace and dislodged the German defenders there. This encounter again betrayed the South African positions and the infantrymen were again subjected to heavy machine-gun fire when flares lit up the darkness. Hardy's men pushed on determinedly and scaled the next two terraces, and then found themselves to the right of the town. The platoon, which was now some distance from the rest of 'A' Company, continued its advance and soon came upon the road leading into Chiusi near a small square. Hardy ordered his platoon, who left their PIAT (Projector, Infantry, Antitank) weapon behind, to work their way back towards the centre of advance and help clear the road into Chiusi.

Once Hardy and his men entered Chiusi itself, they found themselves in a small square near the Teatro Comunale cinema, which stood across the road from a double-storey winery. Working their way up the road, Hardy and his men soon made out the silhouette of an unidentified German tank. Having left their PIAT behind, they rolled a few hand grenades under the tank. This failed to cause any damage but nevertheless prompted the crew to move the tank out of the square. This allowed Hardy to send a runner back to Bartlett and indicate to him

The belfry in Chiusi that was used as a German observation position, bearing the marks of accurate South African artillery fire

South African troops have a drink of Italian wine after their entry into the shell-shattered town of Chiusi

that the road into the town was clear. Shortly afterwards, the whole of 'A' Company established itself in the vicinity of the Teatro Comunale. Before 03:00, Bartlett reported to Flemmer that his company had consolidated their immediate positions in the cinema and two adjoining houses, while another of his platoons had advanced further into the town. At this stage there was no indication that the operation would by anything but a success, even though a prisoner indicated that three companies of the Hermann Göring Division were holding the town, the centre of which had been struck by Bartlett and his men.

The defects of the plan were now becoming painfully apparent. While 'A' Company had advanced into Chiusi, 'D' Company, which was supposed to follow in their wake, had run into difficulties of their own. The immediate assistance of 'D' Company was thus unavailable, as two platoons had lost touch with company headquarters through intense enemy fire and suffered a few casualties from enemy fire, booby traps and anti-personnel mines. While the general impression was that 'B' and 'D' companies were occupying a firm position outside Chiusi, these companies were in fact pinned down by heavy fire and could not support 'A' Company in their attack.

At 03:15 the tactical situation in Chiusi suddenly changed when a German tank started milling about 'A' Company's positions. It had also been two hours since divisional headquarters had heard any further news on the progress of the FC/CTH. The little information that did trickle back up the chain of command came from 8 Field Squadron SAEC, who confirmed that from their vantage point Chiusi was being subjected to heavy shellfire, which was holding up the infantry attack. At 04:40 a further report from the 4/22 Field Regiment, South African Artillery, confirmed that one sub-unit of the FC/CTH had made it into Chiusi and that the remainder were following amid strong enemy resistance. By then it must have been painfully obvious to Poole and his staff that Chiusi was much more strongly held than originally thought. Shortly after 05:00, Poole left for the advance headquarters of 11 SA Armd Bde.

At 05:30, and as a cold, misty and rainy dawn broke over Chiusi, Bartlett and his men could discern enemy movement within and around the square. They succeeded in engaging several infantrymen before enemy tanks again appeared around their positions. Soon one of the tanks, presumably a Tiger, rumbled towards the entrance of the Teatro Comunale and started firing point-blank at the walls of the building. At 05:35, 'A' Company reported that they urgently required assistance, as the enemy had launched a strong counterattack on their positions. Twenty minutes later, Bartlett again reported that enemy infantry were infiltrating all round their positions and that German tanks were still battering the building. With casualties mounting, it was becoming increasingly clear that the South African attack was running into serious trouble. Bartlett's men also tried to engage the tanks with their remaining PIATs, but the rounds simply bounced off the tanks' armour plating.

At about the same time, 'D' Company reached a house next to a high wall on the right of the road leading into the town. They soon identified three more German tanks in their vicinity. While they attempted to call in artillery fire on the German armour, the South African gunners could not succeed in knocking out the tanks. Flemmer now found himself in a tough situation. With all three of his companies engaged, he had no means at his disposal to offer 'A' Company some relief. Moreover, while corps, divisional and brigade headquarters were incessantly pressing for updates on the tactical situation in Chiusi, no orders were given for the ILH/KimR to assist the FC/CTH attack.

By 08:15, Bartlett, still full of determination, reported that enemy infantry were now crossing the rooftops of nearby buildings in broad daylight. 'A' Company nevertheless reported some success at sniping with their Bren guns and rifles. However, their defensive positions were becoming quite untenable, as Panzerfaust projectiles, 75 mm tank shells and machine-gun and small-arms fire were raking the cinema and creating choking clouds of dust and smoke. At 09:18, Flemmer received a report from 'A' Company that the enemy was creeping into their last defences. German troops had managed to break into the Teatro Comunale, and with all the officers and many others of 'A' Company wounded, the situation was desperate. The building was now also on fire. With their ammunition nearly spent, the remaining defenders realised there was no possibility of escaping from the cinema and so they surrendered. At 10:30 Flemmer's communication with 'A' Company ceased.

Having accounted for 'A' Company, the Germans next turned their attention to dislodging 'D' Company from their forward positions on the edge of Chiusi. Both 'B' and 'D' companies were forced to fall back towards Stazione di Chiusi, while Flemmer kept pressing for the promised armour support, which was planned to arrive at first light. However, no tanks arrived. Moreover, even the ILH/KimR positions at the station were now being heavily shelled and harassed by Nebelwerfer fire. Only after 10:00 did the tanks of 'B' Squadron PAG leave their harbouring area for Chiusi to join the attack. The road selected for their advance was nothing more than a goat track and soon became quite impassable. It then transpired that no previous reconnaissance of any approach for armour towards Chiusi had been done. The attempt of the PAG tanks to force an entrance to the town and extricate any possible FC/CTH survivors came to nothing, as heavy rain caused the armour to become bogged down on the steep, muddy slopes. 'B' Squadron PAG would remain in this position for the night.

At midday, 11 SA Armd Bde headquarters reported to divisional headquarters that they were still attempting to drive the German forces out of Chiusi. This was, of course, entirely unrealistic. The frontal attack on Chiusi had been a huge failure and 6 SA Armd Div had suffered its first tactical and operational reverse in the Italian theatre. In late afternoon, XIII Corps intercepted a wireless message from the Hermann Göring Division indicating that the defenders of Chiusi had suffered heavy casualties during the day's fighting. However, this news was of little consolation to Flemmer and his men. During the attack on Chiusi, the FC/CTH suffered 17 killed, 27 wounded and 75 missing. Chiusi was the biggest reverse suffered by the South Africans since the disasters at Sidi Rezegh in 1941 and Tobruk in 1942.

During the next few days, 11 SA Armd Bde marked time outside Chiusi, while the British 24th Guards Brigade struck at Sarteano to their west. Further to the east, the British 4th Infantry Division and 78th Infantry Division managed to break through the Trasimeno Line. On the morning of 26 June, the Royal Natal Carbineers entered Chiusi unopposed after the enemy had withdrawn from their defensive positions the night before.

Despite the gallant attack and resolve shown by the men of 'A' Company FC/CTH, the Battle of Chiusi was an unfortunate tragedy that, in hindsight, could have been avoided. It is evident that there was no thorough reconnaissance, detailed preparation or adequate support given to Bartlett and his men during their attack on the well-defended hilltop town. Moreover, the South African attack was marked by a complete lack of combined-arms warfare, with no real integration or support between the different arms during the battle. The haphazard decision-making within 6 SA Armd Div before the final attack commenced, along with a complete misunderstanding of the tactical situation on the ground, only served to exacerbate matters. While Poole and his staff were under immense pressure from Kirkman to continue with the advance northwards, Furstenburg nevertheless erred when he ordered Flemmer and the FC/CTH to attack Chiusi.

It was unrealistic to expect Bartlett and his men, operating in the dark across unfamiliar urban terrain, to conduct a frontal assault against well-sited defensive positions that they believed were not strongly held. An understrength battalion, without armour support, was inadequate for such an undertaking. Whether or not the FC/CTH could have been supported by the ILH/KimR company in the station area during the attack is also open to debate. There is also the question whether Chiusi should have been occupied in strength on the morning of 20 June, when Hall and his company advanced to the outskirts of the town in broad daylight without meeting any opposition. This is, of course, mere speculation, but many lives could have been saved if the operational initiative had been taken early on to exploit the favourable tactical situation on the ground. In fact, following the reverse at Chiusi, and given the South African aversion to suffering battlefield casualties in the wake of the defeats at Sidi Rezegh and Tobruk, Smuts personally visited Poole and his division in Italy over the following days to see for himself what had happened. Nevertheless, 6 SA Armd Div could learn many lessons from the tragic reverse at Chiusi.

After taking Chiusi, the South Africans continued to meet stiff resistance from the Hermann Göring Division. On 4 August, 6 SA Armd Div was one of the first Allied units to enter Florence, after which they were withdrawn into the Eighth Army reserve. After a mandatory period of rest, recuperation and refitting, Poole's division was ready to continue offensive operations in Italy. However, the South Africans were placed under the command of the Fifth Army for the remainder of the campaign. Under American command, 6 SA Armd Div would continue the advance northwards towards the Apennines. German resistance stiffened considerably during the Allied advance north, with several delaying actions fought as they fell back on a series of successive defensive lines. The fighting on the Gothic Line and in the Apennines was unlike anything experienced by South African soldiers during the entire war. The campaign during the winter of 1944–1945 was static, with the fighting primarily left to the infantry. Indeed, the South African motorised infantry bore the brunt of the fighting from the liberation of Florence until the German surrender in May 1945.

South Africa emerged from the Second World War with an admirable military record, with combat deployments to East Africa, North Africa, Madagascar and Italy. Demobilisation and post-war rationalisation would detrimentally affect the UDF's nature, strength and organisation, as it had after the First World War. However, the defence force would undergo further drastic transformation after the electoral victory of the National Party in 1948. With only a limited deployment during the Korean War (1950–1953), South Africa became increasingly isolated on the world stage owing to its apartheid policies. This was the age of national liberation, decolonisation and the start of the Cold War in Africa, and the South African defence establishment would have to evolve its doctrine and force design to meet these threats across southern Africa over the coming years.

14

ONGULUMBASHE, 1966

The Union Defence Force (UDF) emerged from the victorious campaign in East Africa 1941 with a firm belief in its particular brand of manoeuvre warfare. Highly mobile motorised infantry, combined with armoured cars and armour, supported from the air and working together with the artillery, ran circles around the Italians, who adopted a static defensive position. The South Africans, unconventionally using their armoured cars as fire support for the infantry, would envelop or double-envelop the Italians, who would often flee or surrender after being completely demoralised. Trucks, laden with provisions that would give the infantry independence from conventional logistical lines for days at a time, replaced the horse. But the doctrine of initiative, intuition and independent action in the combat zone harked back to the days of the Boer republican commandos, who were able to frustrate their more conventional British opponents during the South African War.

When the South Africans redeployed to North Africa to bolster the British Eighth Army against the Axis forces, the British concept of combined operations using a balanced all-arms formation in combat was light years behind that of the Germans. The British favoured their armoured formations, which would often venture forth, lacking infantry or artillery support, to seek a decisive battle with the German panzers. Too often, they would be defeated in detail by the more flexible combined-arms formations of their enemy. A more progressive army than the British would have found a natural home for the South African motorised infantry as an integral part of the British armoured brigades. Their high mobility and natural initiative and intuition would have complemented the firepower of the British armoured formations. This was not to be, though, as the British had little idea of how to use infantry effectively in what they saw as a campaign that would be determined by tanks, and tanks alone.

The British were unsure of the infantry's role in a mechanised war, and so the South Africans were often relegated to manning static positions or coerced into making frontal assaults, which was anathema to their manoeuvre doctrine. The British misuse of the South African brigades resulted in the twin disasters of Sidi Rezegh and Tobruk. On both occasions, Erwin Rommel, the doyen of manoeuvre warfare in the desert, tore into and destroyed the British armour, leaving the South Africans isolated and vulnerable. They were ordered to stand fast instead of being able to use their superior mobility to escape from disaster.

The South Africans were once again ordered to stand fast at the first Battle of El Alamein (1–30 July 1942). Although the outcome for the Allies was positive, the South Africans were highly uncomfortable manning static positions in the teeth of enemy armour. At this stage of the war, the clash between British doctrine and South African doctrine strained relationships to breaking point, and the trust between British and South African commanders all but evaporated. The South Africans rather suddenly and unexpectedly repatriated their forces to South Africa after the second Battle of El Alamein, in October 1942. There they were reconstituted as the 6th South African Armoured Division, seemingly convinced that the answer to future survivability in a modern war lay with tanks.

The final irony of South Africa's experience in the Second World War was that there was little opportunity for the 6th South African Armoured Division to express or develop its manoeuvre doctrine in the rugged mountainous terrain of Italy. At the tactical level, the fighting turned out to be about deploying maximum combined firepower and achieving overwhelming odds against an enemy who assumed the defensive, in terrain that very much favoured the defender – as was the case at Celleno and Chiusi. At the operational level, the advance up the spine of Italy was a slow, predictable slogging match in which the enemy could be dislodged only through expensive frontal assaults. This was hardly a scenario that suited the South African way of war or the inherent mobility of an armoured division designed for the wide-open expanses of the desert. The division's officers, who served for a time under American command, must have emerged from this experience with a keen sense of the superiority of firepower and attrition over mobility and manoeuvre. One can speculate that it is these officers, veterans of the Italian campaign, who shaped and perhaps misshaped South African doctrine in the 20 years following the end of the Second World War.

The UDF accumulated a vast amount of knowledge about the conduct of conventional war during the Second World War. A portion of this was lost once large numbers of personnel were demobilised at the war's end. However, those who remained in the defence force taught an operational and tactical doctrine born of their experience in the Second World War. There was a tendency towards detailed command, with officers being required to make battlefield appreciations and plans and then issue detailed orders and fire planning based on the tactical plan. The UDF was seen as a component of a greater Allied deployment rather than as a stand-alone defence force. The initiative, intuition and directive command style that the UDF embraced at the beginning of the Second World War were all but subsumed by the more rigid British and American doctrine of the latter stages of the war. There was no room for the UDF to express its nuanced approach to manoeuvre warfare as a junior partner to the major Allied powers. The UDF emerged from the world conflict with a set of skills that would soon fade into irrelevance when the Border War began in 1966.

The National Party takes over

The electoral victory of the National Party under DF Malan in 1948 ushered in an era of unfettered Afrikaner domination in many spheres of South African life, including defence. Frans Erasmus, the new minister of defence, aimed to create a 'national' defence force in which Afrikaners would feel at home. He embarked on an affirmative action programme to ensure that Afrikaners were placed at all levels of the UDF at the expense of their English counterparts. Within two weeks of assuming office, he announced that the exchange of military instructors between Britain and the Union would be discontinued. During the 1950s, Erasmus dismantled much of the English-speaking and

189

British-oriented elements of the UDF and restructured the ethos, appearance and composition of the defence force. While Erasmus sought a defence force that reflected the Nationalist government's political aims, he was not averse to South Africa's participating militarily with or on behalf of the West's interests against communism. This desire to garner support for the Nationalist regime would lead to the deployment of elements of the UDF to Korea from 1950 to 1953.

On assuming office, Erasmus immediately proceeded to rid the UDF of its English officers above the rank of colonel and replace them with Afrikaners who were sympathetic to the Nationalist vision. His restructuring, based on language and political grounds, had the effect of ridding the UDF of a vast pool of combat-experienced leaders. Political appointments came at the expense of officers with abilities honed by experience during the Second World War. The decimation of the English officer component and British-oriented traditions continued until Erasmus was replaced in 1959 by the more open and amenable Jim Fouché.

The Erasmus era saw the UDF stagnate, with limited acquisition of new equipment or weapons. The only notable arm of service to expand during his term was the navy. The other components of the defence force fell into disrepair, and the poor state of the infantry and armour was demonstrated during an exercise held in 1950. Adding to these woes was the fact that the SAAF commitment of one squadron in Korea was consuming 20 per cent of the entire defence budget. An American assessment of the capabilities of the UDF in 1951 confirmed the lamentable state of the navy as well as a shortage of tanks and antitank weapons in the land forces. Moreover, the SAAF mostly operated obsolete aircraft and morale was generally low in all sectors of the defence force.

Towards an internal security doctrine

A crucial change in defence policy occurred at the end of 1957, when Prime Minister JG Strijdom's cabinet resolved that the Department of Defence should reorient its focus to internal security rather than to providing a task force for overseas deployment. In response, several Active Citizen Force units received their first training in internal stability, with a focus on combating local disturbances. Erasmus had envisaged a more significant role for the commando units in rear-area defence, but in truth the commandos were ill-trained and ill-equipped for the task at hand. The budget, force levels and battle preparedness of the South African Defence Force (SADF), as the UDF was renamed in 1957, were on a downward trajectory.

Just before Erasmus's departure as minister, in 1959, the Department of Defence released its reorganisation plan, in which the primary role of the army and the air force was focused on 'conventional warfare against lightly armed forces of aggression apart from its internal security task'. Intrusion by subversive elements would be discouraged by 'fast, lightly armed security forces'. Erasmus left behind a defence force with no sense of urgency and ill-equipped to meet any of its required tasks. The Sharpeville disturbances of March 1960, a mere nine months after his departure, confirmed the SADF's inability to deploy rapidly to deal with internal threats.

Fouché set about arresting the decline of the Erasmus years, and his tenure saw the formation of English-medium commando units, together with an enhanced training programme for the entire commando system. A contingent was sent to the British Army's parachute training centre that would form the nucleus of a nascent South African paratroop unit. Defence expenditure rose exponentially, from £11 million in 1960 to £105 million in the first four years of Fouché's tenure. New equipment was ordered, such as Saracen armoured personnel carriers, FN semi-automatic rifles and Alouette helicopters. The SAAF benefited from purchases of Mirage IIIC fighters, C-130 Hercules transports and Buccaneer and Canberra bombers. The SADF also took note of the rise in wars of insurgency throughout the world and in Africa, and its emphasis shifted from conventional war towards counter-guerrilla-type warfare.

The Pondoland Revolt

The SADF did not have to wait long to test its counterinsurgency doctrine against an internal threat. The Pondoland Revolt (1960–1961) is probably one of the least known of modern counterinsurgency campaigns. Although relatively small in scale, it contributed significantly to the future air-mobile counterinsurgency doctrine of the SADF. The unrest in Pondoland, part of the Transkei, was sparked when the local population could no longer tolerate the draconian measures implemented by the apartheid government. The South African Police responded in a heavy-handed manner to a gathering of 250 people at Ngquza Hill on 6 June 1960, during which the SAAF dropped tear gas and smoke bombs, and the resulting shootout led to the deaths of at least 14 people. The tragedy came a mere three months after the massacre at Sharpeville and fuelled the flames of unrest throughout the region. The SAP, unable to control the situation, called for the support of the SADF. It is worth noting the clash between the traditional doctrine of the police, as the minimum force, and the doctrine of the military, whose members are trained to use extreme violence to gain superiority over the enemy. A combined police–military operation was not an ideal fit until both disciplines could embrace each other's methods at a later stage in the Border War.

The SAAF and the navy patrolled the coast to prevent outside aid reaching the rioters in Transkei, while the army was deployed for four months to the Pondoland region under Operation Swivel. The SADF component, supporting 280 policemen, consisted of 450 men, including support troops, leaving the 'sharp' end to about 70 men. The small SAAF component fielded four Harvard aircraft armed with tear gas and smoke bombs, along with two reconnaissance planes. Most important for the mobility of the operations were the three helicopters – two Alouettes and one Sikorsky. The rugged and broken terrain of Pondoland, dotted with dense forests and crisscrossed by numerous rivers, and the poor roads hampered traditional vehicular mobility, especially in the rainy season. It made sense to use helicopters in this setting in what became South Africa's first deployment of this type of equipment in a military context. The outlines of the future Fireforce concept were apparent, as heliborne troops could be deployed swiftly to engage fleeing guerrilla targets identified by aerial reconnaissance, having been flushed out from cover by sweeping ground troops.

The experience of Operation Swivel helped shape the future doctrine of counterinsurgency operations in addition to the use of airmobile troops. The helicopter provided a commander with a superior means of battlefield command, allowing him to view the changing circumstances of the tactical battle from an elevated position. The enhanced mobility

Aerial view of the SWAPO positions at Ongulumbashe

South African troops busy mopping up the objective after the attack on the SWAPO base at Ongulumbashe

of the helicopter allowed for the quick deployment, reorientation or redeployment of troops in response to a rapidly changing tactical situation on the ground. The helicopter was also a superb reconnaissance tool that gave a commander a better appreciation of the terrain than any map could provide. It also facilitated the speedy evacuation of battle casualties. General McGill Alexander, a former SADF paratroop commander, sees the airborne operations in Operation Swivel as 'the embryogenesis of what became known as fireforce – the acme of tactical airborne operations during the thirty-year war in southern Africa'. If manoeuvre doctrine encompasses the four pillars of mobility, flexibility, directive command and battlefield intuition, then the SADF had at least rediscovered some of these. However, although the SADF was rapidly acquiring an airmobile capability through its acquisition of helicopters and transport planes and the formation of a paratroop unit, it lacked codified doctrine on the tactical and strategic possibilities offered by these new-found capabilities.

South West Africa and the beginning of the Border War

The South West Africa People's Organisation (SWAPO) was established in 1960 with the aim of terminating South Africa's mandate over the territory and gaining independence for Namibia. The first six SWAPO insurgents entered Ovamboland from Angola in July/August 1965 and possibly even earlier in 1964. The insurgents set up a base in a remote, sandy area dotted with sparse bushes. The camp was referred to as Ongulumbashe and the occupants began to train youths in guerrilla tactics and disseminate their propaganda to the local inhabitants. The SAP were able to gain knowledge of the existence of the guerrilla base at Ongulumbashe after the capture of a second group of insurgents, who revealed its strength and location. A two-month undercover operation then began during which the activities of the SWAPO group at Ongulumbashe were monitored closely. It was decided to attack and destroy the base, with the caveat that the operation would have to appear as a police matter, as the terms of the South African mandate precluded the use of military personnel in the territory.

However, the police did not possess the capability, expertise or equipment to launch such an operation without the support of the

SADF. As a result, the SADF would provide eight Alouette III helicopters, three C-130 Hercules transport aircraft, several light trucks and weapons, and, crucially, eight paratroopers and a senior SADF officer. The SADF officer, a veteran of Operation Swivel, would train the policemen and accompany them into action. Although the police received two weeks of military training, the entire operation remained in essence a police action and most of the advice from the SADF component was ignored. Members were ordered not to fire on the insurgents until police warnings had been issued. The police instruction did not sit well with the SADF contingent, for obvious reasons. The operation got under way on 26 August 1966.

The overall commander of Operation Blouwildebees was a police officer, who commanded a heliborne component of 30 men, divided into six 'sticks' of five men each. Two of these sticks were commanded by SADF paratroopers. An additional helicopter would provide a reserve force stick and another would provide air control and carried an SAAF observation officer. A force of 14 policemen and four paratroopers mounted in trucks was situated 18 km away; it was intended that these men would arrive on foot at the Ongulumbashe base and act as a cordon before the arrival of the helicopters. But the cordon was never used; instead, the helicopters disgorged their sticks all around the base. Those to the north would sweep the area while the others, mainly consisting of paratroopers, would act as stopper groups. Detailed maps of the area were non-existent and as a result the ground forces relied on a member with knowledge of the target area to act as a guide.

The police banked on the idea that the insurgents, once surrounded, would immediately surrender to them. The SADF component were doubtful and sceptical of the police expectations and methodology. From the word go, the operation did not develop as planned, for even before the helicopters landed, they came under fire from the 16 SWAPO insurgents – the first shots of what would become the 23-year Border War. The sweeper group, who expected to make arrests in police fashion, now came under fire and as a result turned into an assault group. The police had not rehearsed for this situation and were not trained in the art of fire and movement and battle discipline. The scene soon deteriorated into chaos. The helicopter pilots, who became nervous under fire, deposited their troops too far away from the objective to ensure an effective placement of the cordon. Some of the airborne contingents were deposited with their backs to a defensive trench and were fortunate that it was unoccupied. Any vestiges of command and control disappeared as the leader group became embroiled in the immediate fighting instead of directing the events. However, the insurgents became even more disorganised than the attackers. The result was inevitable, with one insurgent killed, ten captured and five having escaped. The reserve force brought in by helicopter managed to kill one further insurgent and capture another. The attackers suffered no casualties.

The operation was a partial success, and it was fortunate that the security forces came through the chaotic situation unscathed. Important lessons were learned during Operation Blouwildebees and would be developed and perfected in future operations. One result was that the police began to assume a more paramilitary role in the operational area of SWA and received appropriate training in counterinsurgency doctrine. They were also equipped with the Casspir armoured personal carrier, which afforded its occupants good cross-country mobility with a measure of protection against landmines and small-arms fire. Other developments included the eventual inclusion of helicopter gunships to provide firepower from the air. Aspects of the command-and-control structure were also improved, so that the commander of the operation could control and react to the changing events on the ground via his command helicopter. The development of the final iteration of this type of airborne assault would reach its zenith with the Rhodesian Fireforce concept.

The use of helicopters by the SADF was not a new concept: helicopters had been in military use in a multitude of roles since the last stages of the Second World War. They were used mainly for casualty evacuation in Korea (1950–1953) and for counterinsurgency warfare in Malaya (1948–1960), French Indochina (1946–1954) and Kenya (1952–1960). In the Algerian conflict (1954–1962), the French military introduced the first helicopter gunships and helicopter-borne infantry and paratroopers to engage insurgent groups. The helicopter alone was certainly not a war-winning instrument, but it was undoubtedly a force multiplier when used in a combined-arms approach together with infantry and artillery. The helicopter's unique ability to take off and land vertically in most terrain and weather conditions, combined with an unmatched versatility in choice of cargo, made it a potent weapon in the hands of counterinsurgent forces. The helicopter enhanced mobility and therefore aided the manoeuvre-type warfare much favoured by the South Africans with its ability to place firepower and troops virtually anywhere on the battlefield.

The Rhodesians were able to build on the experience of the various worldwide counterinsurgency operations, including Ongulumbashe, and develop their version of a vertical envelopment combined-arms approach to counterinsurgency operations. Rhodesia, crippled by sanctions and manpower challenges, had to rely on expediency in building the world's most formidable counterinsurgency doctrines. In a reversal of the ideal situation, where doctrine shapes training and equipment procurement, the Rhodesians formulated a solution around their existing irreplaceable hardware. Despite many challenges and limitations, the Rhodesians achieved startling kill ratios at the height of the Bush War (1964–1980). However, as so often in conflicts of this type, a tactical solution alone does not win wars and, despite their impressive military prowess, the Rhodesians finally succumbed to the inevitable political process.

The Rhodesians were able to locate their Fireforce bases in reasonable proximity to insurgent activities. These rudimentary bases contained a makeshift runway for the fixed-wing element of the Fireforce and accommodation for the troops who made up the Fireforce team. Fireforce consisted of a helicopter component made up of 'G-Cars', each carrying a stick of four men. The command-and-control element of the operation was guided by the commander in a 'K-Car' helicopter circling the target area at 800 feet during the operation. The fixed-wing element consisted of one or two light propeller-driven aircraft that would drop high explosive or napalm ordnance to force the enemy to take cover before the G-Cars dispensed their sticks at various locations around the target, directed by the K-Car. In a truly combined operational manner, there was a motorised component designated 'The Tail', which set out to the target area overland as reinforcements for a second trip by the G-Cars or as a backup to the post-contact clean-up operations. Because of their limited number of helicopters, the Rhodesians used vintage Dakota transport aircraft to drop paratroopers as the sweeper element.

The paratroopers would jump at heights of no more than 800 feet to arrive at the target at a location designated by the commander in the K-Car. Fireforce, born out a need for expediency and subject to limited resources, became a deadly counterinsurgency tool in the hands of the capable Rhodesians.

The South Africans, who on occasion provided helicopter pilots for the overstretched Rhodesians, adopted much of the Fireforce doctrine for the SADF, designating their version 'Reaction Force'. Unfortunately, the South African interpretation of the Fireforce doctrine mimicked the name 'Reaction', as the South Africans were far more reactive than the Rhodesians. The Rhodesian Fireforce was driven by intelligence delivered by reconnaissance elements or 'turned' former insurgents who revealed the location of insurgent groups. On many occasions, the reconnaissance element would direct the Fireforce onto the target in what was a particularly proactive doctrine. The South Africans were more prone to react to a terrorist attack than to actively seek out insurgent bases before the guerrillas had a chance to launch an attack or infiltrate deep into the territory.

Ongulumbashe marked a turning point for the South African military establishment. Existing conventional doctrine and the lessons learned at great expense during the Second World War would have to be adapted to meet the demands of irregular warfare. The helicopter, like the aeroplane and tank of the First World War, would have to be integrated within the existing structure as part of a combined operations team. The helicopter added an important dimension to battlefield mobility but was most effective when used in conjunction with and supported by the other arms. South Africa and Rhodesia would go on to develop a potent doctrine of vertical envelopment through the Fireforce concept. Ongulumbashe was an important first step towards the rediscovery and evolution of South Africa's manoeuvre doctrine.

15

OPERATION SAVANNAH, 1975–1976

From the 1960s onwards, southern Africa became an active theatre in the global Cold War. Amid the wave of decolonisation sweeping throughout Africa during this period, the Portuguese, Rhodesian and South African regimes in southern Africa clung to power. The Portuguese remained in Angola and Mozambique, the South Africans occupied South West Africa and Rhodesia enforced its unilateral declaration of independence from Britain. Against the backdrop of Cold War ideologies, all three regimes turned to the West for political and military support, while the nascent liberation movements sought active military and ideological support from the Soviet-dominated Eastern Bloc. Moreover, the various liberation movements in Angola, Mozambique, SWA and Rhodesia concluded that they could achieve their independence only by recourse to violence and military action. As a result, several irregular warfare campaigns were launched across southern Africa.

The subsequent conflicts – the liberation wars in Angola and Mozambique (1961–1975), the Rhodesian Bush War (1964–1980), South Africa's so-called Border War and the broader liberation struggle in South Africa – form part of what is sometimes called the 'thirty-year southern African war' (1959–1989). The late historian Leopold Scholtz further argues that this southern African war had three distinct layers. The first was the civil rights struggle against apartheid within South Africa. The second included the wars of national liberation in Angola, Mozambique, Rhodesia and SWA (irregular warfare), which became fundamentally enmeshed with the third layer, the global ideological Cold War (semi-conventional warfare).

Operation Savannah, 1975–1976

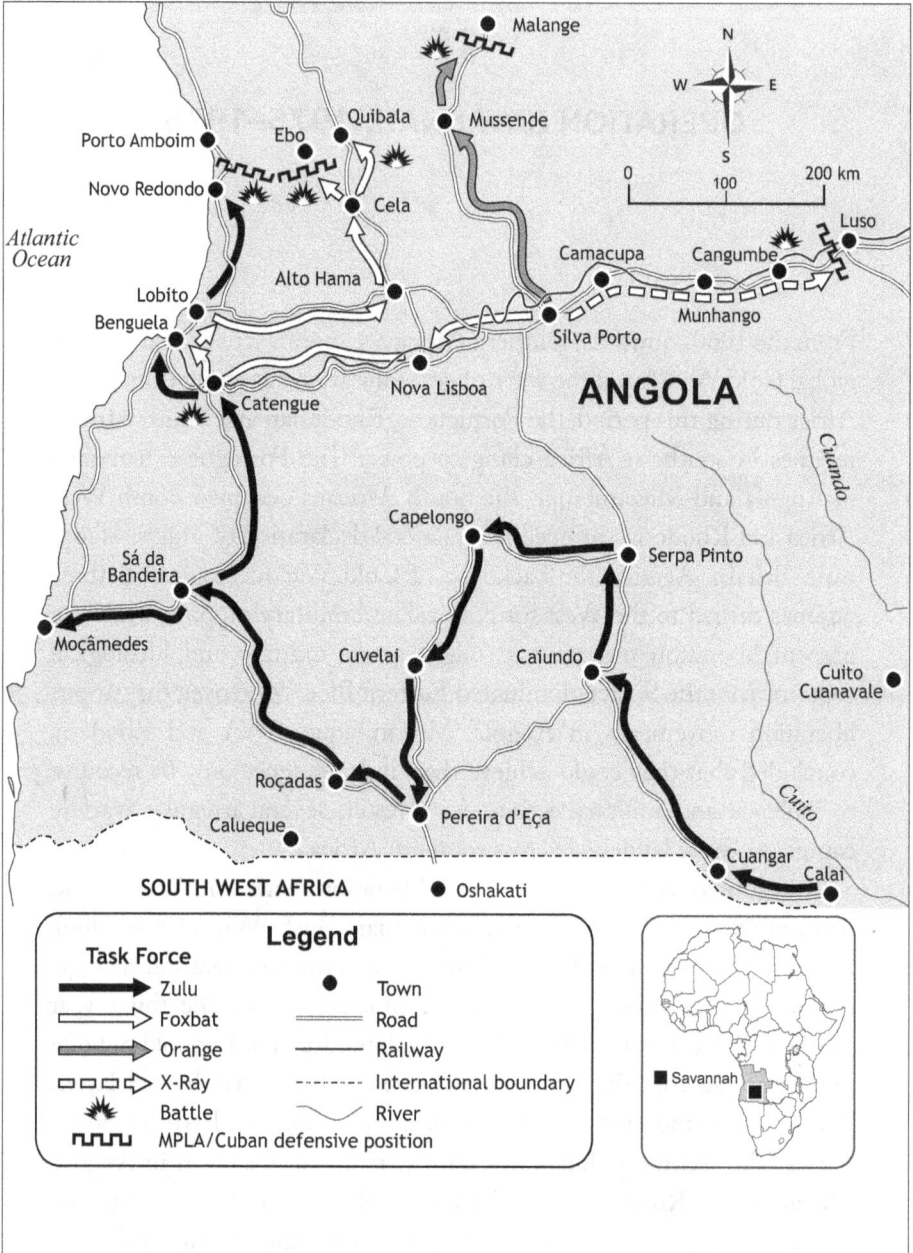

Legend

Task Force
- Zulu
- Foxbat
- Orange
- X-Ray
- Battle
- MPLA/Cuban defensive position

- Town
- Road
- Railway
- International boundary
- River

Savannah

As noted in the previous chapter, South Africa had become increasingly involved in a low-level insurgency war in South West Africa (SWA) from 1960. The South African attack on the SWAPO guerrilla base at Ongulumbashe on 26 August 1966, generally accepted as the start of the Border War, had serious consequences for the South African Defence Force (SADF).

During the late 1960s, the SADF, and specifically the commander Joint Combat Forces, Lt Gen Charles 'Pop' Fraser, began to design a comprehensive strategic doctrine to deal with the various military threats South Africa faced. In this regard, the defence force relied heavily on the strategic thinking of notable counterrevolutionary theorists such as Robert Thompson, JJ McCuen and André Beaufre. During this time, PW Botha, the new minister of defence, inherited a somewhat antiquated defence force that had suffered from years of neglect. However, with Botha at the helm, the SADF would undergo a process of rapid transformation and modernisation. With South Africa facing a growing number of conventional and unconventional threats, the restructuring of the SADF became a priority. The defence force was accordingly reorganised to conduct both conventional and counterinsurgency operations across the southern African battlespace. To account for these organisational changes and offset the greater demand placed on manpower, the SADF would acquire modern weapons and equipment, create new Citizen Force units, extend the call-up period for reservists and institute national service (conscription).

In 1966, however, the SADF was in no position to fight either a conventional or a counterinsurgency war. As a result, the government entrusted the South African Police with fighting the SWAPO insurgency: the SADF would assume complete responsibility for the counterinsurgency war only several years later. Following the defeat at Ongulumbashe, SWAPO incursions into Ovamboland dwindled. Instead, the Caprivi Strip became the main battleground, with SWAPO insurgents infiltrating from Zambia. But there, too, SWAPO struggled to gain a foothold, suffering several reverses during repeated incursions between 1968 and 1974.

Meanwhile, the SADF grew increasingly frustrated. The SAP, rather than the defence force, was afforded the opportunity to gain valuable operational experience during the Bush War in Rhodesia. While there were justified concerns over the SADF's lack of combat experience, the defence force nevertheless gained valuable experience by providing limited support to Portuguese counterinsurgency efforts in southeastern Angola. However, by 1972 the SAP was finding it increasingly difficult both to maintain internal security in SWA and to stem the SWAPO insurgency. The SADF thus began to assume greater responsibility in SWA and – despite its lack of combat experience but given its superior organisation and perceived edge in manpower, weapons and equipment – finally assumed complete responsibility on 1 April 1974.

However, within the space of a few weeks, a peaceful coup d'état toppled Portugal's fascist dictatorship on 25 April. The so-called Carnation Revolution would hold tremendous strategic consequences for South Africa.

A changing geostrategic landscape

The uprising in Lisbon directly affected the geostrategic situation in southern Africa. The new government moved rapidly to end Portugal's long-running colonial wars and grant independence to its remaining colonies. With the independence of Mozambique and Angola scheduled for 1974 and 1975 respectively, South Africa, and to a lesser extent Rhodesia, faced a major problem. The Portuguese colonies had provided a cordon sanitaire that kept the liberation movements and insurgent groups at a distance. Moreover, the new situation led to the collapse of the Alcora Exercise – the military alliance between South Africa, Rhodesia, and Portugal to jointly counter the mutual threat to their territories in southern Africa.

For South Africa in particular the looming independence of Angola would mean the disappearance of a convenient buffer territory. More importantly, the SADF could no longer count on the Portuguese military forces to interdict SWAPO insurgents in southeastern Angola and prevent their infiltration into SWA. Soon the Portuguese military informed the South Africans that they could no longer conduct defensive patrols or 'hot pursuit' operations against SWAPO forces into Angola. On 26 October the last SADF liaison officer attached to the Portuguese forces in Angola vacated his post and returned home. South Africa indeed found itself in a grave situation.

In contrast, however, the changing geopolitical situation in Angola greatly benefited SWAPO's independence struggle. The liberation movement was able to relocate its headquarters from Lusaka, Zambia, to Luanda, the Angolan capital. They also soon benefited from a political pact with Agostinho Neto's vocal and influential Movimento Popular de Libertação de Angola (MPLA). More importantly, SWAPO now had access to cross-border sanctuaries in Angola upon which it could fall back after launching attacks into SWA – a prerequisite for any successful insurgency. It could, in theory, also infiltrate and launch attacks into SWA all along the long border with Angola.

Within a relatively short period, SWAPO seized the operational initiative. Soon after the collapse of Portuguese control in southern Angola, armed SWAPO bands moved into the area and established a number of forward operating bases. From November, SWAPO incursions into northern SWA, and Ovamboland in particular, drastically increased. Between May and June 1974, the SADF launched several clandestine operations into southern Angola to prevent the build-up of SWAPO forces and the establishment of forward operating bases. However, even these preventive operations were not enough to stem the tide of SWAPO incursions. It was apparent that more proactive action was needed to counter the SWAPO insurgency.

On 5 January 1975, the Alvor Agreement was signed in Portugal between the three principal Angolan liberation movements – the MPLA, the União Nacional para a Independência Total de Angola (UNITA) and the Frente Nacional de Libertação de Angola (FNLA). The Alvor Agreement, under which Angola became independent, established a government of national unity drawn from three ethnically and ideologically divided liberation movements. The idea was that the MPLA, UNITA and FNLA would jointly administer the territory until elections were held in November 1975. However, with Angolan independence fixed for 11 November, and amid great political, social and economic competition between the liberation movements to gain political power and popular support, it soon became apparent that the Alvor Agreement would not be honoured. In fact, a civil war was imminent.

As the political situation in Angola deteriorated throughout 1975, the MPLA, UNITA and FNLA increasingly struggled to bolster their political power and secure resources in the run-up to the November elections. In their various bids for power and influence, the liberation movements actively sought foreign support, which, through increased foreign intervention, would escalate the impending civil war. The MPLA came under the sustained influence of the Soviet Union and Cuba, who supported the movement with military equipment and instructors. In early November, a large-scale Cuban intervention, codenamed Operation Carlota, provided the MPLA with additional military equipment and instructors, which led to the deployment of some 36 000 Cuban troops over the coming years. The MPLA soon took the offensive, occupying Luanda and clearing the southern coastal districts and parts of central Angola of the FNLA and UNITA. In due course, an MPLA government was proclaimed.

In contrast, the United States provided financial and military assistance to the FNLA, while South Africa backed UNITA. In doing so, both the FNLA and UNITA secretly received weapons and ammunition from Washington and Pretoria in exchange for their promised support against PLAN. In fact, both UNITA and the FNLA promised to locate and attack known PLAN bases in southern Angola, while allowing South African forces to conduct cross-border 'hot pursuit' operations at will. Thus, by the end of 1975, South Africa had become embroiled in a regional war and a direct confrontation with the Soviet Union and its proxies.

The involvement of the Soviet Union and Cuba in the Angolan civil war was cause for concern for the SADF. For Pretoria, the decision whether to intervene actively in Angola was a difficult one, with the cabinet divided over the issue. The prime minister, John Vorster, was at first unwilling to sanction intervention. Vorster was supported by Gen Hendrik van den Bergh, the influential head of the Bureau for State Security, who argued that SWAPO could be kept at bay by simply securing the Angolan border. However, senior SADF officers disagreed and, through PW Botha, managed to convince Vorster that, despite his misgivings, South Africa needed to take a proactive approach in Angola if it wanted to defeat the SWAPO insurgency.

At the outset, the South African objectives were modest. The SADF was tasked with helping UNITA regain political control over the areas it had previously controlled in southern Angola. During September 1975, senior SADF officers presented a plan for the Angolan intervention that revolved around providing military aid to the anti-Marxist movements; preventing further advances and occupation of territory by MPLA/Cuban forces; and recapturing all areas, including harbours, occupied by the MPLA/Cuban forces during their southward advance. Concurrently, the SADF would conduct operations against SWAPO in southern Angola. The ultimate strategic aim was thus for South Africa to conduct a limited war to exert the necessary pressure on the Organisation of African Unity for the organisation to establish a government of national unity in Angola as stipulated in the Alvor Agreement. Collectively, these developments signalled the beginning of Operation Savannah.

Operation Savannah

South African ground forces became involved in operations on 9 August, when they were deployed to protect the Ruacana and Calueque hydroelectric complex and other installations on the Cunene River, some 50 km inside Angola. On 14 October, these troops, along with armoured support, advanced deeper into Angola towards Roçades (today Xangongo), officially signalling the start of Operation Savannah. From here Task Force Zulu, under the command of Col JS van Heerden and comprising combat groups Alpha and Bravo supported by Eland armoured cars and mortar teams, advanced through southern Angola and northwards along the coast.

During late August, the South African government, under pressure from the US Central Intelligence Agency, agreed to step up the training of UNITA and FNLA forces. At this stage, SADF instructors, with heavy weapons support, were already deployed with UNITA troops at Colombo near Silva Porto (Bié), while FNLA forces were being trained near Mpupa close to the SWA border. However, the situation in Angola continued to deteriorate. By mid-September, most of the towns between the SWA border and Luanda were under the control of the MPLA. Moreover, in the north, the FNLA proved to be no direct threat to the MPLA forces ensconced around Luanda.

The first serious fighting began during the last week of September after information reached Colombo that MPLA forces were advancing south towards Nova Lisboa (Huambo). A hastily organised force, comprising South African-manned light armour and several hundred UNITA fighters, advanced towards contact on 5 October and were ambushed 10 km south of Norton de Matos (Balombo). The SADF/UNITA force fought back and caused significant MPLA casualties while incurring minimal UNITA losses.

This engagement was important for two reasons. First, it dealt a severe blow to MPLA confidence early in the civil war. Second, and far more profoundly, the battle showed that the UNITA troops depended on SADF support. The South African government was therefore faced with a conundrum: either remain neutral and accept an MPLA victory or proceed with a larger SADF intervention. South Africa opted for the latter, with the intervention limited to a maximum of 2 500 men and 600 vehicles. For the SADF, the basic objective remained to place UNITA and the FNLA in a strong enough position by 11 November to prevent a de facto MPLA political victory. This required the MPLA to be pushed out of southern Angola and for UNITA/FNLA control to be established over the strategic Benguela railway line running from the Angolan coast into then Zaire.

On 22 October, a squadron of Eland armoured cars were flown to Silva Porto (Kuito) to join the newly established Combat Group Foxbat, jointly established by Cmdt Eddie Webb and Cmdt Willem van der Waals and comprising three companies of UNITA infantry, 22 Eland 90 armoured cars and a host of heavy support weapons. Its task was to block any western MPLA advance. In doing so, it clashed with advancing MPLA forces on several occasions, inflicting heavy casualties and halting their advance. Near Luimbale (26 October), it destroyed three MPLA armoured vehicles and compelled the remainder of the force to retreat. After Foxbat assisted Zulu during the fighting at Cubal (4 November), it advanced further north and took over positions around Cela and Santa Comba on 11 November.

Meanwhile, Zulu continued its northward advance along the Angolan coast as two separate combat teams, Alpha and Bravo. It was instructed to advance as far north as possible before 11 November and to secure the major ports. On 13 October, and after capturing Pereira D'Eca

*South African artillerymen manning a 140 mm G2 cannon at
Hippo Hill near Bridge 14 in Angola during Operation Savannah
wearing East German helmets*

*SADF troops boarding a C-160 Transall aircraft to escort POWs
back to South West Africa during Operation Savannah*

207

(Ongiva), Zulu advanced to Roçades (Xangongo). After brushing aside the MPLA defences during the attack on Sá da Bandeira (Lubango) on 21 October, the SADF battle groups received two additional FNLA infantry companies plus more armoured cars and mortars. With its confidence surging, Zulu secured the port of Moçamedes (Namibe) on 27–28 October and Catenque on 31 October, despite signs of a significant Cuban presence and improved MPLA defences. At Cubal (4 November), Zulu, in collaboration with Foxbat, destroyed an MPLA force from Nova Lisboa and went on to seize the port of Benguela on 5–6 November.

The heaviest fighting occurred just before Zulu reached Novo Redondo (Ngunza), which coincided with the arrival of Cuban special forces sent to bolster the demoralised MPLA troops. During the advance towards Novo Redondo, elements of Combat Group Alpha, who were acting as the vanguard, were ambushed by an MPLA/Cuban force at the Quicombo River (11–12 November). The SADF force withdrew after taking significant casualties. In due course the South Africans, with the support of a recently arrived SADF 25-pounder artillery troop, drove back the MPLA/Cuban force. Novo Redondo was occupied on 13 November and Zulu advanced to Quibala via Porto Amboim and Gabela. The bridge over the Queve River, and all the other bridges along the intended route of advance, had been demolished by the Cubans. After an unsuccessful attempt to probe the defences on their immediate front, Combat Group Bravo was forced to retreat after coming under intense rocket and mortar fire. Hostilities on this front then became limited and consisted of a few artillery duels and limited actions. By 18 November, Zulu had covered approximately 3 100 km inside Angola. During its advance, Zulu had inflicted many casualties on the MPLA/Cuban forces in an impressive number of engagements. Moreover, the SADF losses were minimal.

On 11 November, Portugal formally handed over political power to the MPLA as the de facto and widely recognised government of Angola. While several socialist and African states recognised the new MPLA government, similar recognition was not extended to the makeshift FNLA/UNITA government established at Nova Lisboa. The MPLA, however, faced serious problems: their forces in southern Angola had been defeated and the SADF/UNITA/FNLA units remained a force that could threaten Luanda.

At this point, events in northern Angola drastically influenced the outcome of Savannah. On 10 November, an FNLA force, supported by 120 Portuguese Angolans, two Zairian battalions, a handful of armoured cars and artillery pieces, and three SADF 140 mm guns and crews, with air support from three SAAF Canberra light bombers, launched a suicidal attack upon Quifangondo, 50 km east of Luanda. While the FNLA attack was a predictable disaster, the MPLA, bolstered by Cuban special forces and troops manning six BDM-21 rocket launchers, put up a staunch fight. More concerning was the fact that the BDMs outranged the SADF artillery and that the high-level aerial bombing proved completely ineffective. Accordingly, further assistance to the FNLA in the north ceased and the SADF personnel were evacuated by sea from Ambriz on 27 November. The remnants of the FNLA were completely routed by mid-February 1976. In the result, the MPLA no longer faced a war on two fronts.

Savannah's command structure was formalised on 12 November only after 101 Task Force was established, with its headquarters at Rundu, in northern SWA. However, the South African government had already taken the decision to withdraw SADF troops from Angola. This was a logical course of action since Cuban reinforcements were streaming into Angola. The SADF was also operating on extremely long lines of communication and it was doubtful whether the defence force could logistically sustain an escalation of the war effort.

Meanwhile, the MPLA/Cuban forces shadowed the SADF troops across the 160-km-wide front, hoping to determine their likely route of advance towards Quibala (Kibala). By this stage of Savannah, the SADF had recaptured virtually all the southern territory lost by UNITA and the FNLA during the previous months.

During the SADF pursuit of MPLA forces towards Qibala, the main bridge over the Mabassa River (later Bridge 14), the most obvious approach to the town, was demolished. Several more clashes with MPLA/Cuban forces occurred in the Ebo/Hengo area, particularly on 18 November, when Foxbat's troops gained the upper hand. Foxbat, reinforced by three more companies of UNITA/FNLA infantry, was then ordered to advance rapidly to Quibala. On 23 November, at Ebo, on the road to Quibala, and in difficult terrain, a mixed force of SADF armour and artillery and UNITA/FNLA infantry encountered an ambush set by a group of 70 Cuban special forces, who were concealed on the northern bank of the Mabassa River near the bridge. The Cubans, armed with rocket-propelled grenade (RPG) launchers and recoilless guns and supported from the rear by BDM-21s and mortars, inflicted several casualties on the combined SADF/UNITA/FNLA force and destroyed several Eland armoured cars. During the battle, the SADF artillery also struggled to locate and engage targets effectively.

The Cubans celebrated the victory at Ebo as one of the most decisive military moments of the war. Moreover, the battle not only damaged South African morale but also shattered their apparent air of invincibility. As a result, SADF reinforcements were urgently moved forward. A lull in the fighting over the following days allowed the Cubans time and space to consolidate their defensive positions and move up reinforcements from Luanda. Further SADF reinforcements, comprising infantry, artillery and armour, arrived in the operational area at the end of November and were immediately sent forward to reinforce Zulu and Foxbat.

The SADF secured a tactical victory at Bridge 14 on 8–12 December, when superior South African artillery fire proved decisive and inflicted particularly heavy casualties on the MPLA/Cuban forces. Despite their setback at Bridge 14, though, the MPLA/Cuban forces regrouped and continued to successfully block the SADF advance along the route from Quibala to Luanda. From this point, the frontline became static.

On 15 December, Lt Gen Magnus Malan, then Chief of the South African Army, visited the front and stated that no further reinforcements would be dispatched to Angola. He also indicated that the SADF would withdraw all its troops in January 1976. However, three days later, the SADF suffered a severe propaganda defeat near Quibala, when four of its soldiers were captured while recovering damaged vehicles. This provided concrete proof to the international community that South African troops were indeed fighting in Angola – a fact that the South African government had denied up to this point. On 20 December, and despite Malan's statement, fresh troops arrived to relieve some of Foxbat's personnel. This brought the total number of SADF troops deployed to Angola to around 3 000, far above the original manpower ceiling determined by the government.

Combat Group Orange, formed as a reserve in late November 1975, was shifted to the central front in December to locate potential river crossings east of Bridge 14, in the hope of forcing a route to Quibala. Unfortunately, these crossings had either been destroyed or were impassable. The SADF's inability to cross the Pombui River proved to be a serious setback. On 20 December, Orange's position became untenable as the MPLA/Cuban bombardments increased and their positions were outflanked. On 23 December, a full-blown artillery duel led to SADF casualties, and two days later South African patrols were strafed by enemy jet fighters. The limitations of the South African artillery resurfaced when the 144 mm guns could again not silence the BDM-21s. Despite inflicting some casualties on their opponents, Orange encountered increasingly strong resistance from the MPLA/Cuban forces, which at times threatened to envelop them. By early January 1976, this central front had become the most precarious of all the SADF positions in Angola. This involved Battle Group X-Ray, under the command of Cmdt AA Kotzé and comprising an infantry company, an armoured car squadron, a 25-pounder battery from 4 Field Regiment and a number of support troops. After capturing Luso further to the east along the Benguela railway line, X-Ray could not exert effective control over the rest of the railway infrastructure.

At the end of 1975, Vorster and Botha championed the decision to withdraw all SADF forces from Angola. At this stage, increasing numbers of Cuban troops, equipped with advanced Soviet weaponry, were arriving in Angola, greatly bolstering the confidence and aggression of the MPLA forces. The stark reality was that if the SADF wished to continue to deploy in Angola, substantial reinforcements from South Africa as well as more advanced weaponry would be required. As it was, at least 5 000 reservists had been mobilised and deployed to northern SWA to cover the gradual South African withdrawal from Angola in January 1976.

On 3 February, Botha confirmed there were up to 4 000 South African troops deployed in southern Angola just north of the SWA border. Meanwhile, the MPLA/Cuban forces continued to advance slowly south in the wake of the retreating SADF. Their advance, like that of the South Africans before, was hampered by severely extended

211

lines of communication, minefields and destroyed roads and bridges. However, the MPLA/Cuban forces did not draw the retreating South African troops into any further battles. On 27 March, shortly after Angola's president, Agostinho Neto, gave assurances that the Calueque dam would not be interfered with, the SADF withdrew its last troops from Angola, bringing an end to Operation Savannah.

Throughout Operation Savannah, several SADF battle groups embarked on a series of impressive northern advances as they conducted a limited semi-conventional war in Angola. During a mere 33 days of operational movement, the SADF battle groups advanced deep into Angola, successfully engaging the MPLA/Cuban forces several times. This was, as Leopold Scholtz states, rapid manoeuvre warfare similar to the German invasion of the Low Countries and France in 1940 and of Russia in 1941. This was the case during the early stages of Savannah, especially during Task Force Zulu's rapid advance up the coast in November 1975, during which it overran several MPLA/Cuban defensive positions. The speed of the South African advance threw the MPLA/Cuban forces off balance, and it took them some time to regroup and redeploy into defensive positions. However, once the frontline became static, attrition-type warfare became the order of the day and the tide slowly turned against the SADF battle groups through late 1975 and into 1976. Overextended logistically and operating in difficult terrain, with limited air support, the SADF's perceived edge in manpower, weapons and equipment was soon disproved. By early 1976, having clashed with MPLA/Cuban forces equipped with advanced Soviet weaponry, most notably superior artillery, the SADF had to reassess its presence in Angola. If South Africa wished to continue its deployment, the defence force would require substantial reinforcements and more advanced weaponry, and would have to improve its conventional force mobilisation and combat capabilities drastically. For the moment, this was both politically unattainable and militarily unrealistic. As a result, all SADF forces were withdrawn from Angola in March 1976.

In hindsight, Savannah provided the SADF with a crucial learning curve that would stand it in good stead as the Border War intensified over the coming years. At the military level, Savannah was a mixed bag of results. Tactically, the SADF performed extremely well. While suffering a battlefield reverse at Ebo, expertly exploited by the MPLA/Cuban propaganda machine, the SADF nevertheless secured a string of tactical victories during which their offensive prowess was unmatched. While the strategic aims of Savannah were clear at the outset, at the operational level the planning and objectives were muddled. In fact, it appears as if the identification of an operational *schwerpunkt* remained elusive during Savannah, which was further compounded by haphazard command and control, the incremental commitment of widely dispersed forces, stronger-than-expected enemy resistance and an adverse military operating environment. However, the operations were also hallmarked by mission command, which allowed the operational commanders in Angola to use their own initiative and facilitated freedom of action and decision-making during combat operations.

During the initial rapid northerly advance, combat operations were characterised by manoeuvre warfare and force projection on a grand scale. When the frontline stagnated, the South Africans lost their operational freedom and initiative. However, at the strategic and grand-strategic levels, the South Africans fared less well. Principally, they were unable to control the fluid geopolitical situation in Angola. South Africa was thus forced to withdraw from Angola not having been defeated militarily but having the lost the political and propaganda battle against the MPLA and their Cuban ally. Moreover, it had been proven that the SADF could be beaten on the battlefield. The myth of the invincible South African war machine had therefore been somewhat exposed. Of far greater concern was the fact that the SWAPO threat remained in Angola. The coming years would see an upsurge in the number of PLAN insurgents trained in Angola and infiltrated into northern SWA.

In 1978, the SADF launched Operation Reindeer, its second major military operation into Angola. The operation targeted three SWAPO base complexes: at Chetequera, Dombondola and Cassinga. The most notable of these, and to some extent the most infamous, was the large-scale airborne assault on Cassinga.

The Attack on Cassinga, 1978

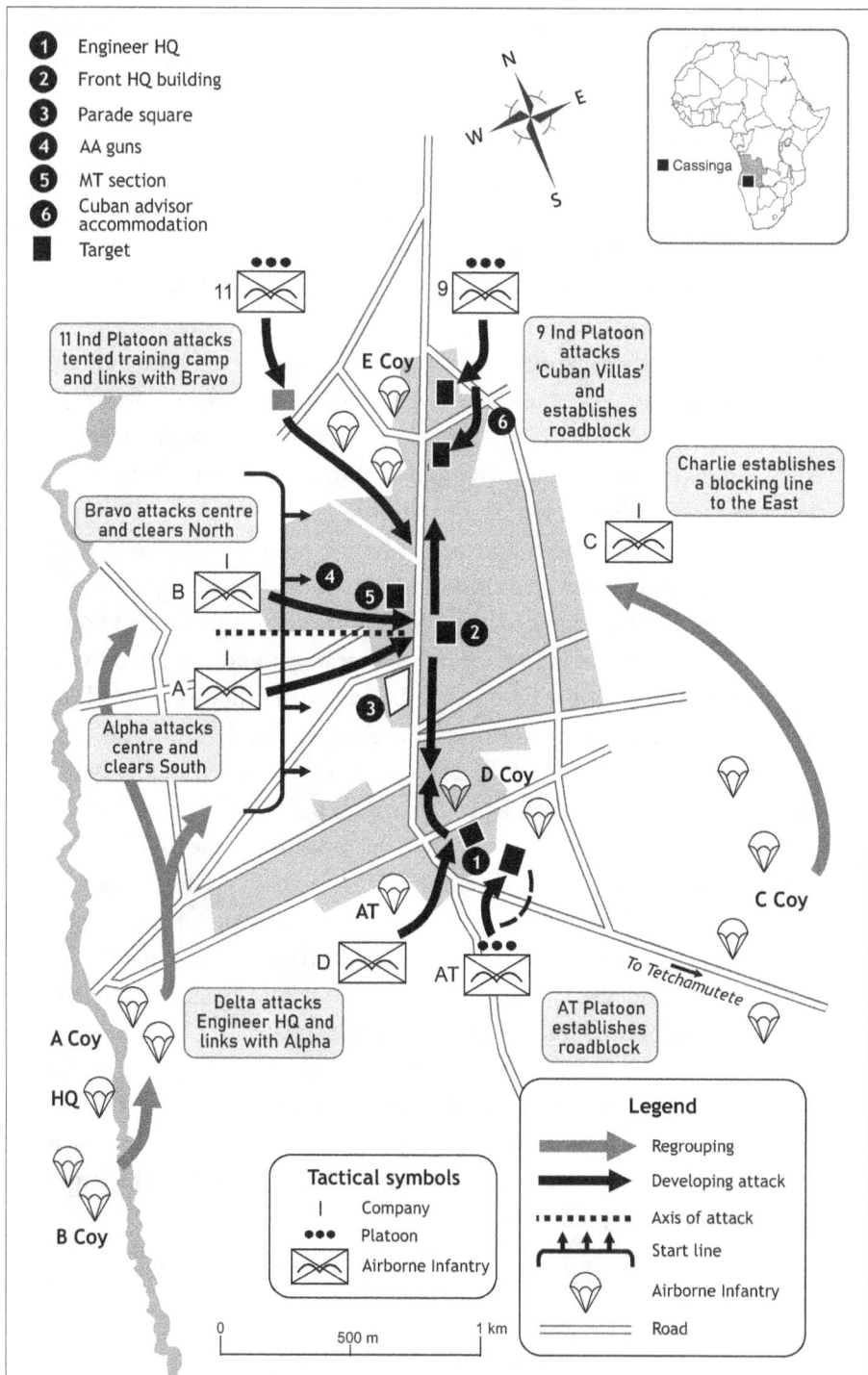

Legend / key:

1. Engineer HQ
2. Front HQ building
3. Parade square
4. AA guns
5. MT section
6. Cuban advisor accommodation
■ Target

■ Cassinga

11 Ind Platoon attacks tented training camp and links with Bravo

9 Ind Platoon attacks 'Cuban Villas' and establishes roadblock

Charlie establishes a blocking line to the East

Bravo attacks centre and clears North

Alpha attacks centre and clears South

Delta attacks Engineer HQ and links with Alpha

AT Platoon establishes roadblock

E Coy

C

B

A

D Coy

C Coy

A Coy

HQ

B Coy

D

AT

AT

To Tetchamutete

Tactical symbols

| Company
••• Platoon
Airborne Infantry

Legend

Regrouping
Developing attack
Axis of attack
Start line
Airborne Infantry
Road

0   500 m   1 km

16

CASSINGA, 1978

Warfare is an ambiguous affair at best, and downright paradoxical at its worst. Militaries have adopted various command styles to deal with friction on the battlefield and the inevitable fog of war. The British Army relied on a detailed command style characterised by voluminous written orders that left little scope for initiative at the lower levels of command. The Germans acknowledged that even the best plans needed alteration as soon as the first shot was fired in anger. The German mission command style, or *Auftragstaktik*, allowed for decision-making to be devolved down to the lowest level of the command structures, provided that subordinates did not alter the overall mission objectives. The German doctrinal approach gave birth to several astounding tactical and operational victories. Ever since the Second World War, armies worldwide have attempted to mimic the German doctrine, with varying degrees of success.

The South African Defence Force (SADF), although rooted in a mission command style, struggled to rediscover its manoeuvre warfare doctrine at the beginning of the Border War. Many years of functioning under the yoke of the British Empire had resulted in a stolid, British-oriented conventional warfare doctrine. The experiences of Operation Savannah, and particularly the defeat at Ebo, were a wake-up call for the SADF, revealing, at significant cost, its command and equipment shortcomings. To meet the challenges of conventional opponents such as the Cubans and the Forças Armadas Populares de Libertação de Angola – the Angolan armed forces – and insurgent groups such as SWAPO, Umkhonto we Sizwe (MK) and the Azanian People's Liberation Army

(APLA), the South Africans turned to several disparate sources to construct a coherent defence doctrine. Conventional advice and co-operation came from the Israelis, especially regarding mechanised warfare. A new breed of South African officers, such as Roland de Vries and Tony Savides, were inspired by the likes of Friedrich von Mellenthin, a capable Second World War panzer general, and the military philosophers, BH Liddell Hart and JFC Fuller.

Although the SADF's historical mounted infantry roots were alluded to, little recognition was given to the UDF's interpretation of manoeuvre warfare in Africa during the two world wars. There was considerable cooperation with the Rhodesian Army, and the many South Africans serving with the Rhodesians helped exchange ideas to benefit both defence forces.

At the strategic level of warfare, the SADF understood that a military victory was impossible in the war of insurgency on the borders of and within South Africa. All the military could hope to achieve was to buy the politicians enough time to find a political solution, or perhaps to inflict sufficient tactical setbacks to convince the enemy to come to the negotiating table. In this regard, the SADF, in partnership with the politicians, was heavily influenced by the French theorists André Beaufre, who developed the theory of total strategy, and David Galula, who analysed the experience of counterinsurgency warfare in Indochina and Algeria. Once again, the ambiguity of warfare, and in this case insurgency-type warfare, would obscure the objectives of many of the role-players who sought to achieve victory.

The dilemma facing the South Africans was that victory at the strategic level remained elusive, despite a string of tactical and operational victories. The opposite was often true: success at the tactical and operational levels resulted in significant setbacks at the strategic level as South Africa lost ground to their opponents' propaganda machines. Operation Savannah is an example of South Africa suffering a diplomatic setback despite achieving much of significance at the tactical level. The Battle of Cassinga is another example: a supposedly well-planned and brilliantly executed plan resulted in a resounding defeat for SWAPO, FAPLA and the Cubans at the tactical level but produced a political disaster of enormous proportions for South Africa at the strategic level.

Cassinga – a military target?

The military historian faces several challenges in assessing the Battle of Cassinga. It is impossible to divorce the purely military aspects from the considerable politics and emotion surrounding the battle. Accusations that the SADF murdered hundreds of innocent civilians at Cassinga mar attempts to assess the operation from a purely military point of view. There is ambiguity about whether Cassinga was a refugee camp, the hub of insurgent activity in southern Angola or something in between. It will be difficult, if not impossible, to prove either case with the passing of time and the absence of incontrovertible evidence. Nevertheless, despite the opposing views and raw emotion that persists even today, the operation is worth studying from a military point of view as an example of the potential of an independent vertical envelopment deep in enemy territory.

South Africa's disastrous withdrawal after Operation Savannah left a vacuum in southern Angola: the absence of the SADF enabled SWAPO to set up bases in Angola. SWAPO was thus in a stronger military position than ever before, with the ability to train and garrison soldiers in a relatively safe rear area before sending them south on incursions. PLAN, SWAPO's armed wing, operated almost with impunity from inside Angola with very little interdiction from the SADF, which conducted sporadic raids into Angola from time to time. Each month there were about 100 contacts between insurgents and the SADF in the East Caprivi, Ovamboland and Kavango regions of SWA, and an estimated 2 000 and 1 400 PLAN fighters were based within 20 km of the border in Angola and Zambia, respectively. The quality of the insurgents and their weaponry improved under the tutelage of the Cubans and with the steady flow of sophisticated weapons from the Eastern Bloc. Adding to the mix were 11 000 FAPLA and Cuban troops, who often shared bases and facilities with SWAPO across southern Angola.

Facing SWAPO and their allies were about 11 000 South African troops on the South West African (SWA) border. In addition to the regular forces was a company of paratroopers, who conducted operations using the Rhodesian Fireforce concept. The SADF and the FAPLA/Cuban forces were reluctant to engage each other, with the South Africans mainly concerned with suppressing the activities of SWAPO while the MPLA busied itself with combating UNITA. The danger facing the SADF was that the Cubans could use the growing strength of SWAPO to infiltrate SWA, thereby distracting and engaging most of the South African forces. The prospect of a SWAPO infiltration at multiple points and locations simultaneously along the border would naturally disperse the fighting power of the SADF, which would seek out the infiltrators using small combat teams based on the Fireforce concept. The dispersal of the SADF to meet the SWAPO threat would lend itself to a concentrated conventional attack by the Cubans and FAPLA across the border and, after that, a deep incursion into the heart of SWA. A logical strategy for the SADF would therefore be to attack a significant SWAPO command centre and logistical hub deep inside Angolan territory. Such an attack would cripple and demoralise SWAPO for many months and dissuade the Cubans from invading SWA. The target identified by the SADF was a SWAPO base at Cassinga, a small town some 265 km from the SWA/Angola border.

The challenge facing the SADF was how to engage and destroy a target so deep inside enemy territory. The tyranny of distance ensured that any ground-based operation would face immense logistical challenges and have to confront numerous enemy strongpoints manned by well-equipped Cuban/FAPLA/SWAPO formations. Once Cassinga had been neutralised, the invading force would have to fight its way out of Angola, with fully alerted enemy formations converging on them from every direction. The solution was therefore to utilise the doctrine of vertical envelopment: airborne troops would adopt a raiding strategy to attack the objective, with light infantry, helicopter gunships and ground-attack aircraft in support. True to a raiding strategy, once the objective had been met, the ground troops would be quickly extracted via helicopter before the enemy had a chance to launch a counterattack.

The case for vertical envelopment

The use of airborne troops comes with its own set of unique challenges. There is the overwhelming psychological aspect of inserting oneself deep into enemy territory and being surrounded by hostile troops. There is a reason why airborne troops are considered elite forces: members are selected only after surviving a punishing selection and training programme designed to sift out the fittest and most mentally capable.

Airborne troops are lightly armed and no match for the armoured and mechanised opponents who will inevitably launch a counterattack once the initial surprise has elapsed. They cannot sustain a prolonged attack and must either be quickly extracted or reinforced from the ground. The element of surprise is essential for an airborne attack to be successful, as the defender will be able to bolster their defences in anticipation of a leaked operation. Airborne troops also rely on fire support from helicopter gunships and ground-attack aircraft to keep the reinforcing enemy at bay while the operation proceeds. All resupply, casualty evacuation and final extraction will come from the air component, necessitating air superiority over the target area for the duration of the operation. Airborne operations that do not adhere to the principles of vertical envelopment can lead to high levels of casualties, as occurred at Crete (1941) and Arnhem (1944) during the Second World War.

Cassinga was first identified as a major SWAPO base via aerial reconnaissance. In March 1978, the then Chief of the Army, Lt Gen Constand Viljoen, noted in a communiqué that Cassinga was the planning headquarters and the recruitment and medical centre of PLAN. An extensive zig-zag trench system surrounding the town, although incomplete on the southern side, lent credence to the belief that the town was a major military base. It was estimated that the camp could provide for some 3 000 soldiers and their camp followers. The proposed attack on Cassinga (codenamed Moscow) was twinned with a simultaneous attack on Chetequera (codenamed Vietnam), a mere 30 km from the border, or 'cutline', which was vulnerable to a lightning-fast armoured and mechanised attack, to be led by Maj Frank Bestbier.

The Cassinga operation would be led by Col Jan Breytenbach, of 1 Reconnaissance Commando and 32 Battalion fame, who estimated that he would need a minimum of 450 paratroopers for the capture and destruction of the base. His men would be recruited mainly from the Citizen Force component of the SADF, adding an element of sensitivity in the event of heavy losses, which would not be well received on the home front. Breytenbach would have to rely on operational manoeuvre, coupled with tactical surprise and superior training, to overcome an enemy estimated to be numerically superior by a factor of at least four to five, which went against the rule book demanding at least a 3:1 advantage.

A further challenge was the limited number of helicopters available, which meant that while the entire force could land simultaneously on the target from fixed-wing transport, the extraction process would be undertaken by 18 helicopters in two waves. This necessitated the establishment of a helicopter administration area (HAA) 19 km away from Cassinga, stocked with fuel and other resources. This would allow for helicopter support during the operation to facilitate the extraction back to Ondangwa in SWA once the operation was over. Logistical constraints meant that Breytenbach was forced to reduce his force to 343 paratroopers, but he was assured that the SAAF would step up their pre-landing bombardment to soften up the target area.

Operations Bruilof and Reindeer: The plan

Operation Bruilof, the prequel to the Cassinga operation, kicked off with an intensive training programme at an isolated camp bordering the Kruger National Park. Citizen Force members of 2 and 3 Parachute Battalions, many of whom were older veterans of the Border War, were called up with the idea of increasing their fitness levels and training. However, a security leak put paid to this first iteration of the operation, and Bruilof was cancelled. The man behind the security breach was the spy Dieter Gerhardt, who passed the details of the operation to the Soviets. A few weeks later, the paratroopers received a call-up for Operation Quicksilver, which would serve as a cover to distract the dignitaries and journalists invited to observe it.

Behind the scenes, the real operation, designated Operation Reindeer, proceeded with a more ambitious plan incorporating Cassinga as the main objective. The SADF believed that Cassinga was an important PLAN military base used to recruit and train insurgents, and to plan and coordinate all incursion operations into SWA. The destruction of the Cassinga base, it was claimed, would disrupt SWAPO's operational activities and logistical systems for at least six months. The date set for the raid on Cassinga was 1 May 1978, the objectives being the destruction of the base, the killing or capture of as many PLAN fighters as possible, including their commander, Dimo Amaambo, and the seizure of as many documents as possible.

The significance of a large-scale parachute jump deep inside enemy-held territory was not lost on the participants, who had previously conducted most of their combat insertions via helicopter. The revitalised training programme incorporated a large-scale sand model depicting every building, trench and weapon site at Cassinga, which allowed the troops to familiarise themselves with all aspects of the target area. The planners also warily assessed the town of Techamutete, 16 km south of Cassinga, which had a Cuban/FAPLA garrison, some armour and MiG fighter jets.

Cassinga was a former Portuguese mining town that SWAPO had opportunistically occupied and developed as a military base. The town had been extensively fortified on its northern, eastern and southern fronts, marked by various trench systems and foxholes. If these trenches were occupied and defended, they would pose a considerable obstacle to any attacking force. The southern section of the trench system was thinner, owing to the presence of the Cuban/FAPLA garrison at Techamutete. South African military intelligence did not identify any heavy support weapons or artillery, and it was believed that these would be provided by the garrison at Techamutete. The trench system did not extend as far as the western side of Cassinga, but the town was flanked on the west by the fast-flowing Culonga River, which would be quite wide at the end of the rainy season. The approaches to Cassinga provided little in the way of cover or concealment, making it difficult for an attacker to advance against well-defended positions. Cassinga was also located on a slight rise, necessitating an uphill advance to the objective. The defences had clearly been constructed to repel a ground attack rather than an airborne assault. In short, the Cassinga terrain favoured the defenders.

The overland route from the SWA border to Cassinga was some 260 km, with myriad villages and settlements along the way. Each of these would have set off the alarm bells should the South Africans attempt to assault Cassinga using ground forces. Therefore, because of the tyranny of distance, the planners settled on a joint airstrike and parachute drop to destroy the SWAPO base. An airborne assault would bypass all the obstacles and resistance en route and provide the important elements of surprise and speed by using the indirect approach. The German airborne attack on Fort Eben-Emael in May 1940 would serve as inspiration in that the element of surprise and the superior quality of the SADF troops would overcome their numerical disadvantage.

A temporary tactical headquarters was established at Ondangwa Air Force Base, in northern SWA, and Maj Gen Ian Gleeson, Chief of Army Staff Operations, assumed overall command of the operation. The fighting forces on the ground at Cassinga were to be led by Col Jan Breytenbach, the former commander of 32 Battalion, who at the time was the most experienced and decorated combat commander in the SADF. He had first-hand experience of airborne operations and an intimate knowledge of the fighting qualities of the Cubans, FAPLA and SWAPO. However, at the outset there seems to have been a conflict as to who was in charge, as Brig MJ du Plessis was the commander of 44 Parachute Brigade. Army Headquarters also failed to issue clear instructions to clarify command and control appointments within the brigade. The rivalry between Breytenbach and Du Plessis would lead to some confusion on and off the battlefield. Adding to the confusion was political interference from above, which led to the operation being delayed for 48 hours, to 3 May, and then for another 24 hours, to 4 May.

The plan of attack was simple enough in its formulation. Yet, it would prove otherwise in the execution. The attack on Cassinga would commence with an airstrike at 08:00, delivering a mixture of anti-personnel and precision bombs to coincide with the camp's morning parade. This would soften up the enemy, and it was hoped that the resulting confusion would mask the arrival of the fleet of aircraft transporting the paratroopers. The airborne assault would proceed within minutes of the airstrike and consist of five companies and an antitank platoon. E Company would deploy to the north of Cassinga, while C and D companies would deploy to the east and south respectively. A and B companies would drop between the Culonga River and the town of Cassinga. After advancing to suitable positions, E, C and D companies would act as stopper groups and intercept the enemy forces being swept from the west by A and B companies. The antitank platoon and D company would also block any attempted advance by the FAPLA/Cuban forces situated at Techamutete.

Cassinga: The attack

In executing the plan, the fog of war descended rapidly over the battlefield and friction played havoc with strict timetables, designated targets and drop zones. The bombing mission, although on time, was less than effective, and up to 1 200 of the cluster bombs failed to explode. Fewer personnel than anticipated were present on the parade ground. The precision bombing component of the airstrike was disturbed by the dust thrown up by the cluster bombs and most of the targets were missed. Despite the relative inaccuracy of the airstrike, it sowed terror and confusion among those on the ground. Directly after the airstrike, the transport fleet descended on Cassinga and made all sorts of complicated manoeuvres to get into the planned 'box' formation before disgorging the paratroopers at a height of 250–300 m.

The first instance of combat friction occurred when A and B companies and the mortar section jumped too late. Breytenbach blamed Du Plessis, accusing him of interfering with the determination marker for the release point. The confusion can be blamed on the fuzzy command-and-control structure of the operation. Another fault lay with the air photo interpreters, who had miscalculated the scale of the aerial reconnaissance photos and as a result misrepresented the size of the drop zone between the Culonga River and Cassinga. Instead of the 3 000 m by 600 m area depicted, the actual size of the drop zone was 1 100 m by 200 m, which was far too small for the size of the force being dropped. The result was that the paratroopers were dropped 2–3 km south of Cassinga and 500 m west of the river.

C Company, destined for the eastern drop zone, also jumped late, leaving them straddling the Cassinga–Techamutete road well to the south of their original target. They immediately began to move north in dense bush and engaged in sporadic and fierce firefights with fleeing SWAPO members. Amid much confusion, C Company managed to reach their designated stop line at 09:45, much too late to act as an effective stopper group for the SWAPO members fleeing to the east. To the north, E Company (9 and 11 platoons) had more success and were accurately dropped on their target, forming a stop line guarding any escape to the northwest. D Company landed some 500 m to the south of their target in wooded terrain and drew sporadic fire from the tree line. They also came under friendly fire from elements of B and C companies before taking up positions on their stop line with the antitank platoon to block the southern escape route from Cassinga. Importantly, the antitank platoon set up a tank ambush position along the road to Techamutete, a decision that would pay dividends later in the day when a convoy was sent along the road to assist SWAPO at Cassinga.

Although much confusion reigned in the South African camp, SWAPO were also overwhelmed by the catastrophic events as they unfolded – it proved impossible for the SWAPO fighters to regroup and counterattack the South Africans in a coordinated fashion. Confused insurgents dashed for any available cover and those who fought back did so as isolated entities, resulting in many casualties due to friendly fire. Nevertheless, C Company's late arrival at its destination allowed many SWAPO fighters to escape out of harm's way in an easterly direction.

It took about an hour and a half for A and B companies to organise themselves after the landing, which included getting those who had landed on the western side of the river onto the correct side. Breytenbach, making the best of a poor situation, changed the main axis of attack from west–east to south–north. He was able to communicate his changed plan to all involved as he had established good radio communications with all the companies. As A and B companies swept into Cassinga they encountered little opposition at first, but resistance stiffened by the time they reached the centre of the town, where they came under sniper fire. Breytenbach reported after the battle that B Company was brought to a complete halt by fire from two 14.5 mm anti-aircraft guns employed in a ground-support role. A Company, on the left flank, was similarly halted for more than two hours. Both companies were now effectively pinned down by the anti-aircraft guns. The situation became so critical that consideration was given to deploying the airborne reserve to deal with the situation. D Company was called on to perform a flanking attack on the west of Cassinga and work their way up to the guns. Meanwhile, Breytenbach called in fire from the mortar platoon and every other available mortar to suppress the anti-aircraft guns.

The guns that had caused much trouble in the South African ranks were finally silenced by the combined effect of small arms and mortar fire. The ferocity of the fighting can be gauged by the 95 dead SWAPO fighters found near the guns. During the action, the guns were recrewed several times when those manning them became casualties. Breytenbach himself was wounded and two South Africans were killed and another two wounded.

The final South African tally was three paratroopers killed, eleven wounded (two critically) and six injured during the parachute drop, with another missing. The casualties among the SWAPO fighters and civilians were massive. The silencing of the anti-aircraft guns marked the end of all significant resistance at Cassinga and the start of the mopping-up operation. There remained the tasks of reorganising the battalion, collecting captured documents and prisoners and preparing for the helicopter extraction.

Word was soon received of the approach of a Cuban armoured column from Techamutete, which resulted in an altercation between Du Plessis and Breytenbach. The former wanted to call in the helicopters for immediate extraction; Breytenbach insisted that a helicopter landing zone (LZ) first be secured and declared safe, but he eventually relented. The extraction process had all the hallmarks of barely controlled disorder. Some extraction plans were modified on the fly, the command-and-control structure adding to the confusion. For example, the two demolition sappers were evacuated before they had completed their job of destroying bunkers and equipment.

At about 13:00 a circling Buccaneer aircraft spotted 30 vehicles advancing from Techamutete and managed to destroy three before returning to base. After the first extraction, the remaining 200 paratroopers, some armed with RPGs, now faced 400 advancing Cuban troops supported by a company of tanks. The antitank platoon had planted mines in the approach road from Techamutete and waited in the predetermined ambush position. After destroying several tanks and armoured personnel carriers and killing 40 Cuban soldiers, the antitank platoon beat a hasty retreat to the LZ to join the final extraction.

Chaos reigned at the LZ, where Breytenbach had all but taken over the lower-level command-and-control structure. He formed a thin defensive line against the approaching Cuban column, which was later reinforced by the retreating antitank platoon. At 14:20 several SAAF planes arrived on the scene and destroyed many tanks and armoured personnel carriers in the Cuban column. However, the Cubans were undeterred and continued to advance on the LZ. The attack lost some momentum when the South Africans opened fire with all they had at the Cubans, who were now no more than 200 m from the LZ. There was an undisciplined scramble for the helicopters as all semblance of order disappeared in the extraction process. Nevertheless, the South Africans were able to extract the remaining defenders, although in the ensuing chaos most of the prisoners had to be released.

It seemed that the SADF had dealt a crippling blow to the SWAPO military infrastructure at Cassinga and it took many months for PLAN to recover. The SADF proved that they could deny SWAPO safe cross-border bases, even when located deep inside Angola. The operation demonstrated once again the difficulty of executing a successful airborne attack, even though the SWAPO defenders were disorganised and unable to launch an effective counterattack. There was considerable international political fallout from the operation, caused by the high number of casualties on the SWAPO side. Together with the vulnerability of such operations deep inside enemy territory, this ensured that the SADF was reluctant to repeat the likes of Cassinga again, just as the Germans had hesitated to mount large-scale airborne operations after the costly invasion of Crete in 1941.

Despite an astounding tactical victory that demonstrated all the hallmarks of South African manoeuvre doctrine, SWAPO made the most of the propaganda war and pushed the narrative that the South Africans had committed a heinous atrocity against innocent civilians seeking safety in a refugee camp. However, despite the political fallout from Cassinga, the scope and intensity of the Border War would increase during the 1980s. In 1981, the SADF would launch Operation Protea, one of the largest and most impressive cross-border operations of the entire Border War.

17

OPERATION PROTEA, 1981

The outcome of the Border War was hanging in the balance by 1981. The South African Defence Force's (SADF) cross-border operations into Angola the previous year had partially relieved the pressure on the hard-pressed counterinsurgency forces battling the People's Liberation Army of Namibia (PLAN) in South West Africa (SWA). However, the combined military and political threat from the South West Africa People's Organisation (SWAPO) was still present. In fact, the military situation was deteriorating, since PLAN continued to receive new recruits and reinforcements and its combatants still clashed regularly with the South African security forces in SWA. After the conclusion of Operation Sceptic (10 June–1 July 1980), a complicated large-scale conventional cross-border operation, the SADF adopted a two-pronged strategy for the Border War. It would continue mounting a classic counterinsurgency campaign within SWA while launching larger pre-emptive semi-conventional strikes, augmented by numerous smaller operations, against SWAPO in Angola.

In 1981, the SADF launched several small-scale operations into southern Angola. During these operations, it became clear to the South Africans that the resolve of the Forças Armadas Populares de Libertação de Angola, or FAPLA, had increased and that it was no longer willing to simply stand aside while the SADF attacked PLAN. However, South African policy clearly stated that FAPLA should not be engaged unless necessary.

The largest of these cross-border operations, Operation Carnation, lasted from June to August. Carnation's purpose was to disrupt SWAPO's

Operation Protea, 1981

Legend
- SADF troop movement
- Contact/Skirmish
- Town
- Road
- Task Force
- Tango Line

Task Force Bravo

Task Force Alpha

Angola

South West Africa

Etosha Pan

Ionde
Embundo
Dova
Nehone
Anhanca
Evale
Mupa
Mongua
Peu-Peu
Humbe
Xangongo
Cahama
Techipa
Calueque
Chitado
Ruacana
Omahenene
Nautila
Cuamato
Mahenene
Okalongo
Okongo
Okankolo
Ondangwa
Eenhana
Oshikango
Oshakati
Oshaka
Omuthiya
Oshivelo
Ongiva
Omupanda
Namacunde

Tango Area

Battle Group 30

Battle Groups 20 and 30

Battle Groups 20, 30 and 40

Battle Group 10

Retreat of Battle Groups 10, 20 and 40

Cunene

N W E S

0 25 50 75 100 km

Protea

logistical infrastructure in the Cunene province of Angola. However, Carnation soon developed into a cat-and-mouse game. When PLAN determined that the South Africans were advancing on their bases, they would evacuate and either disperse into the safety of the bush or take advantage of the security offered by FAPLA bases. As a result, Carnation had achieved negligible operational results by August, with only limited numbers of insurgents captured and killed, a few SWAPO bases destroyed and some logistical infrastructure disrupted. While Carnation succeeded in pushing the SWAPO forward bases deeper into southern Angola, the only noticeable reduction in PLAN activity was in the central and eastern regions of Ovamboland.

The growing integration of SWAPO/FAPLA was of immense concern to the SADF since this allowed PLAN to continue its war effort largely unhindered. In fact, intelligence had picked up a renewed buildup of SWAPO logistics in Cunene province. Small-scale pre-emptive SADF operations were simply not enough to stop the rapid infiltration of PLAN insurgents into SWA. The rate of SWAPO infiltration had grown so much that in July alone at least 217 PLAN fighters were killed in northern SWA. It was evident that more direct action was needed.

In May 1981, Maj Gen Charles Lloyd, the GOC South West Africa Territorial Force, recommended to Gen Constand Viljoen, then Chief of the SADF, that further offensive strikes into Angola were imperative. Lloyd argued that the SADF needed to conduct lengthier operations to dominate a specific area rather than conducting lighting raids to destroy a specific base and then retreating. He also recognised that PLAN bases in Cunene province were generally located near FAPLA-controlled areas or bases. Moreover, FAPLA and SWAPO often shared logistics and lines of communication and their defensive positions were at times also completely integrated. Lloyd therefore urged Viljoen to sanction a cross-border operation aimed at destroying the FAPLA/SWAPO strongpoints at Xangongo, Mongua and Ongiva. It was against this backdrop that Operation Protea was sanctioned.

Planning and preparation

Protea turned out to be one of the largest SADF cross-border operations of the entire Border War. During Protea, approximately 4 000 South

African troops participated in an intricate mechanised operation that saw the large-scale projection of force into Cunene province.

In planning for Protea, the ultimate objective was to neutralise SWAPO's military forces in southern Angola, and specifically to destroy the bases at Humbe, Xangongo and Ongiva. Xangongo was the headquarters for PLAN's northwestern front, while a large SWAPO supply base was located at Ongiva. The planning led to specific guidelines being issued to the effect that FAPLA should not be engaged unless they interfered with the operation or counterattacked. These guidelines would soon prove unrealistic.

South African intelligence reports indicated that FAPLA's 2 Division, with its headquarters at Lubango, was deployed to Cunene province. The SADF planners expected resistance from FAPLA's 21 Brigade at Cahama, 19 Brigade at Xangongo and Peu-Peu and 11 Brigade at Ongiva. The FAPLA defences at Xangongo were known to be elaborate, and military intelligence had identified at least eight clearly identifiable defence complexes, manned by 100–150 soldiers drawn from two infantry battalions. Part of the defences consisted of reinforced-concrete bunkers, many of them facing southwards. These defences were in turn backed up by a squadron of T-34 tanks, a squadron of BTR-23 armoured cars, an artillery battery, three 122 mm rocket launchers, seven anti-aircraft guns and a complement of PLAN fighters. Moreover, at Xangongo, the FAPLA/SWAPO forces were completely integrated, making it extremely difficult to attack the one without engaging the other.

Brigadier Witkop Badenhorst, the OC Sector 10, with its head-quarters at Oshakati in northern SWA, was given overall command of Protea. Badenhorst had three task forces, roughly equivalent in size to a brigade, at his disposal. Task Force Alpha, under the command of Col Joep Joubert, an accomplished commander with a knack for manoeuvre warfare, would bear the brunt of the fighting. Task forces Bravo and Charlie did not play a direct role in Protea and were instead employed in counterinsurgency operations in northern SWA and in conducting area operations in eastern Cunene province, respectively.

Alpha was divided into four battle groups: Battle Group 10, under the command of Cmdt Roland de Vries; Battle Group 20, under Cmdt Dippies Dippenaar; Battle Group 30, under Cmdt Chris Serfontein; and

Battle Group 40, commanded by Cmdt Deon Ferreira. In addition, there was a pathfinder company from 44 Parachute Brigade under the command of Capt Rooies Velthuizen. Task Force Alpha was a force to be reckoned with and consisted of a mixture of mechanised and motorised infantry supported by armoured car squadrons (Ratel 90s, Eland 90s and Eland 60s), 140 mm field artillery, 81 mm and 120 mm mortars, 127 mm Valkiri multiple rocket launchers and combat engineers. At least 142 aircraft, including fighters and bombers, helicopters and various photo-reconnaissance, transport and spotter planes, would provide air support.

The South African plan of attack involved two broad phases. The first phase was an attack on the SWAPO/FAPLA defence at Xangongo. It was decided to launch the main attack from the north, east and southeast, while a stopper group would be deployed to Humbe, to the west of Xangongo, to cut off fleeing forces and prevent possible FAPLA intervention from Cahama. Another group would advance towards Peu-Peu, located northeast of Xangongo, to cover the South African attack, while a paratroop force would deploy further north as an early-warning element for possible FAPLA interference from Techamutete. Collectively, these deployments would completely envelop Xangongo. During the second phase, Task Force Alpha would advance in a southeasterly direction, through Mongua, to attack Ongiva. Once these objectives had been accounted for, the bulk of the South African force would withdraw to SWA.

While it would be impossible for Task Force Alpha to achieve operational surprise, given PLAN's intelligence system, Joubert would nevertheless be able to achieve tactical surprise during the actual offensive operations. Protea, earmarked to last only 14 days, would be a lightning operation. With H-hour set for 11:00 on 24 August, the scene was set for one of biggest, and arguably the most impressive, South African cross-border operations of the Border War.

Operation Protea

On the morning of 23 August, the South African battle groups made for their various assembly points: Battle Group 10 moved to Ruacana in western Ovamboland, while battle groups 20, 30 and 40 journeyed further east to Ombalantu. The deployment ensured that the SADF maintained a presence on both sides of the Cunene River for their advance northwards. The South African forces crossed the cutline (border strip) under cover of darkness during the night of 23–24 August and advanced as far north as possible over difficult terrain before daybreak. Needless to say, progress was slower than what Joubert and his battle group commanders would have liked. Moreover, the South African advance into Angola had not gone unnoticed. PLAN's intelligence structures picked up on the closure of the Ondangwa Air Force Base shortly before the start of Protea and SWAPO used its propaganda to curry international support against and condemnation of the impending South African operation. While the SADF may have lost the element of surprise at the strategic and operational levels early on, SWAPO had no idea of where the first tactical blows would land.

The ground phase of operations was preceded by a pre-emptive airstrike launched by elements of the South African Air Force (SAAF). On 23 August, a formation of Buccaneers, Canberras and Mirage F1s launched several airstrikes against the FAPLA early-warning radar system in Cunene province. Subsequent attacks on the radar installations at Cahama and Chibemba, which eliminated radar cover across the province, proved satisfactory from a South African point of view. In doing so, the SAAF achieved immediate air superiority over the target area and would maintain it for the duration of the operation.

After crossing the Cunene River at Ruacana, De Vries's Battle Group 10 advanced towards Humbe as planned. The attack on Humbe was, however, a bit anticlimactic. After ordering preparatory artillery fire to soften up any possible resistance, and expecting to meet a strong defence, it was discovered that Humbe was deserted. Apart from some fleeing FAPLA soldiers, it appeared that SWAPO had hastily abandoned its positions. De Vries took the initiative and redeployed his troops further west to prevent the FAPLA forces at Cahama from intervening against the main attack on Xangongo.

Meanwhile, the main part of Task Force Alpha had started its advance from Ombalantu. Ferreira's Battle Group 40 operated as the vanguard during the advance, followed by Dippenaar's Battle Group 20 and Serfontein's Battle Group 30. Unfortunately, Ferreira and his troops, comprising motorised infantry companies from 32 Battalion, were less mobile than the other battle groups, and thus slowed down the advance. A frustrated Dippenaar even tried to overtake Ferreira's battle group with his own. However, the thick bush and difficult terrain prevented this altogether. It was soon established that the South African column had strayed too far east and had to be rerouted. Valuable time was thus lost during the morning's advance, which meant that H-hour, and the scheduled SAAF airstrikes on Xangongo, had to be postponed.

Nevertheless, at 11:50 six waves of aircraft bombed the SWAPO/FAPLA defences. The airstrikes were met by intensive fire from Soviet ZU-23-2 anti-aircraft guns. These weapons would soon be turned against the advancing South African ground forces, with devastating effect. Shortly after the airstrikes began, the ground forces commenced their assault. From the north, the infantry from Ferreira's Battle Group 40 advanced on foot and, under the cover of supporting fire from a battery of 120 mm mortars, stormed the defensive positions on their immediate front. FAPLA/PLAN resistance soon ceased and the defenders retreated. From this point, Battle Group 40 was in complete control of the northern defensive positions.

Concurrently, Dippenaar's Battle Group 20 advanced on the enemy trenches on their immediate front from the east. These defensive positions were found to be empty, presumably as a result of the intensive artillery fire that preceded the South African advance. However, the initial momentum of the attack soon dissipated. Dippenaar's troops drew heavy rifle and machine-gun fire and were heavily engaged by a Soviet ZU-23-2 anti-aircraft gun. Dippenaar decided to halt Battle Group 20's attack momentarily while air support was called in to silence the heavy weapon. However, it took nearly 40 minutes for the SAAF to provide air support, which failed to silence the anti-aircraft gun. Dippenaar called in further artillery fire, which also failed to silence the anti-aircraft gun. It was finally silenced after the heroic exploits of Capt Danie Laubscher in his Bosbok observation aircraft, who fired a 68 mm smoke rocket to mark the position and guide in further airstrikes.

Once the anti-aircraft gun was silenced, and nearly two-and-a-half hours after the attack commenced, Battle Group 20 resumed its advance and systematically cleared the FAPLA/PLAN defensive positions on their immediate front. During this action, Dippenaar's men stormed and cleared several trenches and bunkers, and went on to capture the airfield. In late afternoon, a combat team from Serfontein's Battle Group 30 reinforced Dippenaar's force, whose reserves by this time had been committed to the fight. By last light, Ferreira's and Dippenaar's forces were in possession of most of Xangongo. During the day's fighting, the South Africans had suffered three casualties. In contrast, at least 200 FAPLA/PLAN soldiers were killed at Xangongo and a number of tanks and heavy weapons destroyed.

While the attack on Xangongo took place, Serfontein's Battle Group 30 was deployed to the northeast to counter a possible FAPLA advance on Xangongo. Soon, Serfontein reported that a sizeable enemy force, comprising tanks, infantry and artillery, could be observed at Peu-Peu. Without hesitation, Serfontein immediately ordered Battle Group 30 to counterattack and prevent this force from intervening. During the subsequent engagement, the Angolans chose to disengage and retreat rather than stand and fight. Serfontein later occupied Peu-Peu, capturing 200–300 tonnes of ammunition, 120 000 litres of diesel and 90 000 litres of petrol, and destroying a large number of tanks, armoured cars, armoured personnel carriers and anti-aircraft guns.

That evening, the South Africans went into defensive laagers to the north and south of Xangongo. During the night, two FAPLA counterattacks were beaten off. By midday on 25 August, the South African mop-up operation around Xangongo was complete. Joubert then placed Velthuizen's pathfinder company under De Vries's command and ordered De Vries to remain in position to the west of Xangongo, from where Battle Group 10 could cover the SADF forces around Xangongo and prevent any FAPLA interference from Cahama. During the night, a combat team from Battle Group 10, along with Velthuizen's pathfinders, engaged a strong FAPLA force advancing from their rear, trying to break through to Cahama. The South Africans routed the enemy force, capturing several vehicles and heavy weapons. By 26 August, the South African forces had finished their sweep of the area around Xangongo and destroyed all known SWAPO bases in the vicinity. The next phase of Protea was about to commence.

At this point, Task Force Alpha was reorganised. De Vries's Battle Group 10 occupied Xangongo and was tasked with protecting the

SAAF Impala fighter aircraft prepare to take off for a strike mission into Angola during the Border War

A South African convoy during Operation Protea with a captured BM-21 'Grad' Multiple Rocket Launcher

Two BM-21 'Grad' Multiple Rocket Launchers captured by the SADF during Operation Protea

235

task force and preventing any FAPLA interference from Lubango and Cahama. De Vries was also tasked with protecting the bridge over the Cunene River at Xangongo, an important choke point dictating the overall movement of forces in Cunene province. Meanwhile, Ferreira's Battle Group 40 was transferred to Task Force Bravo for area operations in the eastern part of the province. Joubert's remaining troops, comprising battle groups 20 and 30, under Dippenaar and Serfontein respectively, continued their southeasterly advance to Ongiva via Mongua. For this part of the operation, Dippenaar's Battle Group 20 was reinforced by Combat Team Mamba, consisting of a mechanised infantry company and a Ratel 90 antitank platoon under the command of Cmdt Johnny Coetzer.

Combat Team Mamba was tasked with attacking a SWAPO/FAPLA force at Mongua – destruction of the enemy forces at Mongua was imperative in order to clear the route of advance towards Ongiva. During the early morning of 25 August, Coetzer's force attacked Mongua. The main attack was preceded by a barrage from the accompanying 127 mm Valkiri multiple rocket launchers. However, this barrage fell short of the enemy positions and failed to have the desired effect. Coetzer then ordered his Ratels forward through the dense bush, but an Alouette III helicopter that was acting as artillery spotter was shot down by a ZGU-1 anti-aircraft gun. While the South Africans found the going tough, they were yet to spot and engage the enemy. When they reached the open road, Coetzer sped up the advance and charged at the perceived enemy trenches. Upon reaching the trenches, the Ratel 90s destroyed the ZGU-1 anti-aircraft gun. Despite their initial success, the South Africans were soon pinned down by fire from 76 mm field guns. After reinforcing his troops on the frontline, Coetzer managed to silence the field guns with accurate fire from his mortars and Ratel 90s. The South African infantrymen debussed and charged forward on foot under retaliatory fire. With the aid of further mortar fire, the infantrymen cleared the enemy trenches piecemeal. With the enemy defenders at Mongua routed, the route of advance was clear and the main attack on Ongiva by Dippenaar and Serfontein's forces could commence.

South African intelligence had established that Ongiva was well defended by at least two infantry battalions, two anti-aircraft battalions armed with ZU-23-2 guns, a company of T-34 tanks, a BTR-23 armoured car company and an artillery battery comprising 82 mm and 76 mm field guns. The operational intent for the attack on Ongiva would have two phases. During the first phase, Dippenaar's Battle Group 20 would attack towards Ongiva from the northeast. Once Dippenaar had established a secure base of operations, Serfontein's Battle Group 30 would continue the second phase.

The attack was scheduled to begin on the morning of 27 August. The preceding night, the SAAF dropped propaganda leaflets over Ongiva, urging FAPLA soldiers and Angolan civilians to leave the town. While some civilians heeded the warning, FAPLA headquarters at Lubango ordered its troops at Ongiva to remain steadfast. The FAPLA positions at Ongiva were reinforced by some tanks, heavy weapons and at least two infantry platoons. The PLAN fighters at Ongiva were also ordered to harass the South African advance from the rear.

The South African attack on Ongiva commenced early on the morning of 27 August. The attack was preceded by an aerial bombardment of the enemy defences, in particular the airstrip and defensive positions to the west of the town. Heavy FAPLA anti-aircraft fire countered the airstrikes, damaging a Mirage III aircraft. Shortly after the aerial bombardment started, Dippenaar's ground forces commenced their attack. For the attack on Ongiva, they were divided into three combat teams (10, 20 and 30) that would each attack in a different direction, with a further combat team held in reserve (50). Combat Team 30 would advance towards the southeast and occupy the airfield, while combat teams 10 and 20 would head south and southeast.

During the advance of Combat Team 10, commanded by Maj JA Victor, a counterattack by three T-34s was a cause for concern. However, two Ratel 90s, through continuous manoeuvring, managed to knock out two of the tanks and caused the third to retreat. In due course, artillery support helped Victor's infantry silence several anti-aircraft guns. Enemy resistance in this sector soon dissipated, with the remaining FAPLA defenders abandoning their positions and fleeing. Elsewhere, the initial advance of Combat Team 30, commanded by Maj Nel van Rensburg, was soon halted by accurate fire from anti-aircraft guns. Moreover, support from the Ratel 90s was not feasible since it was established that

FAPLA soldiers were armed with RPG-7 launchers. Supporting mortar fire managed to dislodge the FAPLA defenders, which allowed Van Rensburg's troops to occupy the enemy positions successfully at 15:30.

Combat Team 10 next shifted its focus to the airfield, which Victor decided to attack from east to west along the runway. FAPLA resistance was again fierce, with anti-aircraft fire halting the South African advance for two hours. While a Ratel 90 took out a T-34 tank, the accompanying South African artillery fire failed to influence the tactical situation. It was soon established that the enemy guns were being directed from a radio station located on top of a nearby water tower. Accurate fire from a 120 mm mortar battery destroyed the radio station, changing the tactical situation. The South African infantry then continued their advance, and at 14:00 Victor's troops secured the airfield. The South Africans were fortunate that most of the squadron of T-34 tanks at Ongiva played only a limited role in the fighting. FAPLA had foolishly decided to dig in the tanks and employ them in a static role as light artillery. With the capture of the airfield completed, Dippenaar had accounted for his allotted objectives and in doing so provided a secure base from which Serfontein's Battle Group 30 could continue the main attack on Ongiva.

Battle Group 30 duly moved forward and continued with the second phase of the attack. The going was once more tough, with landmines and heavy FAPLA resistance slowing down the advance. When reports were received that several T-34s were threatening Serfontein's force from the east, Joubert ordered De Vries to send forward reinforcements from Battle Group 10 – comprising a mechanised infantry company supported by two Ratel 90s and commanded by Capt Koos Liebenberg. Serfontein called in 120 mm mortar fire to try to halt the advancing enemy tanks, but the T-34s kept coming. As soon as Liebenberg and his troops arrived on the scene, Serfontein ordered him to halt the tanks. Liebenberg moved forward with his Ratel 90s and immediately drew fire from the advancing tanks. With dusk approaching, he deployed his troops on either side of the road leading into Ongiva. Under cover of darkness, Liebenberg's Ratels fired simultaneously on the advancing T-34s, which immediately silenced the enemy fire on their immediate front. Figuring that at least two tanks had been destroyed, Liebenberg pulled his force back some distance and occupied a defensive position for the night from where the final attack on Ongiva could resume the next day.

On the morning of 28 August, and after spending an uneasy night expecting an enemy counterattack, the South Africans discovered that Ongiva had been abandoned. They moved forward and occupied the town, spending the following two days clearing up the battlefield, burying the enemy dead, securing captured documents, burning captured fuel and dealing with the local population. The South Africans also captured vast quantities of military and logistical supplies, which indicated that Ongiva had indeed served as a SWAPO logistical hub. Moreover, in the aftermath of Ongiva, and after engaging a fleeing FAPLA convoy, it was proven beyond doubt that Soviet military advisors were deployed in Cunene province to the FAPLA/PLAN forces. After the attack on Ongiva, Joubert's Task Force Alpha spread out and attacked and destroyed yet more SWAPO bases in the vicinity of Xangongo and Ongiva. However, these locations had all been hastily evacuated. Task Force Alpha crossed back into SWA on 2 September, signalling the end of Protea.

Protea was a highly successful cross-border operation at the operational and tactical levels. Task Force Alpha accounted for all its allotted objectives and in the process occupied Xangongo and Ongiva. The SADF suffered ten soldiers killed in action, with a further 64 wounded, while FAPLA/PLAN casualties were considerably higher, with a suspected 831 combatants killed in action and 25 captured. Joubert's task force also managed to capture 3 000–4 000 tonnes of materiel, including tanks, armoured fighting vehicles, multiple rocket launchers, field guns, a variety of heavy weapons and small arms, and a large assortment of other vehicles. Moreover, a further 250 tonnes of ammunition, along with much petrol and diesel fuel, were captured and later destroyed. The SAAF also destroyed at least 40 vehicles and damaged several more, all for the loss of only one Alouette III helicopter. Surprisingly, given the tough going and the determined enemy defence, only one Ratel was destroyed, with several Buffel armoured fighting vehicles having been damaged by landmines.

Protea further succeeded in disrupting PLAN's command structure, forward operational bases and logistical infrastructure in Cunene province. It was gauged that SWAPO would require at least a year to recover from the blow that Protea had delivered. Moreover, an immediate result of Protea was a sharp decrease in SWAPO acts of intimidation, minelaying, sabotage and contacts with security force personnel in SWA. SWAPO thus suffered a series of major reverses during 1981, losing an estimated 1 500 combatants. However, the South Africans realised that a single operation such as Protea had only a limited effect on the war and that more cross-border operations were needed to keep SWAPO off balance and prevent an escalation of the Border War.

With hindsight, it is clear that Protea demonstrated the merits of manoeuvre-type warfare. In fact, Protea is indicative of the maturation of the SADF's operational and tactical doctrine throughout the late 1970s and early 1980s. The mobile warfare doctrine, as espoused by De Vries and others, time and again threw the enemy forces off balance during Protea. Through the combined-arms approach, and with superior mobility, adequate air support and maintenance of the operational initiative, the SADF demonstrated the superiority of manoeuvre warfare over attritional warfare at Xangongo and Ongiva. This was not surprising at all: it simply reconfirmed the foundation on which the South African way of war was based. Time and again during Protea, the South African forces attacked from unexpected directions and surprised, confused and unnerved the FAPLA/PLAN forces, which remained ensconced in their static defensive positions. The SADF, it would seem, had for the time being perfected the art of manoeuvre warfare.

During the coming years, the Border War would intensify further, and the SADF would conduct more cross-border operations to offset the strength of SWAPO in Angola. During these South African incursions, FAPLA, with Soviet and Cuban support, would intervene forcefully on PLAN's behalf, and in doing so drastically escalate the Border War. In 1987–1988, a series of definitive, and infamous, battles would take place near Cuito Cuanavale that would pit the military might of the SADF against that of FAPLA/PLAN and its Cold War allies.

18

CUITO CUANAVALE, 1987–1988

The Border War (1966–1989) remains a hotly contested space. Long after the guns fell silent, fierce battles raged in the press and in books, with all the participants claiming victory. The final series of battles of the Border War, which became known as Cuito Cuanavale (1987–1988), is perhaps the most contested part of the whole conflict. Logically, it would seem impossible for all the protagonists to claim victory. However, warfare is properly examined at three levels: strategic, operational and tactical. Therefore, it is possible for the ordinary soldier who participated in face-to-face combat with the enemy to feel that he gained the upper hand during the fierce battles. After all, the ordinary soldier views the battlefield through a keyhole and therefore experiences the tactical level of warfare. He remains largely oblivious to the operational and strategic considerations that brought him face to face with the enemy. As one progresses up the hierarchy of command, so one becomes less familiar with the actual combat experiences at the tactical level but more au fait with operational and strategic issues. It is quite possible to defeat an enemy comprehensively at the tactical level of war but ultimately to lose the campaign at the strategic level. This often leads participants to feel that politicians have betrayed them and squandered their hard-earned victory on the altar of political expediency. Cuito Cuanavale is a case where each side claiming victory may have valid reasons for doing so, depending on where their claim is pitched in relation to the three levels of war.

The background to the battle of Cuito Cuanavale is complicated and multilayered but is essential to understanding why the battle took place and how it was conducted in the operational and strategic context. After

The Battle of Cuito Cuanavale, 1987–1988

Cueio

Axis of main attack Combat Group Charlie

Axis of Command Task Force 10

Deception/Mobile/Reserve Combat Group Alpha

4 SAI plus a UNITA battalion and a squadron of Olifant tanks 8 November

7–8 November

Cunzumbia

18–23 November

Main attack on 9 November

61 Mech plus a UNITA battalion 8 November

18–23 November

18–23 November

N E W S

Feint on 16 November

8–10 November

23 November to 5 December

Attack on 16 November

11–18 November

Cuzizi

Catato bush

Probes on 24–25 November

16 Brigade

Attack on 11 November

Chambinga

Objective B

Objective A

Attack on 17 November

Tactical group of 16 Brigade

Supporting attacks 15–16 November

Deception attack 9 November

32 Bn plus a UNITA battalion 8 November

Chambinga high ground

Cuatir

Probes on 25–26 November

66 Brigade (59 Brigade from 14 November)

Chambinga

Hube

Viposto high ground

HQ FAPLA

Operational command post

A battalion of 66 Brigade

59 Brigade

Vimbulo

A battalion of 25 Brigade

21 Brigade

Mianei

20 km

15

10

5

0

Lacaia

Colui

Angola

Dala

Tumpo

Canavale

25 Brigade

Canavale

Cuito Cuanavale

Ferrying logistics from Menongue

Cuito

13 Brigade

FAPLA

8

Tiengo

Legend

SADF troop movements
Enemy troop movements

Thick savannah bush
Open savannah bush
River flood plain
High ground

Town
Road
River

Cuito Cuanavale

Tactical symbols

= Combat Group
x Brigade
xx Division

Mechanised infantry
Headquarters
Defensive position
Tactical headquarters of Task Force 10

the end of colonial rule in Angola in 1975, the South West Africa People's Organisation (SWAPO) was able to use southern Angola as a haven and jumping-off point for its incursions into South West Africa (SWA). The South African Defence Force (SADF) embraced its long history of manoeuvre warfare doctrine during the war and sought to attack and destroy SWAPO bases in southern Angola, dislocating SWAPO's armed wing, the People's Liberation Army of Namibia (PLAN), through a series of lightning, unorthodox and bold cross-border raids. The airborne assault on Cassinga (see Chapter 16) was an early example of such a raid strategy, using vertical envelopment to surprise and destroy the enemy. The SADF, out of political considerations, took care to avoid the Cuban/ Angolan conventional forces where possible and conducted classic counterinsurgency operations against SWAPO. However, such avoidance tactics were not always possible, and as the war inside Angola dragged on without resolution, so the likelihood of an SADF clash with the Cuban/ Angolan military grew more likely, as occurred during Operation Protea.

The forces gather: Manoeuvre or attrition?

The Cuban/Angolan forces were hell-bent on removing Jonas Savimbi's União Nacional para a Independência Total de Angola (UNITA) from their stronghold of southern Angola. South Africa had found a natural ally in UNITA and SWAPO forces avoided UNITA-controlled territory. SWAPO relied on the Cuban/Angolan armies and often placed their bases in proximity to FAPLA bases and sought refuge there when they came under attack from the South Africans. Slowly but inexorably, the protagonists were drawn ever closer to a full-scale conventional battle as they were determined to ensure the survival of their respective proxies – SWAPO and UNITA. From 1983, the SADF's backing of UNITA grew exponentially, going from the provision of clandestine and sporadic air and mortar support to the deployment of considerable artillery, air, naval and Special Forces assets to defend UNITA positions, as took place at Mavinga in 1985–1986 against a concerted Cuban/FAPLA onslaught. In 1987, a looming offensive designed finally to destroy UNITA in southern Angola was the backdrop to the final operation of the Border War, in which South Africa and UNITA met Cuban and Angolan forces in one of the largest conventional land battles in Africa since the Second World War.

243

South African military intelligence became aware of a FAPLA buildup in the vicinity of Cuito Cuanavale in January 1987. It was obvious that the Angolan force was heavily supported by the Cubans and was intent on a large conventional operation using overwhelming force and firepower to finally destroy the UNITA presence in southern Angola. FAPLA's starting point was Cuito Cuanavale and the operation envisaged the occupation of the airstrip at Mavinga to deploy air assets. Gaining air superiority in the combat area would be the springboard for the capture of the UNITA stronghold at Jamba.

Largely following the format of their failed 1985 and 1986 offensives, the Cubans/Angolans launched Operation Saludando Octubre (Salute to October). On 14 August 1987, a force of eight brigades set out from Tumpo to the east of Cuito Cuanavale and the Cuito River. Four brigades formed the spearhead, with 6 000 men and 160 tanks, leaving two brigades behind in Tumpo and Cuito Cuanavale, while another two brigades guarded the supply route from Menongue to Cuito Cuanavale. Facing this substantial force ponderously advancing on Mavinga were 2 600 South Africans and an unknown number of UNITA soldiers.

At the outset, the FAPLA/Cuban advance presented the South Africans with two operational possibilities. The first, an advance to and the capture of Cuito Cuanavale, was a strategy in keeping with the South African reinvigoration of their manoeuvre doctrine, as supported by two of its biggest proponents, Col Roland de Vries and Col Piet Muller, the OC of Sector 30. Their idea was to execute a manoeuvre reminiscent of the German Schlieffen Plan of the First World War, which relied on a revolving-door principle. The more pressure exerted by the FAPLA/Cuban forces in the direction of the Lomba River, the more vulnerable their rear position at Cuito Cuanavale would become. By encouraging the Cuban/FAPLA brigades to advance in the east towards the Lomba River and Mavinga, the South Africans could execute a classic indirect approach and attack Cuito Cuanavale from the rear, west of the Cuito River, thus cutting off four enemy brigades from their source of supply. This was a golden opportunity to inflict a massive and comprehensive defeat on the Cuban/Angolan forces and secure a decisive political advantage.

The powers that be in Pretoria rejected this bold manoeuvre option out of hand, purely for political reasons. They preferred a clandestine intervention out of sight of the international media, a tactic successfully deployed on previous occasions in Angola. Orders emanating from Defence and Army Headquarters made it crystal clear that the intervention, the second of the two operational possibilities, would take place east of the Cuito River, would be of a limited nature and clandestine, and would have zero tolerance for SADF personnel or equipment losses. Finally, any operational success would be exclusively attributed to UNITA. These overriding political considerations destroyed the essential freedom that the military commanders would need to conduct the operation in the most efficient manner. The idea of a classic manoeuvre operation was sacrificed on the altar of political expediency. The SADF abandoned the idea of advancing west of the Cuito River and capturing Cuito Cuanavale in the rear of the enemy forces surging towards the Lomba River.

Choosing to confront the Cubans/FAPLA to the east of the Cuito River would lead to a series of battles of attrition along the Lomba River. There the South Africans would have to rely on their superior tactics to inflict massive losses on the advancing enemy forces rather than the paralysing effect of an operational manoeuvre designed to dislocate rather than destroy the enemy. Again reflecting political considerations, the deployment initially consisted of three motorised infantry companies of 32 Battalion supported by a Valkiri rocket battery, with 61 Mechanised Infantry Battalion Group (61 Mech), together with air support, kept in reserve.

The concept and structure behind the formation of 61 Mech reflected the SADF's homage to combined-arms warfare. This battalion group contained elements of armour and mechanised and motorised infantry, supported by artillery and engineers, in a single entity. It was the physical expression of the doctrine of manoeuvre warfare using a combined-arms approach: 61 Mech was highly mobile, with all elements moving at the same speed and acting in mutual support. It was only on 28 August 1987 that 61 Mech was finally released for offensive operations, thus signalling the end of any hope of keeping the operation clandestine.

Once again, exponents of the SADF's doctrine of manoeuvre warfare clamoured for an offensive operation to the west of the Cuito River, aimed at Cuito Cuanavale in the rear of the enemy force making its way to the Lomba River. Here, South Africa would be able to pit its strength against the enemy's weakest point. But the fear of becoming embroiled in a full-scale confrontation and the possibility of suffering intolerable casualties once again torpedoed the idea. The SADF would release its forces into the fray piecemeal, going against Guderian's dictum of 'Klotzen, nicht Kleckern' (Strike together, not divided), but also contradicting an immutable concept of warfare – concentration of force. The SADF's cautious approach to the operation ensured that they were sluggish in concentrating in time and space, which would eventually negatively affect the operational outcome of the battle.

First clashes on the Lomba River: Operation Moduler

The SADF force facing the enemy, designated as 20 Brigade, grew rapidly and included 61 Mech (sans its tank component), three companies from 32 Battalion, two companies from 101 Battalion and G5 155 mm and 120 mm mortar batteries. Marching inexorably towards the Lomba River were the four FAPLA brigades with more than adequate artillery and air support. The two westernmost brigades deployed to the east of the Cuito River; acting in mutual support were FAPLA's 47 and 59 brigades, with 16 and 21 brigades further east. Events began to unfold rapidly when FAPLA's 47 Brigade took a route around the source of the Lomba River to arrive south of the river. The other brigades were rapidly approaching the northern bank of the river, where they would attempt a crossing.

To meet the threat during Operation Moduler, the South Africans were organised into three combat groups: Alpha (the bulk of 61 Mech), Bravo (elements of 32 and 101 battalions combined) and Charlie (the remainder of 61 Mech, in reserve). Support came in the form of an understrength artillery regiment and air support. The South African plan was to juggle forces by concentrating effort on one FAPLA brigade at a time, with the overall objective of preventing them from crossing the Lomba and advancing on Mavinga. The first task was to prevent 47 Brigade and 59 Brigade from joining south of the Lomba River.

The first South African attack went in on 9 September 1987, with Combat Group Bravo advancing against 21 Brigade, which had established a bridgehead south of the Lomba River. A furious attack supported by artillery persuaded 21 Brigade to abandon its bridgehead positions and flee back across the river, suffering enormous casualties in the process. The South Africans registered just two wounded in total. Combat Group Bravo now turned its attention to 47 Brigade, only to be rebuffed by the larger force even when Combat Group Charlie joined the fray as reinforcements. Although the South Africans were able to destroy five tanks for one Ratel infantry fighting vehicle destroyed, suffering four dead, the attack failed to dislodge the stubborn enemy and was broken off. An attack on 47 Brigade was resumed on 19 September using 61 Mech, but here too the South Africans were frustrated by the dense bush, which made headway impossible. On the same day, 21 Brigade attempted to cross the Lomba River again in the exact same location as before, only to be decimated by the South African artillery, which wreaked havoc among the FAPLA infantry.

FAPLA, despite numerous setbacks, still retained a stubborn presence to the south of the Lomba River, in the shape of 47 Brigade. The South Africans gathered combat groups Alpha and Charlie, comprising the entire 61 Mech, in an attempt to dislodge 47 Brigade and force it back across the river in what would be the final phase of Operation Moduler. The attack took the form of a charge, with Ratel 90s in the lead, causing havoc and devastation among the FAPLA defenders. It was a case of the thinly armoured Ratel 90s, with their low-pressure 90 mm guns (having limited armour-penetration qualities), versus FAPLA's heavily armoured T-54/T-55 tanks, with their 100 mm high-velocity guns, which could easily destroy a Ratel at 100 m or more. Were it not for the dense, bushy terrain, the Russian-built tanks would have had a significant advantage in protection and firepower. The Ratel prevailed where visibility was down to 30 m in places and combat took place at close range. These conditions suited the lower-velocity gun, as the Ratel's superior height gave it an advantage in reduced visibility. A group of Ratels acting in unison would often take on a single T-54/T-55 and destroy the tank with multiple group shots. Equally, the Ratels equipped with 20 mm guns wreaked havoc among the FAPLA infantrymen.

The action ended at 17:00 with 47 Brigade routed, leaving behind 600 dead. FAPLA had no choice but to effect a retreat northward, having lost more than 60 tanks, a similar number of armoured personnel carriers, 20 rocket launchers and more than 1 000 men killed and nearly 2 200 wounded. It was an astounding victory, achieved by a numerically inferior force and at relatively little cost, and a vindication of South African tactical and technological superiority.

Beyond the Lomba River

The SADF's successful prevention of FAPLA from crossing the Lomba River introduced a more dangerous phase of the campaign. To all intents and purposes, the SADF had achieved its initial objective of preventing FAPLA from capturing Mavinga and Jamba, preserving UNITA as a bulwark against SWAPO in southern Angola. The South Africans were cognisant that they would soon face the same threat once FAPLA rebuilt its strength. At a conference held on 21 September 1987 near Mavinga, attended by President PW Botha, Minister of Defence Magnus Malan and top military brass, the SADF received what amounted to a blank cheque to comprehensively destroy FAPLA as a future threat. Botha authorised whatever reinforcements were needed, including heavy Olifant tanks. Unfortunately, Gen Jannie Geldenhuys, the Chief of the SADF, did not take full advantage of the president's offer and made the modest addition of 61 Mech's sister unit, 4 South African Infantry Battalion (4 SAI), with its single Olifant squadron. Once again, the question of advancing west of the Cuito River towards the lightly garrisoned Cuito Cuanavale, thought to be defended by a FAPLA company, was raised. The chief proponent of this option, Col Roland de Vries, would lead the offensive while Col Deon Ferreira would hold the line and the five FAPLA brigades in the east.

The 'western approach' option made perfect operational sense as it seemed that FAPLA did not consider a South African attack in this direction to be likely. With most of the FAPLA strength deployed east of the Cuito River and withdrawing from the Lomba River in disarray after their recent trouncing, it seemed obvious to capture Cuito Cuanavale from the west and cut off the five FAPLA brigades. Any excuse that this approach would unnecessarily escalate the war and draw in more Soviet and Cuban military support had surely disappeared with Botha's 'blank cheque'. An eastern approach, in the teeth of most of the

A column comprising Eland armoured cars and Ratel IFVs passing by a destroyed Angolan T-54 tank during Operation Askari later, 1984

The Ratel IFV – an ideal force multiplier for the SADF during the Border War

A Ratel IFV during one of the many cross-border operations into Angola during the Boder War

Final operational orders are given before the commencement of a cross-border operation into Angola during the Border War

249

FAPLA strength, was certainly not more clandestine than the capture of Cuito Cuanavale.

At this juncture, it is important to note that Cuito Cuanavale was not a strategic objective but merely an operational or tactical objective for the SADF. Its capture was considered only in the context of destroying the FAPLA brigades to the east; once the western-approach option was discarded, the SADF made little reference to the town. Once the SADF adopted the eastern approach, the objective was to destroy all the FAPLA brigades east of the Cuito River and then hand over the territory for UNITA to occupy. Therefore, the South Africans, in adopting the eastern approach, chose to rely on a series of tactical envelopments and attritional frontal attacks rather than an operational envelopment that would have delivered Cuito Cuanavale and dislocated the entire FAPLA contingent without the need for a major confrontation.

Even though FAPLA had suffered serious defeat on the Lomba River, it remained a force in being that was numerically superior to the SADF. The South Africans would now attempt to concentrate their forces and take on the FAPLA brigades one at a time using a sequence of manoeuvres. The first target was the isolated 16 Brigade at the Chambinga River. An exhausted 61 Mech (Combat Group Alpha) would launch a feint attack and fix 16 Brigade from the south. While the Angolans were distracted, 4 SAI (Combat Group Charlie) would launch its main attack from the north. Then the battle groups would make their way westward towards the source of the Hube River and cut off the remaining FAPLA brigades to the south. The attack was launched on 9 November 1987 and for the first time since 1945, South African tanks saw action in fierce battles. Despite several spirited Angolan counterattacks, the surviving members of 16 Brigade began to flee from the battlefield in disorder. However, instead of seizing the advantage, the South Africans decided on an operational pause to regroup and take care of their logistics, thus failing to exploit their tactical victory by cutting off the enemy.

The South Africans attempted the same manoeuvre two days later but reversed the direction of the feint. Alpha would feint from the north while Charlie launched the real attack in the south. Charlie's main attack in the south encountered dense bush, slowing down the attack considerably and enabling the Angolans to lure them into an ambush.

The South Africans were able to fight their way out of the ambush using their superior tactical handling and concentration of overwhelming fire-power. The Angolans retreated in some disarray, but the South Africans failed once again to exploit their victory with a quick and decisive attack on a demoralised force, choosing instead to regroup and replenish. The following days were marked by the failure of the SADF to engage decisively with the retreating FAPLA forces, who proved remarkably resilient in being able to retreat to the bridge over the Chambinga River and to relative safety on 17 November.

The final South African attack went in on 25 November using national servicemen who were due to be demobilised after completing their two-year stint. One can only imagine their trepidation at the thought of becoming casualties a few days before rejoining their families. They were expected to launch an attack on foot through the dense bush on the high ground north of the Chambinga River with little in the way of tank support, since the difficult terrain inhibited the movement of armour. The entire concept of this infantry attack, into the teeth of well-defended FAPLA positions, was not only bereft of imagination but contrary to the principles of South African manoeuvre doctrine. When the time came, the plan of attack was executed with little enthusiasm and amounted to nothing. The entire operation to date had left FAPLA severely mauled but intact as a fighting force, having avoided complete destruction on several occasions. Fortunately for the Angolans, towards the later part of Operation Moduler the SADF were often caught hopelessly out of position when in hot pursuit.

Operations Hooper and Packer

The nature of the battlefield now changed significantly from the wide-open spaces between the Lomba and Chambinga rivers, which favoured manoeuvre-type warfare. The Angolans retreated into a smaller area defined by the Cuito River in the west, the Chambinga River in the south and the Cuatir River in the north, enabling FAPLA to mount a continuous defence with natural terrain multipliers on three sides. The South Africans, unable to use manoeuvre, would have to dislodge FAPLA using a frontal attack and resort to the kind of attrition tactics that went against the grain of their doctrine. It can be strongly argued that the original South African failure to attack Cuito Cuanavale from the west created the predicament where they faced a well-defended area with few options other than a costly frontal attack, and with little in the way of reserves.

The SADF now embarked on Operation Hooper, adding another tank squadron to the mix. The men of 32 Battalion were reassigned on a clandestine mission to interdict FAPLA communication lines to the west of the Cuito River in an operation that can be summed up as 'too little, too late'. The brunt of the campaign would increasingly fall on the mechanised and armoured elements of 61 Mech and 4 SAI in what can be described as a heavyweight slugging match. The FAPLA forces, increasingly aided by the Cubans, were organised in three defensive lines arranged in depth. It was near impossible to outflank their positions, especially as they enjoyed both numerical superiority and the terrain modifiers of a defensive advantage. Inconceivably, the South Africans were conducting the operation without a reserve, a cardinal sin in the immutable rules of warfare. Without a viable reserve, it was almost impossible for the SADF to conduct its affairs at the operational level of warfare; instead, it had to rely on a series of tactical victories to dislodge the enemy and drive them back over the Cuito River. With no chance of exploiting opportunities with a reserve, the South Africans were handed an impossible task in the face of insurmountable odds.

It took the South Africans another five weeks to reorganise their forces and orientate the newcomers to the operational area. They were confronted with the problem of operating on external lines of communication, with their substantial advance taking them further away from their logistical hub. The Angolans, operating on internal lines and having retreated towards their bases, had shortened their lines of communication. The South Africans on the ground were short of everything and operating under extremely hot and humid conditions, and their morale began to suffer accordingly. Constant interference from higher up the command chain adversely affected operational and tactical command and control and played havoc with the doctrine of mission command, according to which subordinates were supposedly encouraged to act independently and on their own initiative, subject to their superiors' overall mission objective. Orders took the form of a detailed command structure in which subordinates were micromanaged in all aspects of the operational and tactical levels.

The devolution of decision-making up the hierarchy accompanied a reluctance at the lower levels to commit to an aggressive plan of action. Instead, all tactical and operational plans took on a decidedly cautious approach, where boldness was called for instead. This type of warfare, involving frontal attacks on prepared positions, was not part of the DNA of South African warfare, which favoured manoeuvre to dislodge an enemy from the ground of their choosing.

An artillery bombardment opened proceedings on 2 January 1988 in the forlorn hope that the Angolans would flee the battlefield. UNITA's attack on the strong enemy defences was easily repulsed. On 13 January, against the hopes that UNITA would bear the brunt of the actual combat, the SADF was forced to commit to the fight. Despite some success with the attack, a lack of SADF reserves ensured that the exploitation phase was limited. Captured FAPLA positions handed over to UNITA were easily reoccupied when UNITA abandoned them at the first sign of a FAPLA counterattack. All the time, the Cuban presence in the frontline and in the organisation grew with Fidel Castro's determination to defend Cuito Cuanavale at all costs.

The SADF launched another attack on 14 February, which resulted in a tactical victory despite a spirited but ill-conceived Cuban counter-attack with tanks. Losses since 1 January reflected the SADF's tactical superiority, with the Cubans/FAPLA losing 532 dead and 27 tanks destroyed for four South Africans killed and one Ratel destroyed. The Angolans, supported by the Cubans, had managed to retain a toehold on the eastern bank of the Cuito. This would mark the end of the series of South African tactical victories in the operations to date. From this point the Cubans took over tactical command of the defences surrounding Cuito Cuanavale and Castro personally directed many aspects of the forthcoming battles. The defences were bolstered with extensive minefields, coordinated artillery barrages and well-directed air attacks. Both sides were determined to gain or maintain control of the real estate known as the Tumpo Triangle on the east side of the Cuito River. On 25 and 29 February 1987, Operation Hooper continued with two successive SADF attacks against the Tumpo Triangle. These were rebuffed by the defenders, ensconced behind fortified positions and minefields and supported by artillery and airstrikes that successfully interdicted the South African attacks.

Operation Packer commenced after the Cubans took the opportunity afforded by a three-week break in the fighting to enhance and improve their defences at Tumpo. The SADF planning lacked imagination and would essentially be a repeat of the previous attacks using the same approach. South Africa's inability to obtain unrivalled air superiority would also hamper their desire for unfettered manoeuvrability on the ground. Inevitably, the attack on 23 March ended in failure, with several SADF tanks becoming immobilised in minefields. Three tanks would end up in enemy hands, scoring a great propaganda victory for Castro and the Cubans and marking the end of the South African efforts to dislodge FAPLA from Tumpo.

At the outset of the campaign, the SADF missed an operational opportunity to capture Cuito Cuanavale deep in the rear of the Angolan forces descending on the Lomba River. Political constraints overrode sound military judgement and the SADF opted for a series of manoeuvres, using their tactical superiority first to halt and then to force the Angolans to retreat to the Tumpo Triangle. The option to direct forces to the west of the Cuito River presented itself to the SADF on numerous occasions during the campaign, but, unfortunately, the political will was lacking to deliver a decisive blow based on the indirect approach and South Africa's doctrine of manoeuvre warfare. Instead, the South Africans became progressively mired in a war of attrition, with their command-and-control structure resorting to detailed command from the top. Long-cherished mission command tactics were discarded in favour of rigid directives from senior generals far from the battlefield. Despite doctrinal and command-structure setbacks, the South Africans were able to claim that they had ensured the survival of UNITA, which was their primary objective. The skewed combat results were a vindication of the overwhelming tactical superiority largely afforded by the formation and deployment of 61 Mech and 4 SAI, which represented a balanced combined-arms team at the battalion group level. Nevertheless the Battle of Cuito Cuanavale amounted to a missed opportunity to destroy several FAPLA brigades and deliver the SADF's most decisive victory in its history.

South Africa's protracted Border War ended with mixed strategic, operational and tactical results. During this period, South Africa was able to build a formidable war machine that embraced and practised a long-established brand of manoeuvre warfare. For the first time, mechanised infantry were carried into battle in the remarkable Ratel infantry fighting vehicles as part of a sophisticated combined-arms team, best represented in the structure of 61 Mech. Officers such as Roland de Vries fought hard to rediscover and implement South African manoeuvre and directive command doctrine and were able to demonstrate its effectiveness when given the opportunity. South Africa's sensitivity to losses and a tendency to tread a cautious political path ensured that political considerations often took precedence over purely military ones. Placing politics above the military has been a familiar aspect of the South African way of war for at least a century and has often led to a diminution of fighting power on the battlefield. This trend would continue after the 1994 democratic elections and the formation of the South African National Defence Force (SANDF). Politics would again play a hand in the conduct of the SANDF when it intervened in Lesotho during Operation Boleas in 1998.

19

OPERATION BOLEAS, 1998

South Africa's intervention in Lesotho in 1998, a mere four years after the transition to democracy, was in many respects a milestone in the country's military and political history. Operation Boleas was launched at the behest of the Southern African Development Community (SADC) and as such it enjoyed a legitimacy not afforded to the South African military for decades prior to 1994. It was also conducted together with the Botswana Defence Force (BDF) and, for this reason, was the first occasion since the Korean War that South Africa cooperated militarily with another sovereign state on foreign soil. Operation Boleas was also the first operation for the fledgling South African National Defence Force (SANDF), which was an amalgamation of former enemies from the protracted liberation struggle and included both statutory and non-statutory components Therefore, the entire enterprise became a litmus test for the effectiveness and cohesion of the SANDF under the new democratic dispensation. Here was an opportunity to measure whether the doctrine of the new defence force was in line with that of the SADF or whether the SANDF had absorbed the doctrines of the amalgamated non-statutory forces, which were heavily influenced by the Eastern Bloc and irregular warfare.

Many of the documents pertaining to Operation Boleas remain classified and therefore gaining an in-depth understanding of the operation is challenging. Jean-Pierre Scherman, at the time a junior officer, has published the only detailed account of the military events at the tactical level. His work relies heavily on interviews with participants and his personal experience of the operation, in which he was severely wounded. The political aspects of the campaign have received greater attention via the media and scholarly articles. Both sets of sources are solidly united in presenting South Africa's intervention in Lesotho as an unmitigated disaster from the military and political points of view. Criticism ranges from whether SADC had the legal authority to approve the operation to gaps in military intelligence and the SANDF's failure to protect Maseru from widespread looting and rioting. Despite the adverse criticism, much of it deserved, valuable lessons were learned that are pertinent to South Africa's future role as an important contributor to peacekeeping and peace enforcement duties in Africa.

Lesotho: A history of resistance to invasion

Lesotho is a small, landlocked enclave surrounded by South Africa. Its people have a fierce history of resisting colonialism, having successfully warded off the Orange Free State Boers in three wars during the long reign of King Moshoeshoe I (1823–1870). In the last of these wars (1867–1868), Moshoeshoe appealed for military aid from the British, who dispatched a small force to restore order. The Boers had no wish to engage the British and withdrew, leaving the British to annex Basutoland (also known as Basotholand). The territory became part of the High Commission Territories but was overtly and covertly coveted by the Boer republics. In May 1910, the passage of the South Africa Act by the British Parliament led to the birth of the Union of South Africa. The Act contained provisions for the incorporation of the High Commission Territories and Rhodesia into the Union at some future date. From Union in 1910 until Basutoland gained its independence from Britain (as Lesotho) in 1966, successive South African governments pressed the British government for the territory's incorporation into the Union and later the republic. After independence, Lesotho had an uneasy relationship with the apartheid government until South Africa embraced its democratic dispensation in 1994.

The transition to democracy saw certain forces within Lesotho and South Africa proposing the reintegration of the kingdom into South Africa. Lesotho has always been economically reliant on South Africa, with its citizens providing a significant percentage of the migrant labour force on South African mines. Lesotho also contains the Katse and

Mohale dams, part of the Lesotho Highlands Water Project, which provides the Witwatersrand with the bulk of its water needs. However, there remains within Lesotho society a powerful faction with a strong sense of national identity created by the country's history of resistance and independence. Lesotho also never came under the yoke of apartheid and enjoyed international recognition. Its political system developed apart from South Africa's, and it has incorporated a monarchy within its institutions. Those wishing to remain politically independent have long been wary of their larger neighbour's acquisitive nature. Operation Boleas cannot be examined without consideration of South Africa's expansionist history.

Lesotho: Political strife

Lesotho has been a politically troubled country since its independence. The Kingdom of Lesotho was ruled by the Basotho National Party (BNP) from independence until 1970. Having lost the elections to the Basotho Congress Party (BCP), Prime Minister Lebua Jonathan refused to cede power and imprisoned the BCP leadership. A military coup in 1986 forced him out of office and installed the ceremonial monarch King Moshoeshoe II, giving him executive powers. The king, having overstepped his powers, was soon forced into exile, and replaced by his son, King Letsie III, in 1987. The military junta eventually handed over power to a democratically elected government of the BCP in 1993. King Letsie III sought to persuade the BCP government to reinstate his father as head of state, but without success. In August 1994, Letsie III staged a military-backed coup that deposed the BCP government. After protracted negotiations, the BCP government was reinstated and Letsie III abdicated in favour of his father in 1995, only to ascend the throne again when Moshoeshoe II died in 1996.

In 1998, the newly formed Lesotho Congress for Democracy (LCD) comfortably won the general election, though there were accusations of electoral fraud from some quarters. The BCP, with several alliance partners, began demonstrations outside the Royal Palace in Maseru, calling for the king to dismiss the government. For several days there were running battles between the security forces and the demonstrators. The security forces were divided in their loyalties and there was a strong possibility of conflict erupting between different factions within the military. It was at this stage, and with tensions mounting, that South Africa, with Botswana and Zimbabwe, decided to intervene. The Lesotho government lost control of the situation when armed opposition supporters took over Maseru and several units of the Royal Lesotho Defence Force (RLDF) mutinied.

South Africa was still emerging from the dark clouds of colonialism and apartheid. In 1994, the SADF had become the SANDF, with the statutory and non-statutory forces amalgamated under its umbrella. The process was more akin to the other forces being subsumed within the SADF rather than a true amalgamation. This was because the SADF was the only force with the infrastructure to effect the complicated transformation and amalgamation process. Therefore, in its early stages, the SANDF closely resembled the SADF in its structure, equipment and, importantly, doctrine. The SANDF in 1998 had a strong institutional history of counterinsurgency and conventional doctrine from its 30 years of experience during the Border War. Its technical ability ensured that it was able to conduct extended operations and maintain vehicles and equipment to a high standard. Perhaps the one area lacking was the doctrine pertaining to peacekeeping and peace enforcement in a foreign country, a skill fundamental to its new role as a democratic country with obligations in the rest of Africa. The process of transformation was designed to make the defence force, at every level, representative of South African society. Although transformation proceeded relatively smoothly, it had a negative impact on fighting power and efficiency.

Operation Boleas: The plan

On 16 September 1998, the rapidly deteriorating situation in Lesotho prompted Prime Minister Pakalitha Mosisili to request Botswana, Mozambique, South Africa and Zimbabwe to 'come to the rescue of the Government and the people of Lesotho'. South Africa's acting president, Mangosuthu Buthelezi, sealed South Africa's intervention in Lesotho on 21 September. South African forces would deploy as part of a joint SANDF-BDF initiative within 24 hours.

The mission was planned around four phases. In the first phase, once the SANDF force was assembled in the vicinity of Ladybrand, the Maseru Bridge border post would be secured. The next phase would be to secure the king's palace, government buildings and other military installations around Maseru. The third phase was to stabilise military targets and to disarm rebel elements within the RLDF. The last phase involved continuous stabilising operations, followed by relief and demobilisation.

Three priorities were identified. First, there was the creation of a stable environment in Maseru by securing the Maseru Bridge border post, the RLDF bases, the Radio Lesotho broadcasting station and the foreign embassies. Second, the Royal Palace and the Lesotho Defence Force Air Wing bases had to be secured. The third priority was to secure the Katse Dam. Intelligence indicated that dissident elements of the RLDF might mount an attack in the vicinity of the dam, where there were two villages housing 198 South African workers.

The planning for this type of operation was not a complete surprise, as members of the SANDF's Rapid Deployment Force had gathered in 1997 to plan for just such an occurrence in Lesotho. The planners had analysed various scenarios, from hostage rescue to a full-blown invasion to restore the elected government in the event of a coup. The results suggested that the SANDF would be able to complete its mandate successfully if called upon to restore order in Lesotho.

The potential for political unrest in Lesotho increased after the swearing-in of the new prime minister from the LCD in May 1998. The SANDF accordingly began preparations by putting together a reaction force. This task fell to Brig Gen MJ Grobler, the GOC Free State Command. Grobler selected elements of the Permanent Force, namely 1 Special Service Battalion (1 SSB), based at Tempe in Bloemfontein. This was an armoured car regiment under the command of Lt Col Butch Williamson and its Ratel infantry fighting vehicles, some armed with 90 mm guns, and Rooikat armoured reconnaissance vehicles, with their 76 mm high-velocity guns, could provide both mobility and protection. Added to the force was a mechanised infantry company in Ratel 20s, drawn from 1 South African Infantry Battalion, and a company of paratroopers from 1 Parachute Battalion, both also based at Tempe.

Williamson spent the next four months drafting a workable plan for the mission. The SANDF completely lacked essential intelligence, having no informer network in Lesotho, and Williamson did most of his planning on maps he bought from a local garage. A Presidential

Minute, issued on 16 September, provided the SANDF with the legal framework for an intervention operation, designated as Operation Boleas. Williamson's preparations thus far (Operation Kitso) did not completely encompass the expanded requirements of Operation Boleas. Critics pointed out that a new plan should have been developed rather than an adaption of Operation Kitso.

In 1997, the SANDF had formed a Joint Operations Division to plan and coordinate all the necessary components of an operation. This was an innovation over the traditional planning system, in which operations staff worked under the command of the Chief of Staff. Under the new regime, each arm of service was obligated to supply adequately trained and equipped forces for a particular mission under the command of the Joint Operations Division, led by Lt Gen Deon Ferreira. The exception was the Special Forces Brigade, which fell directly under the command of Chief of the SANDF but was allocated permanently to the Joint Operations Division.

General Siphiwe Nyanda, the Chief of the SANDF, ordered the mobilisation of SANDF units for the Lesotho intervention through the Joint Operations Division. The proposed deployment represented a balanced all-arms force, restricted by a cap placed on deployment numbers, where mechanised, motorised, artillery, antitank and air assets were represented under joint operational command. Added to the available forces was a company of mechanised infantry from the BDF. Numerical restrictions were once again a case of political considerations overriding military necessity – a formula that usually favours expediency over efficiency.

On 19 September, at a formal briefing delivered by Colonel Robbie Hartslief, the commander of the newly constituted Combined Task Force Boleas, it was clear that major opposition from the RLDF was not expected. For this reason, the SANDF contingent earmarked for the operation represented a force in possession of overwhelming firepower, with a peace mission to restore law and order rather than an invasion force. It was also hoped that a mere show of force at the border would suffice instead of an invasion, as had been the case four years earlier in similar circumstances. The intervention was, after all, at the request of Prime Minister Mosisili. Moreover, it was expected that

The RLDF Makoanyane Base with damaged buildings after the South African attack

A Ratel IFV alongside captured arms and ammunition at the RLDF Makoanyane Base

Remnants of the RLDF Mohali Base after the South African attack

The BDF contingent made a favourable impression on their South African counterparts

An SAAF Allouette III helicopter operating from the RLDF Sekoaing Base

the entire operation would be over in 72 hours. Not for the first time in military history have the resolve and fighting power of an opposing force been severely underestimated. The extensive preparations for the operation were no secret to the RLDF mutineers because of the close connections between the citizens of both countries. Naively, the intervention force hoped that their preparations would dissuade the RLDF mutineers from offering resistance.

Operation Boleas in execution

After securing a bridgehead over the Caledon River and seizing the Maseru Bridge border post on 22 September 1998, the first objective was to neutralise the Ratjimose Military Base located on the outskirts of Maseru. The base was identified as the *schwerpunkt* and source of the recent unrest. If there was to be any armed opposition to the incursion, then it was expected from this quarter. Hence, a considerable amount of the task force's heavy fighting power was allocated to the task of subduing the base and securing all its weapons stores. The remainder of the task force was earmarked to secure key points in Maseru, such as the radio station, embassies, government buildings and the Royal Palace. Vertical envelopment would be conducted by paratrooper teams carried in four SAAF Oryx helicopters, escorted by two Alouette III helicopter gunships, who would secure the Makoanyane Military Base. This was the main military installation in Maseru, housing two motorised RLDF infantry battalions. Finally, two paratrooper teams, comprising 24 men, were earmarked to secure the all-important Katse Dam by disarming any RLDF soldiers in the vicinity and safeguarding South Africans working at the dam construction site.

Incredibly, considering that the intervention had been under consideration for four months, there were no aerial maps of Maseru from which to plan the SANDF's route into the city. Instead a Special Forces operative familiar with the city would meet the advancing convoy in Ladybrand and guide the soldiers to the Ratjimose base. Hartslief established an observation post and a radio relay station on high ground on the South African side of the border, giving a view over Maseru. It did not take long for elements of the RLDF to mortar the observation post in what would be the first shots of the operation.

Shortly after midnight on the night of 21–22 September, the armoured convoy departed from Tempe for the 150 km journey to Ladybrand and Maseru. Several vehicles suffered minor breakdowns, and a wrong turning was soon rectified. At sunrise the armoured convoy passed over the bridgehead established by the engineers and entered Maseru en route to the Ratjimose base. The convoy, with hatches battened down, entered the base through the open gates and formed an all-round defence. The paratroopers emerged from the infantry fighting vehicles with the intention of neutralising any RLDF soldiers in the vicinity.

A worrying sign was the absence of any evidence of RLDF personnel. A further concern was that the base was dominated by high ground on two sides, giving a full view of the entire area. It soon became apparent that RLDF soldiers had taken up positions on the high ground when those inside the base came under accurate and effective machine-gun fire. According to radio reports, all the elements of the SANDF intervention force, at Katse Dam, the Maseru central business district (CBD) and the Makoanyane Military Base, had come under fire. Permission to fire back at the RLDF was not granted immediately; once again, political considerations overrode what should have been a simple military decision at the lowest levels of the command structure. When permission came, it was for small arms only, which precluded use of the Ratels' 90 mm guns and support from the mortars. Despite being hamstrung by an order not to deploy the greater part of their firepower, the paratroopers were able to storm the RLDF positions on the high ground, covered by the machine guns of the supporting Ratels. Other elements of the convoy outside the base began to come under fire from RLDF soldiers who had taken up positions in civilian dwellings surrounding the base.

After the initial RLDF ambush had dissipated, with its members disappearing into civilian areas, the SANDF force regrouped and was tasked with regaining order in the Maseru CBD, which had descended into anarchy. A violent scene of looting, arson and rioting greeted the soldiers as they entered the CBD, and it took the heavily outnumbered and exhausted SANDF troops more than five hours to restore a semblance of order.

While the SANDF had gained some control over the Ratjimose base and the Maseru CBD, a fierce battle involving the 54 heliborne para-troopers and the RLDF raged at the Makoanyane Military Base. The paratroopers took casualties as they approached the base from the east and west but managed to subdue some of the defenders with mortar fire. However, resistance was determined and stiff and the casualties on the South African side began to mount. Hartslief detached the mortar group, consisting of five Ratel 81s from the CBD operation, to support the hard-pressed paratroopers at the Makoanyane base. Despite the arrival of the mortars, the paratroopers remained in a vulnerable position as the RLDF controlled the high ground as well as the dominant multistorey building within the base. The SANDF assault force of little over a platoon with mortar support was overwhelmingly outgunned and outnumbered by the RLDF and a 14.5 mm anti-aircraft gun. Reinforcements were a priority if the SANDF was to have any hope of dislodging the defenders, who were well ensconced and determined to resist at all costs.

It was now decided to add a squadron of Ratel 90s to the assault on the Makoanyane base to bolster the firepower of the attackers, especially after the mortar element had withdrawn owing to a mechanical failure with the command vehicle. The squadron had to be regrouped after being dispersed in Maseru. The approaching Ratel 90s soon came under small arms and mortar fire from the defending RLDF soldiers and were halted. After withdrawing to regroup, the Ratels formed up in a line-abreast attack formation and the South Africans resumed the attack using the concentrated firepower offered by the Ratels and their machine guns. After some tactical reorientation of the direction of the attack, the Ratels at last made contact with some of the paratroopers and, after picking them up, exited the base. Armed with intelligence gathered by the paratroopers, they then re-entered the base through the main gate. Even then the superior SANDF firepower was limited, and the supporting armour was initially restricted to firing blanks. At last, the Ratel 90 squadron received permission to utilise their main armament, which up to now had been prohibited due to political considerations.

After the Ratel 90s fired their main guns in anger at identified targets – for the first time since the end of the Border War – and through combining their attack with the paratroopers in a combined-arms approach, the South Africans began to subdue the defenders and soon overran five buildings in the base. From the extent of the defensive preparations, it was evident that the RLDF had got wind of the South African operation well before the intervention. Retreating RLDF members continued to offer resistance, taking up new positions after giving ground. The fighting continued after sunset despite the losses inflicted on the defenders. A white flag was spotted over the headquarters building at Makoanyane base, but the five-man SANDF delegation came under fire when they approached the single RLDF member who claimed to be the OC of the base. As darkness approached, Alouette III helicopter gunships attacked and flushed out the remaining defenders on the high ground, while the paratroopers and Ratels, in conjunction with the air support, prepared for a final assault on the headquarters building. Rather than risk casualties in a night-time attack, the SANDF attackers decided to withdraw to the south of the base, where they assumed an all-round defence for the night.

Darkness brought about an opportunity for the South Africans to reorganise, and two serious casualties were evacuated at first light. Fortunately, their equipment and vehicles had held up. Some RLDF members used the cover of darkness to storm one of the South African armoured vehicles but were dispersed with light machine-gun fire. At midnight Hartslief instructed the South Africans at the Makoanyane base to abandon their positions and the entire force withdrew to the Ratjimose base where, after a rest and refit, they would receive a new mission. The withdrawal was conducted without incident and the force arrived at the Ratjimose base at 01:00 on 23 September. Meanwhile, the BDF complement arrived on the evening of 22 September, and quickly impressed the South Africans as a disciplined and professional outfit.

While events were unfolding in the Maseru CBD and at the Makoanyane base on 22 September, the paratroopers at the Katse Dam also faced difficult challenges. The paratroopers were deployed simultaneously at three different locations at Katse Dam, with protecting the dam and neutralising RLDF members at the Mohali Military Base as their objectives. As a stick of five South African paratroopers approached the Mohali base, they came under fire from a force of 26 RLDF members. The heavily outnumbered South Africans soon received heliborne reinforcements and began a fire-and-movement manoeuvre on the RLDF positions, sending several of their adversaries in full flight up the mountain. With most of the RLDF members neutralised, the paratroopers moved towards the base buildings, of which two were found to be empty. Fire erupted from the third building, killing two South African medical personnel; all three RLDF members were killed when the South Africans stormed the building. Not wishing to take any more casualties, the South Africans swept the remaining buildings with 20 mm cannon fire from two Alouette II helicopter gunships. By the time the guns fell silent, 23 members of the RLDF had been killed in the entire action.

Securing the Katse Dam marked the end of the military enforcement phase of Operation Boleas and direct conflict with the RLDF. The members of the task force would spend the next seven months as occupation troops. South Africa finally pulled out its forces from the mountain kingdom in May 1999.

The South African death toll for Operation Boleas amounted to eight soldiers, with more than 70 RLDF members and Lesotho civilians killed. What was originally foreseen as a peacekeeping or peace enforcement operation had descended into a full-blown shooting war. The fact that the SANDF was unable to stamp its authority in Lesotho quickly and completely control the unfolding situation was due in part to the inadequacy in numbers of the 600-strong SANDF force deployed. The high level of RLDF resistance was not anticipated and Butch Williams's original plan for Operation Kitso had been for a much smaller affair, requiring far fewer troops. A further consideration was that, despite many months of planning for Operation Kitso, there was insufficient time to plan Operation Boleas as the requirements for the operation were more challenging.

Another limitation placed on the SANDF was the requirement of minimum force to be exercised during the operation. This hamstrung the SANDF; on several occasions when South African soldiers came under heavy fire, they had to wait for permission from higher up to respond with lethal force. This had the effect of prolonging the RLDF resistance. Overwhelming firepower applied in the initial stages, along with overwhelming aerial support, might have ended resistance much earlier. Armies in a conventional environment are typically not suited to the application of minimum force, on account of either their doctrine or their fighting equipment. Peace operations call on a different skill set, one that the fledgling SANDF may have been ill-suited to at this stage. In addition, the SANDF soldiers sent into Lesotho had not received the proper training for the operation they were asked to execute. Although peacetime operations were a priority task for the SANDF in 1998, a thorough doctrine had not yet been devised, nor had the required training or equipment been made available.

In the following years, the SANDF would deploy its troops on peacekeeping operations across Africa – principally to Burundi, the Democratic Republic of Congo and Darfur in Sudan. Apart from peacekeeping operations, which included traditional peacekeeping and peace enforcement, the SANDF also deployed troops to the Central African Republic (CAR) from 2006 onwards to help train the country's defence force, rebuild its defence infrastructure and provide VIP protection to President François Bozizé. However, in 2013, matters came to a head during the infamous Battle of Bangui, when a small group of South African soldiers found themselves in a precarious position, heavily outnumbered and alone, facing an overwhelming rebel threat, thousands of kilometres from home.

The Battle of Bangui, 2013

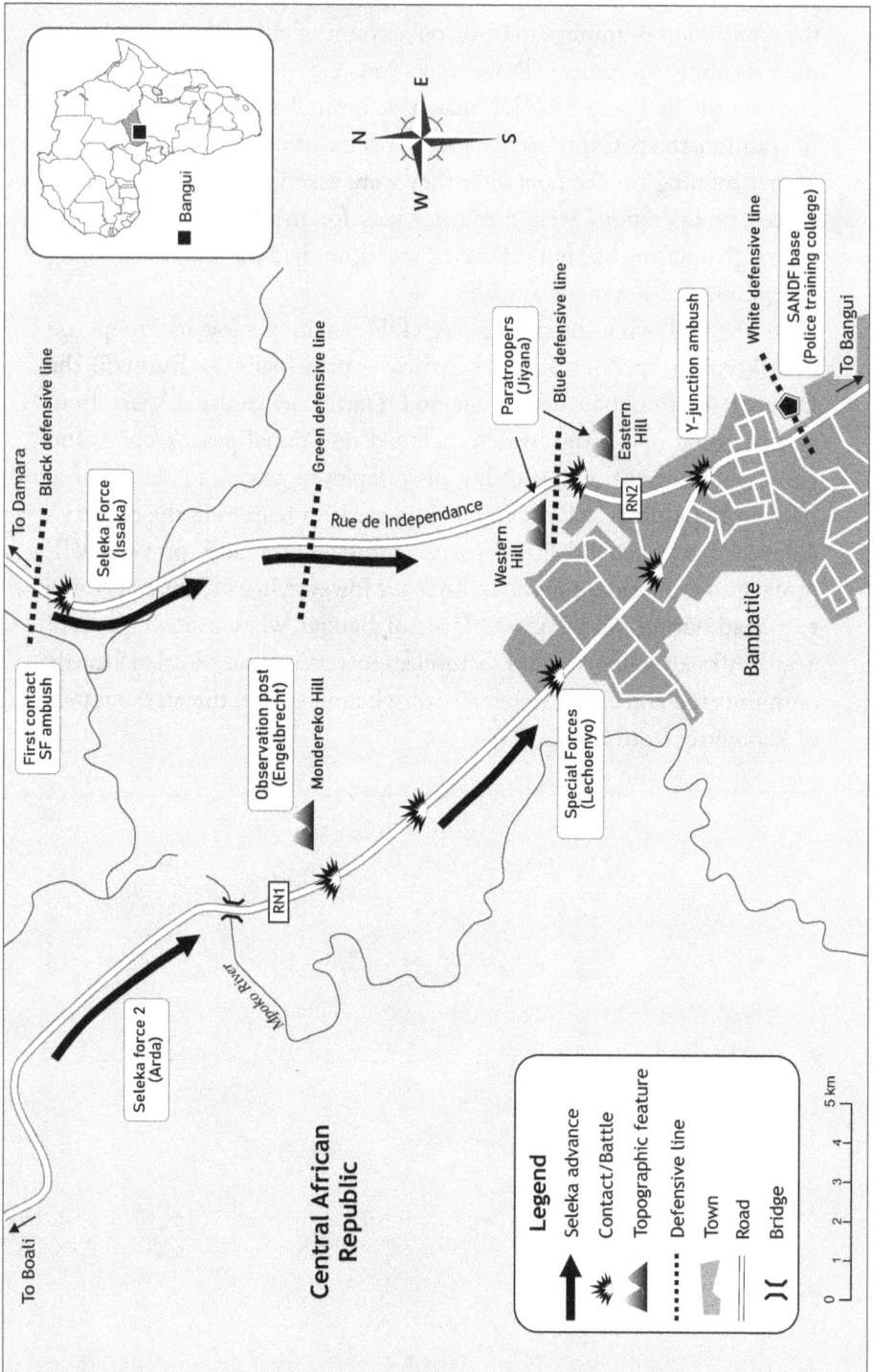

Legend

- Seleka advance
- Contact/Battle
- Topographic feature
- Defensive line
- Town
- Road
- Bridge

0 1 2 3 4 5 km

Central African Republic

Bangui

To Damara

Black defensive line

Seleka Force (Issaka)

First contact SF ambush

Green defensive line

Rue de Independance

Observation post (Engelbrecht)

Mondereko Hill

RN1

Mpoko River

To Boali

Seleka force 2 (Arda)

Special Forces (Lechoenyo)

Western Hill

Paratroopers (Jiyana)

Blue defensive line

Eastern Hill

RN2

Y-junction ambush

White defensive line

SANDF base (Police training college)

To Bangui

Bambatile

20

BANGUI, 2013

In October 2012, Jean-Francis Bozizé, the defence minister of the Central African Republic and special envoy of President François Bozizé, travelled to South Africa to meet with then President Jacob Zuma. The rapidly deteriorating security situation in the country, and more especially the rapid advance of the Seleka rebel movement, prompted President François Bozizé to seek direct military intervention to ensure his regime's survival. Since he did not have the support of France, Gabon, Cameroon and other regional actors, and after Nigeria, Angola and Uganda refused to provide military assistance, Bozizé turned to South Africa. However, South Africa had been involved in the CAR since late 2006 under the auspices of the SANDF's Operation Vimbezela, a mission centred on training the Forces Armées Centrafricaines (FACA) and helping to rebuild the country's defence infrastructure. Later on, through a second, more contested, mission, Operation Morero, South African Special Forces provided VIP protection to Bozizé. While these two deployments were based on bringing peace and stability and building capacity, it is beyond the scope of this chapter to unravel the intricacies underpinning the deployment of South African troops to the CAR.

During 2009, and following the unravelling of the Libreville peace accords, Bozizé opened further negotiations with South Africa regarding military aid. As a result, Operation Vimbezela's mandate was revised, force levels increased and the SANDF deployment extended. All the while, Bozizé benefited politically and militarily and strengthened his grip on power. However, by the beginning of 2012, rebellion was stirring in the country – fuelled by broken promises, extreme dis-satisfaction and evident fraud and corruption.

Bozizé responded heavy-handedly, arresting and imprisoning several opposition leaders. He also alienated the Chadian president, Idriss Déby, who gave support to the political opposition, especially the powerful Seleka alliance of Mohamed Moussa Dhaffane, Moureddine Adam and Michel Djotodia, which was bolstered by disgruntled FACA members. The Seleka alliance quickly transformed itself into a viable threat and a strong military force, including seasoned professional fighters and mercenaries from Chad and Sudan.

In October 2012, shortly after Jean-Francis Bozizé returned from Pretoria, the major Seleka advance commenced. As the rebel force rapidly gained territory, several armed groups joined the rebellion to overthrow Bozizé's regime. While the rebels soon delivered their demands, Bozizé was unwilling to negotiate. By the end of the year, the Seleka rebels had advanced more than 500 km into the CAR and controlled approximately two-thirds of the country. They halted their advance just short of Damara, the last major town before the capital, Bangui. Damara was declared a red line by the Central African Multinational Force (FOMAC), the regional peacekeeping force set up by the Economic Community of Central African States. Any attempt to cross the red line would evoke a military response.

These events prompted South Africa into action, especially to prevent the small SANDF training team and their weapons stores from being captured. As a result, and despite clear intelligence on the Seleka alliance's strength and objectives, several high-level meetings were held at Joint Operations (JOPS) and Special Forces Brigade headquarters at Speskop in Pretoria. On 30 December, Zuma was briefed on the developing situation and the options open to him: either pull out the training team or deploy an additional contingent of troops to defend South African interests in the country. Zuma opted for the latter and thus sanctioned the deployment of an additional protection force to the CAR.

Colonel Doibi Coetzee, then chief of staff of the Special Forces Brigade, scurried to find a suitable officer to lead the operation. Colonel William Dixon, a seasoned paratrooper and veteran of the Border War, then employed at the South African Infantry Formation, was approached to lead the force, which was later designated Operation Vimbezela Protection Task Group. Dixon decided to include Maj Michel Silva, also an experienced paratrooper, as his second in command. While the legal basis for the further deployment of SANDF troops to the CAR was being ironed out, Dixon and Silva reported to Speskop, along with a host of other role-players, to receive detailed instructions.

Dixon had at his disposal a small intervention force consisting of crack troops drawn from 5 Special Forces Regiment in Phalaborwa and paratroopers from 1 Parachute Battalion in Bloemfontein, plus ancillary troops, including intelligence teams, signallers and medics. Dixon's force was about 200 strong, though the actual figures remain unclear. After ironing out the purpose of the mission, Dixon was ordered to collect and secure all South African assets in the CAR, including equipment and ammunition, and prepare an evacuation plan should the tactical situation on the ground deteriorate. Dixon was also ordered to liaise with FACA, FOMAC and the French military to monitor the developing situation. Finally, he was ordered to draft a contingency plan for the defence of Bangui in case the Seleka rebels attacked the capital.

On the evening of 1 January 2013, Dixon and the advance elements of his force boarded a heavily laden SAAF C-130 Hercules transport plane at Air Force Base Waterkloof, destined for Bangui. The remainder of the South African force would arrive in the CAR over the following days.

The gathering storm

Dixon and his advance team arrived in Bangui on 2 January and met with Col Mbongwa Dhlamini, the head of the Operation Vimbezela training team. After scouting around for a possible base, Dhlamini took Dixon to meet Bozizé. During the meeting, Bozizé sketched the deteriorating geopolitical situation and indicated that rebel forces could soon advance on Bangui. Dixon established that there was no multi-national, operational-level headquarters to coordinate the responses of the various foreign forces in country – comprising troops from France and FOMAC. At the suggestion of Dhlamini, Bozizé agreed that Dixon's force be accommodated at the police college in northern Bangui. After the meeting concluded, Dixon and some of his staff attended a further meeting with Dhlamini at the Operation Vimbezela headquarters, the content of which is beyond the scope of this chapter. From this point, cooperation between Dixon and Dhlamini was limited.

After the meetings concluded, Dixon and his advance team were escorted to their base at the École Nationale de Police. Situated in an urban area just off the main route into Bangui, the police college was not ideally located and largely indefensible. While Dixon suggested an alternative location, the far more suitable Barthélemy Boganda sports stadium, Bozizé turned down his request. Making the best of the situation, Dixon set about organising the defence of his new base. He immediately ordered Maj Peet Venter, a weapons expert from 5 Special Forces Regiment, to develop a protection and fire-support plan for the base and oversee the construction of a series of foxholes and defensive positions.

On 3 January, Maj Stephen Jiyana, along with Charlie Company of 1 Parachute Battalion, arrived in Bangui. Another group, under Michel Silva, arrived the next day. Therefore, by 4 January, Dixon's entire force was on the ground. In due course, Dixon, along with Coetzee in South Africa and a FACA liaison officer assigned to him, started planning the details of his operation. He would start with regular live-fire exercises as a show of force and the establishment of observation positions on the high ground near the base. The South Africans would also help retrain Bozizé's bodyguards and conduct regular combined patrols with FACA. Finally, South African Special Forces operators, along with Jiyana's paratroopers, would conduct further patrols within the Bangui city limits. In the hope of gathering credible intelligence, Dixon and his mobile headquarters, often accompanied by a Special Forces detachment, conducted regular reconnaissance patrols towards Damara to monitor the situation on the frontline.

While Dixon and his men were settling in to life at Bangui, there were several major political developments from 8 January onwards. The collapse of the so-called Libreville accord, the product of peace negotiations held in Gabon between Bozizé and Michel Djotodia, and the formation of a new unity government and its subsequent collapse, changed the climate in Bangui. The continued presence of South African troops, for whatever political or economic reason, became a cause of concern, as they were perceived as propping up Bozizé. In the eyes of Seleka, Dixon and his troops were an unwanted and antagonising presence in the CAR.

For Dixon and his troops, life in Bangui continued as the fragile ceasefire held. Despite conducting regular reconnaissance patrols towards Bouar and Damara and being aware of the severity of the rebel threat, Dixon and his staff saw no signs of a buildup of strong rebel forces. During the period leading up to the outbreak of hostilities, Dixon and his staff kept receiving conflicting, non-credible reports on the presence and strength of the Seleka forces. Moreover, without adequate intelligence, air support or aerial reconnaissance at his disposal, Dixon remained 'blind' as to the developments on the ground. Several requests from Dixon to higher headquarters for additional equipment, such as armoured personnel carriers, heavy artillery, fighter aircraft and Oryx and Rooivalk helicopters, among others, were either ignored, lost or simply denied. As a result of this travesty of little to no support forthcoming, a sense of disillusionment affected the South African soldiers on the ground as their deployment was extended time and again.

By March, renewed tensions between Bozizé and Seleka drove matters to a head. The South Africans had been warned not to take sides and to avoid any possible future conflict between Bozizé and his adversaries. On Sunday 17 March, Seleka issued a final 72-hour ultimatum to Bozizé, calling on him to meet their demands or face war. They demanded, for instance, that he release all political prisoners, integrate their members into the army with appropriate ranks and send the South Africans home. For Dixon and his troops, this was the first indication of real trouble on the horizon.

Dixon's contingency plan for the defence of Bangui contained elements of mobile defence and a fighting withdrawal (of sorts). The plan centred on establishing a series of stop lines, each with a colour-coded name, along the road from Damara into the capital (see map). Three factors influenced Dixon's operational intent. First, it was a priority to defend the major access road into Bangui, particularly from Boali and Damara. Second, deploying off-road was not an option, and fighting in jungle terrain was not preferable for the South Africans. Third, fighting in urban terrain was to be avoided at all costs, because of the inhibiting nature of built-up areas, for fire and movement as well as manoeuvre, and the likely high number of casualties. Dixon was thus clear that any fighting had to occur beyond the city limits where there was ample room to fire and manoeuvre – albeit with limited mobility.

The first line of defence was the black line, which would act as an early-warning and delaying position roughly halfway between Bangui and Damara. The black line would be manned by Special Forces, whose orders were to initiate contact with the enemy and delay them, thus giving the remainder of Dixon's troops time to redeploy. After the brief, initial firefight, the Special Forces would break contact and fall back on Bangui. After resupplying their ammunition, they would join Dixon's mobile reserve for the next phase of the battle. Moreover, in the event of an attack, Dixon would deploy his mobile headquarters close to the black line to monitor the fight on his immediate front and ensure that he could communicate with the black and green lines of defence. The operations room at the base would be manned by Dixon's second-in-command, Lt Col Dugmore Mziki, who would coordinate matters in the rear to support and sustain the troops in the frontline.

The second line of defence was the green line, located approximately 10 km closer to Bangui along the Damara road. The second delaying position, manned by a platoon of paratroopers from Charlie Company, was located on a hill overlooking the road. From this position, the paratroopers could engage an advancing rebel force along the Damara road with their heavy machine guns.

The last line of defence was the blue line, located close to the outskirts of Bangui and less than five kilometres from the South African base. The remaining paratroopers of Charlie Company occupied this position, backed up by Special Forces in their Hornets (a light reconnaissance vehicle) and Land Cruisers. A series of hills straddling the road at the blue line offered the defenders elevated positions from which to engage any advancing rebel forces.

The next line of defence was the white line, located at the South African base. However, this position could be held only against a light attack. If the preceding lines of defence failed to halt the rebel advance, then Dixon would move his force to the yellow line of defence, located outside the French base at the Bangui M'Poko International Airport.

On Wednesday 20 March, the Seleka ultimatum expired. Although Bozizé agreed to some of their demands, Seleka considered this to be too little, too late. In a final bid to shore up his position, Bozizé even flew to South Africa the following day to request that Zuma deploy additional South African troops to shore up his defences. However, these reinforcements never materialised.

On Friday 22 March, the tense situation took a turn for the worse. Dixon was informed that the FACA post at Damara was under attack and that civilians were fleeing the general area. Rather alarmingly, Damara's defenders appeared to have been overwhelmed without offering any resistance, or they had switched sides and joined the rebel advance. The FOMAC peacekeepers were non-committal and simply stood aside. Bangui's defence in depth had effectively been breached. Thus, only Dixon and his men, and what remained of the FACA forces, could offer viable resistance and prevent Seleka from taking Bangui. These developments collectively signalled the start of the Battle of Bangui.

The Battle of Bangui

After receiving reports of the fighting at Damara, Dixon contacted JOPS and requested permission to deploy his forces and activate his defensive battle plan. Once Coetzee granted permission, Dixon deployed a group of 28 operators from 5 Special Forces Regiment, under the command of Lt Col Solomon Lechoenyo, to the black line of defence. This group arrived 30 minutes later, followed by Dixon and his mobile headquarters some 20 minutes later. Concurrently, the 36 paratroopers from Charlie Company's Platoon 1 moved to the green line, where they deployed with two 12.7 mm heavy machine guns in support. Finally, Maj Jiyana, Charlie Company's commander, and the remainder of his troops deployed to their defensive position at the blue line. Over the next 24 hours, the South Africans would be involved in intense combat – possibly the most intense since Operation Boleas.

Approximately an hour after arriving at the black line, Dixon ordered Lechoenyo to conduct an aggressive reconnaissance towards Damara. The heavily armed Special Forces convoy initially advanced without incident. However, about 10 km before Damara, the tactical situation suddenly changed. Lechoenyo and his force drove straight into an ambush and immediately drew heavy fire from rebel forces concealed in the dense bush along the road. Activating their counter-ambush drills, the Special Forces engaged the rebels on their immediate front with hand grenades, heavy machine guns, small arms and mortar fire. While laying down suppressive fire, Lechoenyo turned his convoy around and broke contact with the enemy. The Special Forces group fell back on Dixon's position, where the wounded were transferred back to base before being evacuated to South Africa. Lechoenyo and his force also returned to base to resupply their ammunition.

Meanwhile, Dixon relocated his mobile headquarters to the green line, which was manned by the paratroopers of Platoon 1. Major Peet Venter, who had been involved in the earlier ambush, joined Dixon's force with one of the Special Forces Hornets fitted with a multiple rocket launcher. Venter's additional firepower at the green line would soon prove invaluable. At the same time, Silva tried to contact FACA to obtain reinforcements; however, none were forthcoming. To the South Africans it soon became apparent that neither FOMAC nor FACA was involved in the fight. This drastically altered the dynamics, since Dixon's token force was now basically the only line of defence left against the advancing Seleka forces.

At the green line, there appeared to be a lull in the fighting and the Seleka advance for the remainder of the day. Silva used this opportunity to encourage the local population to evacuate the area, while Venter returned to base to resupply ammunition. Venter also managed to hitch a 14.5 mm heavy machine gun to his Hornet and arrived back at the green line just before midnight. For the defenders at the green line, the tense night passed without real incident.

Early on Saturday 23 March, a group of fleeing FACA soldiers confirmed to Dixon and his men that Damara had indeed fallen. The South Africans abandoned the green line and fell back towards Bangui. Dixon dropped off Platoon 1 of Charlie Company at the blue line, where he ordered them to join Platoon 2 and to help shore up its defensive position on the western hill. Dixon's heavy machine gunners also joined Jiyana's heavy machine-gun group and Platoon 3, which were occupying the eastern hill at the blue line.

Dixon and his mobile headquarters now raced into Bangui, making for the French embassy. While Dixon had hoped to persuade the French to come to their aid in the defence of Bangui, this was not to be. The French would not get involved. However, they did concede that any SANDF casualties could be brought to the French base for casevac back to South Africa. Dixon had no time to be despondent, since the ever-changing tactical situation on the ground now demanded his full attention as reports filtered in that Jiyana's force at the blue line was under attack.

By 08:00 on Saturday morning the enemy attack on the blue line materialised. One of Jiyana's forward observation posts reported a huge contingent of rebels advancing along the Damara road. The sound of gunfire and exploding mortars also moved steadily closer to the South African positions. Amid the chaos and disorder of the thousands of fleeing civilians, Jiyana's troops readied themselves for the impending attack. Soon the Seleka forces started firing RPGs into the South African positions and the paratroopers responded with heavy and accurate machine-gun and mortar fire. As a result, Jiyana's force managed to destroy three enemy 'technicals' (modified light trucks) carrying heavy anti-aircraft guns, either killing or wounding their occupants. Eventually, the enemy realised the futility of continuing their attack along the Damara road. The spirited South African defence encouraged the remaining FACA defenders to join the action, but these forces soon panicked, disengaged and retreated.

In the meantime, the Seleka rebels deployed off-road and started attacking the defensive positions manned by the paratroopers of Platoon 1 and Platoon 2 on the western hill on foot. Amid heavy rebel fire, the South African paratroopers clung to their positions and returned fire. However, the rebel advance forced the paratroopers from their defensive positions, and they retreated downhill under covering fire. The men regrouped at the base of the hill and returned the mounting rebel fire with small arms and RPGs. All this time, the South African mortar group, deployed behind the western hill, along with the heavy machine gunners, maintained pressure on the advancing Seleka forces. However, these positions soon also drew heavy fire, injuring some South Africans. The injured were transported back to base under difficult conditions.

Amid the desperate and drastically changing tactical situation at the blue line, Dixon and his mobile headquarters, accompanied by two Special Forces Hornets equipped with multiple rocket launchers and four Land Cruisers, arrived on the scene after 11:00. No sooner had they arrived than they came under heavy fire. Venter ordered the rocket launchers to be dismounted and readied for action. While this was taking place, a heavy machine gun mounted on one of the Hornets delivered suppressing fire on the rebel forces advancing along the slopes of the western hill. This counteraction temporarily halted the enemy advance, and so Dixon ordered Silva to take charge of platoons 1 and 2 and retake the western hill. Venter also took charge of the mortar group and redeployed the mortarmen a short distance back towards Bangui, ordering them to be ready to deliver fire on the high ground of the western hill.

As soon the multiple rocket launchers were made ready, the accompanying Special Forces group noticed a group of approximately 40 rebels advancing down the slopes of the western hill. These rebels had not observed the camouflaged South African positions and had advanced to within 400 m of them. Once permission was obtained, Venter unleashed a ripple (similar to a salvo) from the 107 mm multiple rocket launchers that tore through the advancing Seleka forces. This immediately halted the Seleka advance, and the rebels soon retreated north over the high ground, where they were met with accurate fire from the South African mortarmen. Concurrently, Silva seized the initiative and led the paratroopers back up the hill, engaging any remaining rebels they encountered. Through these gallant actions, the western hill was recaptured within the space of 30 minutes without incurring any further casualties.

Despite a further counterattack by some Seleka rebels on the left flank, the enemy was forced to retreat back down the Damara road, having incurred heavy casualties during the firefight at the blue line. Dixon immediately ordered a Special Forces group to pursue the retreating rebels. This group returned shortly afterwards without incident. With the fight at the blue line over for now, Dixon consolidated his position by noon, and then handed command back to Jiyana. At this point, Dixon and his mobile headquarters returned to base to rearm and take stock of the developing situation.

Later, a South African forward observation post along the Boali road, located approximately 10 km from the northern outskirts of Bangui, reported a large force of technicals with heavily armed rebels advancing on the capital. Captain Henk Engelbrecht and his surveillance team from 1 Tactical Intelligence Regiment in Potchefstroom had occupied the observation post on the Madereko hill overlooking the crucial bridge over the Mpoko River, near Bafinli, since the previous day. It was appreciated that whoever controlled this vital bridge would command the second major route of advance into Bangui. It now dawned on Dixon and Silva that that the rebel actions along the Damara road had merely been diversionary attacks, and that the main rebel advance was in fact occurring along the Boali road. The Boali and Damara roads met at a Y-junction to the north of Bangui, with the South African base located a further 2 km from there alongside the road. From here it was another 10 km to the centre of the capital. Dixon ordered Lechoenyo and his Special Forces group, comprising two Hornets and four Land Cruisers, to advance rapidly along the Boali road and confront the major new rebel threat head-on. Dixon and Silva followed Lechoenyo's group and tried to persuade the remaining FACA forces to join them in halting the rebel advance.

The South Africans established a skirmish line some distance from the bridge, which included Venter with his 107 mm multiple rocket launchers. Lechoenyo and another group established an ambush closer to the bridge. From his position atop the Madereko hill, Engelbrecht fed real-time intelligence to Lechoenyo regarding the rebel movements. The first wave of enemy troops, comprising some 20 technicals and several hundred fighters on foot, brushed past a haphazard FACA roadblock and crossed the bridge over the Mpoko River. However, they soon ran into the ambush set by Lechoenyo, whose men tore into the enemy convoy with their machine guns. After Lechoenyo and his advance element broke contact, Venter fired a ripple from his rocket launchers that tore through the rebel ranks and destroyed their vehicles. Once Lechoenyo and his group returned to the stop line, Venter continued to fire deadly ripples of 107 mm rockets towards the enemy lines. The heavy machine guns mounted on the Land Cruisers were also brought to bear on the enemy, to great effect. However, the combined heavy and accurate South African fire failed to halt the enemy advance. The rebels simply kept surging forward with speed, aggression and determination.

With the situation soon becoming untenable, and with their FACA allies rapidly disappearing, the South Africans broke contact and fell back down the road towards Bangui to set up a new skirmish line. Realising that they needed more firepower to stem the enemy advance, Dixon and Silva raced to Jiyana's blue line to gather reinforcements – specifically mortars. As soon as the reinforcements arrived at the front, the mortarmen deployed and started firing on the advancing rebels. The mortar barrage managed to at least keep down the direct rebel fire. With ammunition starting to run short, great was the relief when the remainder of Lechoenyo's Special Forces group, who had just arrived from South Africa along with supplies, arrived at the skirmish line with six Hornets.

Despite the arrival of the token reinforcements, though, the tactical situation along the Boali road was perilous. The enemy continued their relentless advance towards Bangui, despite the strong South African resistance offered. Moreover, the South African position at the skirmish line was soon being outflanked, with heavy enemy small arms fire making it impossible to hold the position. The ineffective air support offered by a FACA Mi-24 Hind attack helicopter along the Boali road also failed to change the tactical situation. After nearly two hours of fighting a delaying action, and in the face of a relentless rebel advance, Dixon realised that his troops were vastly outnumbered and running out of ammunition. He ordered them to fall back to the last defensive line on the outskirts of Bangui. To compound matters, Dixon received a report that a fresh rebel attack had materialised on Jiyana's blue line.

While Dixon returned to base to direct operations from there, Lechoenyo redeployed his troops to an intermediate defensive line. No sooner had they arrived than they encountered a renewed rebel attack. During the close-quarters fighting in built-up terrain, the South Africans held their own against persistent rebel attacks. However, fearful of being completely enveloped and realising that his immediate position was being outflanked, Lechoenyo ordered his men to break contact and fall back to base. Having successfully broken contact, and while providing covering fire to each other, the Special Forces group limped back into the base. Despite being engaged in a sustained firefight throughout most of the afternoon, South African casualties amounted to just three wounded.

By late afternoon, the rebels had renewed their attack on Jiyana's positions. The reinvigorated rebel attack, supported by Seleka fighters who had advanced cross-country from the Boali road, soon drove the South Africans off the western hill. Despite returning fire, Jiyana and his men found themselves in a difficult position. The rapid rebel advance down the Boali road towards the Y-junction, and the fact the Lechoenyo and his men had retreated to the base in Bangui, meant that the South Africans at the blue line faced the grave risk of being completely cut off and overrun. Dixon, who at that stage was still on the Boali road, ordered Silva to return to base. After collecting all available vehicles, he advanced with his convoy to the blue line to extricate Charlie Company. However, by the time Silva and his convoy arrived at the blue line, after 17:00, Jiyana and his troops were nearly surrounded. Silva ordered a general withdrawal, and, under covering fire, the men of Charlie Company extricated themselves from their defensive positions under heavy enemy fire and mounted the waiting vehicles.

By the time Silva's convoy started moving, dusk had settled in. As they approached the Y-junction, amid an eerie silence and the gathering darkness, the convoy suddenly drew heavy fire as it drove into a predetermined rebel ambush. The South African soldiers immediately dismounted from their exposed positions, took cover and started to return the enemy fire. As Charlie Company became engaged in an intense close-quarters firefight in the built-up terrain, casualties mounted. The fighting intensified, and some paratroopers even became engaged in hand-to-hand combat with the enemy. With their positions being surrounded, Silva obtained permission from Dixon to abandon the vehicles and conduct a fighting retreat across the broken, peri-urban terrain towards the nearby South African base. He ordered the paratroopers to break out of the encirclement and move eastwards across the high ground so they could approach the base from the southeast.

During the night, the paratroopers scattered and split up into smaller groups. Unfortunately, the difficult decision had to be made to leave behind the critically wounded, who stood little chance of surviving. Some of the wounded bravely held the line and provided covering fire to their comrades until their ammunition ran out and their positions were overcome. Under this covering fire, the paratroopers fought their way out. Silva, personally leading a group of approximately 40 paratroopers, broke out of the encirclement and made it back to base by midnight. After midnight came Jiyana and some men who had also managed to break free and move from house to house. Some stragglers, having faced various heroic ordeals, trickled into the base in the early hours of Sunday morning.

While Silva and the men of Charlie Company had been fighting their way back to the base, Dixon had been facing his own perils. At 18:00 on Saturday night, the rebels started firing on his indefensible base. From their exposed positions, and with their ammunition nearly expended, the South Africans found themselves in a dire situation. However, Dixon's immediate priority was to ensure that Silva and the rest of Charlie Company returned safely to base. His staff, and especially his intelligence officers, tried various channels to contact the Seleka leadership. Shortly after 22:00, contact was successfully made with General Arda Hakouma, one of the Seleka leaders. However, he was unwilling to negotiate and threatened to attack the South African base first thing on Sunday morning. The South Africans nevertheless reached out to Hakouma throughout the night, and shortly before midnight negotiations recommenced. The South Africans requested the fighting to stop for the night, for them to be allowed to collect their wounded, and for the remainder of Charlie Company to be permitted to return to base. They also emphasised that this wasn't their war. Hakouma indicated that he would be at the base at 05:45 the next morning to discuss ceasefire terms. Throughout the remainder of the tense night, and as Silva, Jiyana and their men returned to base, the South Africans were unsure of what the morning would bring.

At 05:45 on Sunday 24 March, instead of negotiations, the Seleka rebels launched a direct assault on the South African base. With the base surrounded and Dixon and his men severely exposed, small arms fire, along with rockets and grenades, raked the South African defensive positions. Dixon ordered his men to hunker down and not to return the enemy fire in the hope that it would prevent a full-force attack. Within a few minutes, the Seleka attack halted. Hakouma meanwhile had contacted the South Africans, indicating that he would shortly arrive to start discussions. Concurrently, an estimated 7 000 heavily armed Seleka fighters with technicals streamed into Bangui.

Within an hour, Hakouma arrived at the base. And after a tense standoff with Dixon, Silva and Venter, and the medical treatment of some of the Seleka fighters, serious negotiations commenced. A temporary truce was agreed and hostilities ended immediately. Hakouma also demanded that Dixon and his contingent leave the CAR post-haste and indicated that his fighters would help themselves to South African vehicles and stores. Dixon agreed to Hakouma's demands, based on the precondition that he would leave none of his troops behind, and that the South Africans be granted safe passage to the French base at the airport. Hakouma would also allow unarmed South African medical personnel to leave the base in medical vehicles to collect the wounded and the bodies of their fallen comrades. Once Hakouma departed, the Seleka rebels left behind to protect the South Africans started to loot the base in earnest. During that tense morning, more stragglers and wounded troops returned to the base, while the bodies of the fallen South African soldiers were collected.

At mid-morning, Dixon contacted JOPS and requested the necessary permission to abandon the base. Since the Seleka rebels had swept through Bangui and he was short on ammunition and without the hope of reinforcements arriving, Dixon realised the futility of his immediate situation. Moreover, FOMAC and the French had agreed to escort his forces to the airport. However, Pretoria initially denied his request. Only after another request to Pretoria amid the continued deteriorating security situation in Bangui was Dixon given permission to withdraw.

By midday, and amid intermittent small arms fire, a FOMAC convoy under French command arrived at the base to begin the withdrawal of Dixon's force. Concurrently, a SAAF C-130 Hercules landed in Bangui to evacuate the most seriously wounded to 1 Military Hospital in Pretoria. The FOMAC convoy also extricated Dhlamini's training team, who had been holed up in the Morero building in central Bangui. Between 16:00 and 21:00 the South African troops were escorted to the airport in convoys, taking with them what equipment they could – including trucks, Gecko all-terrain vehicles, Hornets and heavy weapons.

However, Dixon was forced to leave behind some equipment and at least three tons of small arms ammunition. By 21:00, Dixon and his troops, barring some missing men, were all safely ensconced at the French base at the airport.

The Battle of Bangui, fought between 22 and 24 March, pitted a handful of resolute South African soldiers against overwhelming numbers of Seleka fighters. While the developing threat in CAR may have been underestimated, the South Africans were at a distinct disadvantage from the start due to insufficient intelligence, inadequate manpower and a lack of air and artillery support. However, the leadership, initiative and resolve shown by men such as Dixon, Lechoenyo, Silva, Venter and others, along with the countless acts of personal bravery and determination displayed by the rank and file, ultimately carried the day. Moreover, Dixon's inspired decision to establish several predetermined defensive lines ultimately paid dividends as the battle unfolded.

The combination of good leadership, individual initiative, collective determination and dogged resistance are the positive aspects of the battle. However, in hindsight, there are several criticisms that can be levelled at the South African deployment. The fact that Dixon and his staff received conflicting, non-credible intelligence reports on the presence and strength of the Seleka forces was unacceptable. Without adequate intelligence, air support and aerial reconnaissance at his disposal, Dixon and his staff remained in the dark about developments on the ground in the days before the Seleka attack on Bangui. This naturally affected their ability to conduct an intelligence-driven operation and negatively affected South African planning. Thus, their defence could only be reactive in nature. Also, the fact that Dixon's requests to higher headquarters for additional equipment were either ignored, lost or simply denied was unacceptable. Dixon had to conduct the defence of Bangui against overwhelming odds, with an understrength and somewhat poorly equipped force, in the face of a relentless Seleka advance. As a result, South African morale suffered in the days before the battle. Altogether, the Battle of Bangui claimed the lives of 13 SANDF soldiers, with 27 wounded, two of whom would later succumb to their injuries.

Several stark lessons were learned. First, the SANDF had to drastically upgrade its strategic airlift capability and establish a series of forward staging bases in Africa. Bangui demonstrated the difficulties of operating on extended exterior lines of communication, which led to problems with the throughput of logistical and military supplies from South Africa to distant CAR. Second, the value of adequate air support and aerial surveillance, drastically lacking at Bangui, was emphasised, along with artillery support, as critical success factors for future SANDF deployments. Third, the availability of adequate personnel carriers, such as Casspirs or Mambas, was non-negotiable, as was the provision of better body armour. Fourth, the establishment of safe, dependable forward operating bases, with adequate defences and firepower, was important. The South African base in Bangui had none of these attributes and was therefore extremely difficult to defend. Finally, the lack of coordination or cooperation between the various military forces deployed to the CAR was worrisome. At Bangui, FOMAC simply stood aside, FACA largely disappeared and the French were non-committal, which left the South Africans as the last line of effective defence. These were mistakes, Dixon argued, that could not be repeated in future SANDF deployments.

Fortunately, the SANDF took heed and implemented some necessary changes. These could be seen in the successful deployment of the UN Force Intervention Brigade (FIB) to the eastern Democratic Republic of Congo in 2013–2014 to combat the notorious M23 rebels. Consisting of nearly 3 000 troops drawn from South Africa, Malawi and Tanzania, the FIB was better armed, equipped and supported. Moreover, Dixon and some of the veterans of Bangui were instrumental in preparing the South African troops for combat and the exigencies of jungle warfare. The Battle of Bangui, and the ultimate sacrifice of the South African soldiers, which some might see as having been in vain, nevertheless served as the catalyst needed for change in the defence force.

CONCLUSION

A golden thread runs from the formation of the Union Defence Force
(UDF) in 1912 to its successor, the South African Defence Force
(SANDF), and to its present-day incarnation, the South African National Defence Force (SANDF). Many of the challenges faced by Jan
Smuts in the formation of the UDF remain valid for the SANDF today.
Defence is never a priority during peacetime, and the economic hardships
and neglect suffered by the armed forces of South Africa in 1912–1914
and 1919–1939, and again in 1946–1966, are similar to those that have
faced the SANDF since its inception in 1994. Another golden thread is
that the amalgamation of former enemies is not a new concept in South
Africa. The formation of the UDF, SADF and SANDF all involved a
process of reconciliation, and each iteration emerged more representative
than its predecessor, reflecting a growing inclusiveness of all population
groups that culminated in the democratic dispensation in 1994.

The manoeuvre war doctrine adopted early by the fledgling UDF had
its roots in the Boer republican commando system. Although the various
South African defence forces have strayed from this doctrine on occasion
– sometimes with dire results – it remains very much an integral part of
a South African way of war. Manoeuvre warfare doctrine was codified
only in the mid to late 1990s, but since then little progress has been made
in the study of its concepts at the operational level of war. The battles
selected for inclusion in this book focus on the development of that
doctrine, even when there is evidence that the generals and commanders
involved often suffered from historical amnesia and discarded, or were
forced to discard, their manoeuvre roots.

The book opens with the complicated considerations behind the
formation of the UDF in 1912. Many of the same factors inhabited

the mind space of the architects of the SADF and the SANDF. Smuts wanted a modern, disciplined defence force representative of its citizens, albeit in his time restricted to Englishmen and Afrikaners, with its major manpower component being via national service or a volunteer system. The defence force was primarily concerned with internal stability during peacetime and the threat of an external force seemed as remote in 1912 as it does today. Little has changed in threat perceptions in the century of warfare the book covers. The complacency that was present in 1912 has recurred several times in South African military history, so that when South Africa is called upon to meet an external threat it has often been caught militarily unprepared.

Nevertheless, the first challenge the UDF faced was an internal threat presented by the 1913 and 1914 Witwatersrand strikes. Unable to muster enough strength to meet the threat by deploying the standing army and new conscripts, Smuts had little option but to rely on the ex-Boer republican commandos, who had, by design, been languishing in the Defence Rifle Associations. At a stroke, Smuts resuscitated the old commando system and its unique structure and style of command, ensuring that the mounted infantry would have a major role in shaping the future doctrine of the UDF. This was a turning point that was anathema to Smuts's desire to have a UDF based largely on British doctrine. The 1914 Afrikaner Rebellion reinforced the doctrinal trajectory towards a Boer way of war when Louis Botha and Jan Smuts once again relied on the former Boer republican commandos to suppress the sprawling insurrection across the then Transvaal and Orange Free State. The last stages of the GSWA campaign in 1915, well represented by the battle of Otavifontein, set the UDF on a path that embraced manoeuvre warfare, favoured single and double envelopments over frontal attacks, abhorred unnecessary casualties in the pursuit of victory and pursued a directive command structure by which those in command were expected to display extraordinary initiative in achieving the goals set by their superiors.

The UDF reached the pinnacle of its manoeuvre warfare in Smuts's sweeping operational movements at Kilimanjaro in 1916 and in the battles that followed. These prime examples of South African doctrine have all but been lost to history. The fluid, expanding torrent of Smuts's operational advances was then applied to the static trench warfare of the Western Front. At Delville Wood in 1916, a vastly outnumbered South African contingent held their own against great odds and despite heavy losses in static, attritional warfare. Delville Wood went against the grain of the South African way of war. Ironically, it is Delville Wood, along with the sinking of the SS *Mendi*, that has captured the historic attention of South Africans rather than the dramatic First World War campaigns in Africa.

Once again, peacetime brought about the dismantling of the massive manpower structures necessary for a full-blown conventional war, and the necessity of meeting internal threats overtook the unlikelihood of an external one. The post-war period was marked by restructuring, rationalisation and retrogression in the defence force and also by a marked increase in internal threats from syndicalised white labour and African nationalists. The UDF, using a combined-force approach, including airpower, mobilised to supress the strikers on the Witwatersrand during the Rand Revolt of 1922. The defence force had to adapt its doctrine, previously shaped by rural deployments in wide-open expanses, to combat strikers in an urban environment. Moreover, as was the case during the 1913 and 1914 strikes, Smuts once more relied on reserves, particularly the Active Citizen Force and the former republican commandos, to shore up the strength of the Permanent Force of the UDF.

The actions against the Bondelswarts in 1922 indicated that the threat of internal instability was ever-present and that the government would not hesitate to deploy the military against its own or its mandate's citizens. In South West Africa, the Union authorities once more relied on local inhabitants to volunteer for service during the rebellion. The use of volunteers again provided key manpower that could rapidly deploy and supplement the security forces. During both the Rand Revolt and the Bondelswarts Rebellion, the deployment of airpower in an 'air policing' role was also notable. Moreover, these counterinsurgency deployments were also marked by increasing and effective ground–air cooperation, which would come to fruition during the Second World War.

The interwar years, and specifically the 1930s, inevitably saw an erosion of the UDF's conventional capabilities, a condition that would repeat itself whenever South Africa found itself relatively at peace. What was remarkable was the country's ability to mobilise its considerable economic resources in a short space of time and place the UDF on a war footing. Such was the situation when South Africa found itself at war on 6 September 1939.

The first test for the UDF during the Second World War came during its deployment to the East African theatre of operations to face the Italian threat in Ethiopia and Somalia. The South African deployment to southern Ethiopia was generally marked by a high degree of mobility, mission command, operational initiative and combined-arms operations in which infantry, armour, artillery and airpower deployed in unison. As a result, the South African way of war matured and found its expression in manoeuvre warfare marked by a string of tactical and operational envelopments effected across a favourable military operating environment. However, after the occupation of Addis Ababa in April 1941, the open flanks so conducive to manoeuvre warfare disappeared, and the South Africans were faced with an infantry slog through the mountains. Operating in unfamiliar terrain, and without an appropriate doctrine, organisation or experience of mountain warfare, the South African infantrymen nevertheless acquitted themselves well during the battles of Combolcia and Amba Alagi. However, the high-altitude fighting also demonstrated some of the hallmarks of the South African way of war: specifically resolve when operating in difficult, unfamiliar terrain and the importance of mission command to make key decisions as the battle unfolded.

Flushed with victory after defeating the Italians in East Africa, the UDF deployed in support of the hard-pressed British in North Africa. Here, the South Africans would meet their nemesis in the form of General Erwin Rommel and his Afrika Korps. The British, following a half-baked armoured doctrine, failed to include the highly mobile South Africans as an integral part of a combined-arms armoured brigade. Instead, the increasingly frustrated South Africans were on many occasions robbed of their mobility, prohibited from manoeuvring and forced to man static positions, which led to the twin disasters of Sidi Rezegh and Tobruk. The South Africans were able to redeem themselves at Alamein, when the Eighth Army inflicted a decisive tactical defeat on the attacking Axis forces. Ironically, they did so while uncomfortably manning static positions. What emerged from North Africa was the UDF's deep mistrust of the British manoeuvre doctrine in general and of British generalship in particular.

The deployment of a South African armoured division to Italy in 1944 was another landmark for the UDF. However, the actual deployment to Italy, which was considered largely 'untankable', differed vastly from the division's training in North Africa, which was so conducive to large-scale manoeuvre warfare. In Italy, the South Africans faced a challenging military operating environment which limited the deployment of an armoured division in manoeuvre-type operations. In fact, the entire armoured brigade of the 6th South African Armoured Division could deploy in unison only on a single occasion, at the Battle of Celleno. Moreover, at Celleno, the South African tanks mainly operated against German infantry and antitank weapons, with hardly any tank-on-tank engagements. For the most part, the South African infantry bore the brunt of the fighting during the Italian campaign, supported by the armour and artillery when possible. The South African infantrymen, as evident at the Battle of Chiusi, often had to operate in unfamiliar urban and semi-urban terrain, terrain that was defended resolutely by German forces. The battlefield reverse suffered at Chiusi was the product of inadequate intelligence, negligible combat support, questionable decision-making and the incremental commitment of South African forces to attack a well-defended village. Moreover, for the casualty-averse UDF, and considering the earlier reverses suffered at Sidi Rezegh and Tobruk, the defeat at Chiusi was unacceptable. Nevertheless, the deployment to Italy brought modern fighting vehicles and equipment, which ensured that the defence force emerged from the Second World War as a modern military capable of projecting offensive power across Africa if needed. However, what had suffered markedly during the Second World War was South Africa's penchant for manoeuvre warfare – stymied first by the British in Africa and then by the mountainous terrain in Italy.

Almost 20 years passed before the SADF was called upon to conduct a counterinsurgency operation against the South West Africa People's Organisation's first armed incursion into SWA at Ongulumbashe in 1966. The operation was not a complete success and highlighted shortcomings in police–army cooperation and the glaring difference between military and police 'combat' doctrines. However, the introduction of the helicopter into the SADF's combined-arms arsenal considerably enhanced mobility at the tactical level and opened new operational possibilities via vertical envelopment. The nascent elements of Fireforce, later perfected in the Rhodesian Bush War, were present at Ongulumbashe and would culminate in one of the largest airborne operations since the Second World War, at Cassinga in 1978.

During Operation Savannah, several SADF battle groups conducted a limited semi-conventional war into Angola in 1975–1976. In a mere 33 days of operational movement, the SADF battle groups advanced deep into Angola, successfully engaging the MPLA/Cuban forces in rapid manoeuvre warfare on several occasions. However, once the MPLA/Cuban forces had regrouped, the frontline became static and attritional warfare began. The tide slowly turned against the SADF battle groups through late 1975 and into early 1976. Operating on extended lines of communication in difficult terrain, along with limited air support, the SADF's perceived edge in manpower, weapons and equipment was soon dispelled. In early 1976, all SADF forces were withdrawn from Angola. If South Africa wished to continue its military deployment to Angola, the SADF would require substantial reinforcements and more advanced weaponry and would have to improve its conventional force mobilisation and combat capabilities drastically. By early 1976, this was both politically unattainable and militarily unrealistic.

In many ways, the raid on Cassinga was the ultimate expression of South African manoeuvre warfare. The objective of the raiding strategy was not to occupy Angolan territory but to degrade the opponent's fighting power. The operation relied on surprise, using the indirect approach deep in the rear area of enemy-held territory, using vertical envelopment to overcome the tyranny of distance and bypass areas of resistance on the way to the target. But Cassinga also demonstrated the military's inability to 'win' wars in the absence of a political settlement. Cassinga may have been a tactical victory for the SADF, but SWAPO was able to assert its narrative and claim that an atrocity had been committed, notching up a decisive victory in the propaganda war. The action at Cassinga certainly demonstrated what was possible to achieve via vertical envelopment, but it also brought into focus the SADF's often dysfunctional and confused command style, which was exacerbated by the friction of battle and the fog of war. Troubling signs began to emerge of directive command style in the middle management of the SADF but a tendency towards detailed command in the higher echelons.

Operation Protea, conducted in 1981, was a highly successful cross-border operation conducted by the SADF into southern Angola. The SADF was able to project force deep into Angola, demonstrating the merits of manoeuvre-type warfare. In fact, Protea is indicative of the maturing of the SADF's operational and tactical doctrine throughout the late 1970s and early 1980s. The mobile warfare doctrine, as espoused by Roland de Vries and others, time and again threw the enemy forces off balance during Protea. Through the combined-arms approach, and with superior mobility, adequate air support and the maintenance of the operational initiative, the SADF demonstrated the superiority of manoeuvre warfare over attritional warfare at Xangongo and Ongiva. However, this was not really surprising, and simply reconfirmed the foundation on which the South African way of war was based. Time and again during Protea, the South African forces attacked from un-expected directions and surprised, confused and unnerved the FAPLA/PLAN forces, which remained ensconced in their static defensive positions. The SADF, it would seem, had for the time being perfected the art of manoeuvre warfare. An immediate result of Protea was the sharp decrease in SWAPO activity in SWA. However, it soon became apparent that a single operation such as Protea had only a limited effect on the war and that further continued cross-border operations were needed to keep SWAPO off balance and prevent an escalation in the Border War.

The last battles of the Border War took the form of a conventional engagement in the heart of southern Angola between 1987 and 1988. The Cubans and FAPLA were determined to capture the territory held by UNITA in southern Angola, thus ending their hegemony in that area and removing them entirely from the political picture. The South Africans were equally determined to prop up UNITA and remove the Cuban/FAPLA threat in southern Angola. FAPLA's offensive was first halted in September 1987 and then reversed on the Lomba River when the heavily outnumbered South Africans used their superior agility and tactical prowess to deliver a decisive blow. However, the South Africans discarded their manoeuvre option to attack west of the Cuito River and capture Cuito Cuanavale, deep in the rear of the enemy, thus placing FAPLA in the horns of a dilemma delivered by a classic indirect approach. Instead, the SADF fought a series of successful tactical battles to the east of the Cuito River that eventually descended into a static or attritional slogging match in the Tumpo Triangle. Cuito proved to be a missed opportunity to deliver a decisive blow at the operational or strategic level using manoeuvre doctrine, and instead resulted in stalemate and political defeat.

Operation Boleas, ten years after Cuito Cuanavale, was the first large-scale operation conducted by the newly formed SANDF. What was intended as a peacekeeping operation soon descended into a full-on engagement between the SANDF and the Royal Lesotho Defence Force (RLDF). The South Africans were caught unprepared by the resistance offered by the RLDF and by the hostile reception of the local population, who went on a looting rampage in Maseru. The RLDF took advantage of South Africa's peaceful intentions and inflicted early casualties on the invading force. When the South Africans fought back in earnest, the RLDF began to take serious casualties. It was an unsatisfactory campaign, for which the SANDF was heavily criticised by journalists and academics. Once again, South Africa found itself in the unenviable position of having too few boots on the ground for the task at hand. The SANDF paid a heavy price for underestimating its RLDF opponents.

The Battle of Bangui, fought on 22–24 March 2013, pitted a small South African force against overwhelming numbers of Seleka fighters in the Central African Republic. Not for the first time in their military history did the South Africans find themselves heavily outnumbered and outgunned. They were at a distinct disadvantage from the start due to insufficient intelligence, inadequate manpower and lack of air and artillery support. While the South Africans acquitted themselves with great bravery, the Battle of Bangui also revealed several weaknesses in the SANDF, including political interference, questionable deployment mandates, insufficient combat support and poor intelligence. Never-theless, Bangui may have served as the catalyst for positive change in the defence force for future combat deployments in Africa.

The reader of *20 Battles* may be forgiven for arriving at the conclusion that South African forces were often caught in situations from which they extricated themselves only with great difficulty. The book has demonstrated that, on many occasions, friction and the fog of war have rapidly descended after the first shots have been fired. However, this is not unique to the South African defence establishment but rather an inevitable aspect of warfare through the ages. The confusion and heat of battle often rob the best of plans of their efficacy early on, and events usually unfold contrary to expectations. Military institutions through the ages have designed their command styles to combat friction. The two different and opposing command styles are mission (directive) command and detailed command. The fact that South African soldiers have found themselves in difficulty on several occasions is not surprising, but the real subject of our investigation has been the military's ability to extricate itself from precarious situations. A good portion of the South African military's ability to survive and succeed can be attributed to its early embrace of a mission command style. An important aspect of *20 Battles* has been to highlight the positive and negative results on the battlefield when South Africans follow or stray from their command style and manoeuvre doctrine.

The South African way of war is inextricably linked to the historical interplay between the physical environment (climate and terrain) and warfare. When the military operating environment and operational conditions were favourable, the South African penchant for manoeuvre warfare found expression in the ensuing offensive operations. This was clearly demonstrated at Otavifontein (1915) and Kilimanjaro (1916), in southern Ethiopia (1941) and during operations Savannah (1975–1976) and Protea (1981). However, when the military operating environment and operational conditions became restricted, the South African forces lost their freedom of action and initiative and were forced into an unfavourable and at times a static type of warfare. This is what happened at Sandfontein (1914), Delville Wood (1916), Sidi Rezegh (1941) and Tobruk (1942), during Operation Boleas (1998) and at Bangui (2013). In other instances, the defence force was utilised in an asymmetrical role during rural and urban counterinsurgency operations to deal with sprawling internal unrest that threatened the security and legitimacy of the state, most notably during the industrial strikes of 1913 and 1914, the Rand Revolt (1922), the Bondelswarts Rebellion (1922) and the Pondoland Revolt (1960–1961), and at Ongulumbashe (1968).

Combined-arms warfare, underpinned by unity of action and command, where and when applicable, also forms a cornerstone of the South African way of war. Manoeuvre warfare, as practised by the UDF and SADF during both world wars and the Border War, was underpinned by combined-arms operations conducted by mounted, motorised or mechanised infantry acting in unison with armour, artillery and, from the 1920s, airpower. Prime examples include the latter half of the campaign in German South West Africa (1915), the campaign in German East Africa (1916–1918), offensive operations in southern Ethiopia (1941) and operations Savannah (1975–1976), Reindeer (1978), Protea (1981) and Moduler, Hooper and Packer (1987–1988).

From the 1920s onwards, the UDF and SADF regularly used airpower to help curb internal unrest, provide strategic and tactical lift capability, maintain air supremacy and provide fire support to ground combat operations. While air–ground cooperation proved tenuous to start with, especially during the Rand Revolt and the Bondelswarts Rebellion, such cooperation matured over time with the development of appropriate doctrine. Moreover, airpower, when deployed in an 'air policing' role, provided the defence force with a force multiplier in rapidly responding to internal unrest across South Africa and SWA. During the Second World War, and particularly the deployment to East Africa (1940–1941), South African air–ground cooperation in combined-arms warfare matured and provided a distinct edge to offensive operations in southern Ethiopia and Somalia. By the early 1960s, and especially during the Pondoland Revolt (1960–1961), the South African Air Force was increasingly called upon to assist the army in responding to episodes of internal unrest. In this regard, the addition of new platforms such as helicopters and parachute infantrymen added distinct new dimensions to air–ground cooperation. Helicopters would in future carry soldiers into combat in a trooping role and allow commanders to direct operations from the air. Moreover, helicopter gunships could also provide soldiers on the ground with ample fire support during combat operations.

This was the case during Operation Blouwildebees (1968). During the Border War, parachute infantry added a further dimension to the battlefield, that of vertical envelopment. Paratroopers, acting in conjunction with ground combat forces, could be strategically dropped over an objective. When operating in conjunction with ground forces and helicopters, airborne troops allowed the SADF to complete far bigger and bolder operations inside Angola, overcoming the tyranny of distance and avoiding areas of resistance, as took place in the infamous attack on Cassinga. Moreover, until about the mid-1980s, the SAAF dominated the airspace of southern Angola, giving the ground combat forces unprecedented freedom of action during cross-border operations. This facilitated the SADF's rather brash and bold manner, emboldened by the lack of enemy aerial activity. When the SADF lost air superiority later in the Border War, the South Africans could no longer conduct their specific brand of manoeuvre warfare. The limited use and complete absence of airpower during Operation Boleas (1998) and the Battle of Bangui (2013), respectively were also noteworthy and adversely affected the nature and outcome of operations. Thus, the South African way of war, especially during the Border War, was inextricably linked to the development, availability and use of airpower.

On several occasions, South African soldiers have shown a steady resolve and dogged determination to offer resistance when pushed into a corner against formidable enemies. When the tactical and operational outcomes were not favourable, this led to capitulation and defeat, such as at Sidi Rezegh (1941) and Tobruk (1942). Nevertheless, South Africans acquitted themselves even under the most adverse conditions – at Delville Wood (1916), Sidi Rezegh (1941), Chiusi (1944) and Bangui (2013). Unfortunately, for the casualty-averse South Africans, losses incurred during attritional-type warfare, however negligible, are unacceptable and typically evoke a public outcry and political fallout. Typically, when the military was allowed freedom of action to conduct manoeuvre-type operations on their own terms, battlefield casualties were far fewer and easier to stomach by the defence force and the public at large.

Historically, the defence force has always relied on a small permanent force that could be bolstered by the calling up of reserves during wartime or when needed to deal with internal unrest. Reserves, particularly in the form of the UDF's Active Citizen Force and Defence Rifle Associations, along with their successors in the SADF and SANDF, have always acted as a strategic force multiplier when needed. Prime examples are interspersed throughout the book, especially in the deployments to deal with internal unrest, the two world wars and the Border War. In fact, the SANDF still relies on the reserve force to bolster its manpower requirements for both internal and external deployments.

Crucial to understanding the development of a distinct South African way of war is to recognise and get to grips with doctrinal development within the UDF, SADF and SANDF. Throughout the period under investigation, doctrinal development occurred in a unique fashion, with key tenets borrowed from various other defence forces – the British, Germans, Israelis, and so forth. However, by adopting foreign doctrines, the South African way of war often regressed and remained uncodified. Moreover, time and again, as was the case during the Rand Revolt and at the battles of Combolcia (1941) and Chiusi (1944), for instance, the prevailing doctrine made no allowance for specific scenarios such as urban and mountain warfare. Doctrinal development was thus largely linked to tactical and operational innovation, often accrued during so-called first battles. However, between the 1960s and the 1980s, South African doctrine and a distinct way of war matured under the leadership of officers such as Roland de Vries, Tony Savides, Jan Breytenbach and others. In fact, the early to mid-1980s was the highwater mark of the South African way of war, as demonstrated during Operation Protea (1981) and its successors. However, to date the South African way of war remains largely uncodified, with only snippets contained in military manuals such as the *South African Staff Officers' Operational Manual*. Moreover, since 1994, very few of these doctrinal and operational manuals have been updated, leading one to speculate that either the SANDF accepts its manoeuvre warfare roots or there is a doctrinal disconnection in the defence force without the required skill or interest to resolve it adequately. Therefore, instead of turning towards South African military history to confirm our way of war and build on the available doctrine in the defence force in the context of 21st-century warfare, one gets the distinct impression that the SANDF remains unsure of its doctrinal future.

The South African military has all too often deployed without a coherent strategic plan and with less than adequate operational planning. Throughout the Border War, operational-level planning was weak. Poor strategic and operational planning was, however, a hallmark of the Boers in the early stages of the South African War, and this same weakness is almost a trait of the South African way of war. Moreover, operational doctrine is largely uncodified in the modern SANDF and operational concepts are not the main emphasis of the South African military. Should the SANDF reorient its doctrine, structure and force design to respond to the current strategic realties and prevailing threat perceptions in South Africa and the region? Or does the defence force remain in stasis, unsure of its doctrinal outlook and unwilling to respond to the ever-changing changing nature of warfare? These are serious issues that deserve to be read about, debated in the SANDF and academia, and lectured on at the various services, war and defence colleges. Only by doing so can we sensitise the current and future crop of South African soldiers about the uniqueness of the South African way of war and explain its doctrinal roots and development.

SOURCES

This book is the product of several years of primary archival research and the critical reading of secondary sources. Since this is a general military history, we have avoided cluttering the book with the usual scaffolding of scholarly endnotes. Thus, we have kept our references limited mostly to the more accessible primary and secondary sources for inquisitive readers who wish to explore some of the case studies and themes raised in the book.

Chapter 1: Industrial Strikes, 1913–1914

Fokkens, AM. (2006) '*The Role and Application of the Union Defence Force in the Suppression of Internal Unrest, 1912–1945*'. [Master of Military Science thesis, Stellenbosch University].

Geyer, R. (2104) 'The Union Defence Force and the 1914 strike: The dynamics of the shadow of the burgher'. *Historia*, vol. 59, no. 2, pp. 136–151.

O'Quigley, A. (1981) *The 1914 Strike: Collected Seminar Papers* (London: Institute of Commonwealth Studies).

Union of South Africa. (1911) *Debates of the First Session of the First Parliament of the House of Assembly 1910–1911* (Cape Town: Cape Times Limited).

Union of South Africa. (1914) *Correspondence Relating to the Recent General Strike in South Africa* (London: J.J. Keliher and Sons).

Chapter 2: Sandfontein, 1914

Collyer, JJ. (1937) *The Campaign in German South West Africa 1914–1915* (London: Imperial War Museum and Battery Press).

Katz, DB. (2021) 'Sandfontein: An operational re-examination of the battle, contextualised within General J.C. Smuts' first phase of the German South West African campaign 1914'. *Journal of African Military History*, vol. 5, no. 2, pp. 77–120.

Lange, G. (1991) *Urgent Imperial Service: South African Forces in German South West Africa 1914–1915* (Johannesburg: Ashanti).

Stejskal, J. (2014) *The Horns of the Beast: The Swakop River Campaign and World War I in South-West Africa 1914–1915* (Solihull: Helion).

Ungleich, TR. (1974) '*The Defence of German South-West Africa during World War I*'. [Master's thesis, University of Miami].

Chapter 3: Otavifontein, 1915

Adler, FB. (1927) *The History of the Transvaal Horse Artillery* (Johannesburg: Regimental Association of the THA).

Katz, DB. (2022) *General Jan Smuts and His First World War in Africa 1914–1917* (Johannesburg: Jonathan Ball Publishers).

Rayner, WS & O'Shaughnessy, WW. (1916) *How Botha and Smuts Conquered German South West* (London: Simpson, Marshall, Hamilton, Kent & Co.).

Strachan, H. (2004) *The First World War in Africa* (Oxford: Oxford University Press).

Von Oelhafen, H. (1923) *Der Feldzug in Südwest 1914/1915: Auf Grund Amtlichen Materials Bearbeitet* (Berlin: Safari-Verlag).

Chapter 4: Kilimanjaro, 1916

Collyer, JJ. (1939) *The South Africans with General Smuts in German East Africa* (Pretoria: Government Printer).

Fendall, CP. (2014) *The East African Force 1915–1919: The First World War in Colonial Africa* (n.p.: Leonaur).

Hordern, C. (1941) *Military Operations East Africa, Volume 1, August 1914–September 1916* (London: Her Britannic Majesty's Stationery Office).

Katz, DB. (2022) *General Jan Smuts and His First World War in Africa 1914–1917* (Johannesburg: Jonathan Ball Publishers).

Paice, E. (2008) *Tip & Run* (London: Phoenix).

Chapter 5: Delville Wood, 1916

Anonymous. (1924) *The Union of South African and the Great War 1914–1918: Official History* (Pretoria: Government Printer).

Buchan, J. (1920) *The History of the South African Forces in France* (London: Thomas Nelson & Sons Ltd).

Digby, PKA. (1993) *Pyramids and Poppies: The 1st SA Infantry Brigade in Libya, France and Flanders 1915–1919* (Rivonia: Ashanti Publishing).

Nasson, B. (2007) *Springboks on the Somme: South Africa in the Great War 1914–1918* (Johannesburg: Penguin Books).

Uys, I. (1991) *Rollcall: The Delville Wood Story* (Johannesburg: Uys Publishers).

Chapter 6: Rand Revolt, 1922

Fokkens, AM. & Visser, GE. (2003) 'Die Rol van die Unieverdedigingsmag in die Onderdrukking van die Nywerheidsonluste aan die Rand, 1922'. *Acta Academia*, vol. 35, no. 1, pp. 124–153.

Fokkens, AM. (2006) *'The Role and Application of the Union Defence Force in the Suppression of Internal Unrest, 1912–1945'*. [Master of Military Science thesis, Stellenbosch University].

Kleynhans, E. & Delport, A. (2023) 'Urban counterinsurgency: The Union Defence Force and the suppression of the 1922 Rand Revolt'. *Small Wars & Insurgencies*, vol. 34, no. 2, pp. 452–493.

Krikler, J. (2005) *White Rising: The 1922 Insurrection and Racial Killing in South Africa* (Manchester: Manchester University Press).

Union Government (UG 35-22). (1923) *Report of the Martial Law Inquiry Judicial Commission* (Pretoria: Wallach).

Chapter 7: Bondelswarts Rebellion, 1922

Fokkens, AM. (2006) *'The Role and Application of the Union Defence Force in the Suppression of Internal Unrest, 1912–1945'*. [Master of

Military Science thesis, Stellenbosch University].

Kleynhans, E. & Garcia, A. (2023) 'The Union Defence Force and the suppression of the Bondelswarts Rebellion, 1922'. *Small Wars & Insurgencies*, vol. 34, no. 2, pp. 422–451.

Lewis, GLM. (1977) '*The Bondelswarts Rebellion of 1922*'. [Master's thesis, Rhodes University].

Union Government (UG 30-22). (1922) *Report of the Administrator on the Bondelzwarts Rising of 1922* (Cape Town: Government Printer).

Union Government (UG 16-23). (1923) *Report of the Commission Appointed to Enquire into the Rebellion of the Bondelzwarts* (Cape Town: Government Printer).

Chapter 8: Southern Ethiopia, 1941

Birkby, C. (1987) *Uncle George: The Boer Boyhood, Letters and Battles of Lieutenant-General George Edwin Brink* (Johannesburg: Jonathan Ball Publishers).

Kleynhans, E. (2014) *Armoured Warfare: The South African Experience in East Africa, 1940–1941*. [Master of Military Science thesis, Stellenbosch University].

Kleynhans, E. (2018) 'The South African Offensive Operations in Southern Abyssinia, 1940–1941'. *International Journal of Military History and Historiography*, vol. 38, no. 1, pp. 34–66.

Orpen, N. (1968) *South African Forces World War II, Volume I: East Africa and Abyssinian Campaigns* (Cape Town: Purnell).

Stewart, A. (2016) *The First Victory: The Second World War and the East Africa Campaign* (London: Yale University Press).

Chapter 9: Combolcia and Amba Alagi, 1941

Hartshorn, E. (1960) *Avenge Tobruk* (Cape Town: Purnell).

Kleynhans, E. (2021) 'Combat at High Altitude: The South African Experience in East Africa, 1941'. *International Journal of Military History and Historiography*, vol. 41, no. 1, pp. 74–108.

Orpen, N. (1968) *South African Forces World War II, Volume I: East*

Africa and Abyssinian Campaigns (Cape Town: Purnell).

Pollock, A. (1943) *Pienaar of Alamein: The Life Story of a Great South African Soldier* (Cape Town: Cape Times Ltd).

Stewart, A. (2016) *The First Victory: The Second World War and the East Africa Campaign* (London: Yale University Press).

Chapter 10: Sidi Rezegh, 1941

Agar-Hamilton, JAI & Turner, LCF. (1957) *The Sidi Rezegh Battles, 1941* (Cape Town: Oxford University Press).

Barnett, C. (1961) *The Desert Generals* (New York: Viking Press).

Katz, DB. (2018) *South Africans Versus Rommel: The Untold Story of the Desert War in World War II* (Johannesburg: Delta Books).

Monick, S. & Baker, OEF. (1991) *Clear the Way ('Faugh-A-Ballagh'). The Military Heritage of the South African Irish 1880–1990* (Johannesburg: South African Irish Regimental Association).

Playfair, Maj Gen ISO. (2004) *History of the Second World War: Mediterranean and the Middle East Volume I*, edited by Butler, JRM. (Uckfield: Naval and Military Press).

Chapter 11: Tobruk, 1942

Agar-Hamilton, JA. & Turner, LCF. (1952) *Crisis in the Desert: May–July 1942* (London: Oxford University Press).

Hartshorn, E. (1960) *Avenge Tobruk* (Cape Town: Purnell).

Katz, DB. (2018) *South Africans Versus Rommel: The Untold Story of the Desert War in World War II* (Johannesburg: Delta Books).

Orpen, N. (1971) *South African Forces World War II, Volume III: War in the Desert* (Cape Town: Purnell).

Stewart, A. (2008) 'The "Atomic Despatch": Field Marshal Auchinleck, the Fall of the Tobruk Garrison and Post-war Anglo-South African Relations'. *Scientia Militaria*, vol. 36, no. 1, pp. 78–94.

Chapter 12: Celleno, 1944

Bourhill, J.F. (2011) *Come Back to Portofino: Through Italy with the 6th South African Armoured Division* (Johannesburg: 30 Degrees South).

Fielding, WL. (1946) *With the 6th Div* (Pietermaritzburg: Shuter & Shooter).

Kleynhans, E. (2012) 'The First South African Armoured Battle in Italy During the Second World War: The Battle of Celleno – 10 June 1944'. *Scientia Militaria*, vol. 40, no. 3, pp. 250–279.

Orpen, N. (1975) *South African Forces World War II, Volume V: Victory in Italy* (Cape Town: Purnell).

Steenkamp, W. (2017) *The Black Beret: The History of South Africa's Armoured Forces, Volume 2: The Italian Campaign 1943–45 and Post-war South Africa 1946–1961* (Solihull: Helion).

Chapter 13: Chiusi, 1944

Griffiths, R. (1970) *First City: A Saga of Service* (Cape Town: Howard Timmins).

Murray, LG. (1945) *First City/Cape Town Highlanders in the Italian Campaign: A Short History, 1943–1945* (Cape Town: Cape Times).

Orpen, N. (1975) *South African Forces World War II, Volume V: Victory in Italy* (Cape Town: Purnell).

Orpen, N. (1986) *The Cape Town Highlanders, 1885–1985* (Cape Town: The Cape Town Highlanders History Committee).

Punt, C. (2022) '*The Experiences of the Infantry of the 12th South African Motorised Brigade in the Italian Campaign of the Second World War*'. [Master of Military Science thesis, Stellenbosch University].

Chapter 14: Ongulumbashe, 1966

Alexander, EGM. (2016) '*The Airborne Concept in the South African Military, 1960–2000: Strategy Versus Tactics in Small Wars*'. [Doctoral dissertation, UNISA].

Alexander, EGM. (2019) 'Operation Blouwildebees, 1966: The Helicopter Assault on Ongulumbashe'. in van der Waag, IJ & Grundlingh, A (eds), 'In Different Times: The War for Southern Africa, 1966–1989'. *African Military Studies*, vol. 2 (Cape Town: African Sun Media).

Els, J. (2007) *Ongulumbashe: Where the Bushwar Began* (Wandsbeck: Real Publishers).

Scholtz, L. (2013) *The SADF in the Border War, 1966–1989* (Cape Town: Tafelberg).

Wood, G. (1993) '"The Horsemen are coming": Rethinking the Pondoland Rebellion'. *Contree*, vol. 33, pp. 27–34.

Chapter 15: Operation Savannah, 1975–1976

Du Preez, S. (1989) *Avontuur in Angola: Die Verhaal van Suid-Afrika se Soldate in Angola 1975–1976* (Pretoria: Van Schaik).

Scholtz, L. (2013) *The SADF in the Border War, 1966–1989* (Cape Town: Tafelberg).

Spies, F. (1989) *Angola: Operasie Savannah, 1975–1976* (Pretoria: SADF Directorate Public Relations).

Van der Waag, IJ. (2015) *A Military History of Modern South Africa* (Johannesburg: Jonathan Ball Publishers).

Warwick, R. (2012) 'Operation Savannah: A Measure of SADF Decline, Resourcefulness and Modernisation'. *Scientia Militaria*, vol. 40, no. 3, pp. 354–397.

Chapter 16: Cassinga, 1978

Alexander, EGM. (2003) '*The Cassinga Raid*'. [Master's thesis, UNISA].

Baines, G. (2009) 'Memories, Competing Narratives and Complicating Histories: Revisiting the Cassinga Controversy'. *Journal of Namibian Studies*, vol. 6, pp. 7–26.

Breytenbach, J. (2008) *Eagle Strike: The Story of the Controversial Airborne Assault on Cassinga 1978* (Sandton: Manie Grove Publishing).

McWilliams, M. (2011) *Battle for Cassinga: South Africa's Controversial Cross-Border Raid, Angola 1978* (Solihull: Helion).

Scholtz, L. (2013) *The SADF in the Border War, 1966–1989* (Cape Town: Tafelberg).

Chapter 17: Operation Protea, 1981

Barnard, L. (2006) 'The Role of the South African Air Force (SAAF) During the SADF's Cross-border Operations in Angola,

1978–1981: A Historical Exploration'. *Journal for Contemporary History*, vol. 31, no. 3, pp. 267–282.

Monick, S. (1993) 'The Forging of a Strike Force (Part I)'. *Militaria*, vol. 23, no. 3, pp. 20–56.

Scholtz, L. (2013) *The SADF in the Border War, 1966–1989* (Cape Town: Tafelberg).

Steenkamp, W. (1989) *South Africa's Border War 1966–1989* (Gibraltar: Ashanti).

Steenkamp, W & Heitman, H. (2016) *Mobility Conquers: The Story of 61 Mechanised Battalion Group 1978–2005* (Solihull: Helion).

Chapter 18: Cuito Cuanavale, 1987–1988

Bridgland, F. (2017) *Cuito Cuanavale: 12 Months of War that Transformed a Continent* (Cape Town: Jonathan Ball Publishers).

De Vries, R. (2013) *Eye of the Firestorm: Strength Lies in Mobility* (Cape Town: Naledi).

Scholtz, L. (2020) *The SADF and Cuito Cuanavale: A Tactical and Strategic Analysis* (Johannesburg: Delta Books).

Steenkamp, W. (1989) *South Africa's Border War 1966–1989* (Gibraltar: Ashanti).

Steenkamp, W &Heitman, H. (2016) *Mobility Conquers: The Story of 61 Mechanised Battalion Group 1978–2005* (Solihull: Helion).

Chapter 19: Boleas, 1998

De Coning, C. (2000) 'Lesotho Intervention: Implications for SADC. Military Interventions, Peacekeeping and the African Renaissance'. *Africa Dialogue Monograph Series*, vol. 1, no. 1.

Neethling, T. (1999) 'Military Intervention in Lesotho: Perspectives on Operation Boleas and Beyond'. *The Online Journal of Peace and Conflict Resolution*, vol. 2, no. 2.

Pherudi, M. (2003) 'Operation Boleas under Microscope, 1998–1999'. *Journal for Contemporary History*, vol. 28, no. 1, pp. 123–137.

Scherman, JP. (2015) '*The Utilisation of South African Armoured Forces in a "Peace Support Mission": The Intervention in Lesotho, 1998*'.

[Master's thesis, University of the Free State].

Williams, C. (2019) 'Political Imperatives and Military Preparations: New Insights into why South Africa's 1998 Intervention in Lesotho went Awry'. *South African Journal of International Affairs*, vol. 26, no. 1, pp. 25–51.

Chapter 20: Bangui, 2013

Heitman, H. (2013) *The Battle in Bangui: The Untold Inside Story* (Parktown: Parktown Publishers).

Janse van Rensburg, W, Vreÿ, F & Neethling, T. (2020) 'From Boleas to Bangui: Parliamentary Oversight of South African Defence Deployments'. *Scientia Militaria*, vol. 48, no. 1, pp 1–21.

Phetha, RH. (2015) '*Peacekeeping and Conflict Resolution: An Examination of South Africa's Role in the Central African Republic*'. [Master of Science thesis, University of KwaZulu-Natal].

Thompson, W, Hofstatter, S & Oatway, J. (2021) *The Battle of Bangui: The Inside Story of South Africa's Worst Military Scandal since Apartheid* (Cape Town: Penguin Books).

Vreÿ, F & Esterhuyse, AJ. (2016) 'South Africa and the Search for Strategic Effect in the Central African Republic'. *Scientia Militaria*, vol. 44, no. 2, pp. 1–27.

ACKNOWLEDGEMENTS

Collaboration projects owe far more to the many dedicated and generous people behind the scenes than merely the authors. Our first thank you must be to our ever-patient wives, Marit and Adina, who are ever-present to bolster flagging resolve when the occasion demands. Annie Olivier and her professional team, especially Nicole Duncan, Jan Booysen, and Alfred LeMaitre, have offered all the tools necessary to produce a substantial book on South African military history. The crew at Jonathan Ball are a delight to work with – cool, calm, expert in all phases of the enterprise and know how to throw a party or two when the occasion demands. We owe a debt of gratitude to the institution that has nurtured both of us, the Faculty of Military Science of Stellenbosch University. We also owe a special thanks to the Dean, Professor Sam Tshehla and the Director of Faculty Management, Andries Fokkens, who have always vigorously encouraged and supported our initiatives.

A book such as this relies heavily on the resources and expertise housed at the various archival depots in South Africa. We have used the Department of Defence Archives in Irene, the National Archives in Pretoria and the facilities at the University of the Witwatersrand, the University of South Africa and Pretoria University. All of these essential facilities and their staff have generously assisted us in producing the book. Our final thanks are reserved for Acting Director Alan Sinclair and Curator Anzel Veldman of the Ditsong National Museum of Military History located in Saxonwold. Anzel ably helped us with locating and making available some of the beautiful pictures reproduced in the book.

We sincerely hope that *20 Battles* will be the first in a series of collaborative efforts aimed at (re-)introducing our military history to ordinary South Africans. Through understanding their history, those who have fought one another will learn to live side by side in peace as worthy former opponents.

INDEX

Note: Page numbers in italics indicate a photograph or a map

ABOUT THE AUTHORS

DR EVERT KLEYNHANS is a senior lecturer in the Department of Military History at the Faculty of Military Science at Stellenbosch University (SU). He is the author of *Hitler's Spies: Secret Agents and the Intelligence War in South Africa* (2021) and *The Naval War in South African Waters, 1939-1945* (2022). He is also the editor of *Scientia Militaria: South African Journal of Military Studies*.

DR DAVID BROCK KATZ is an author and historian, in addition to being a part-time lecturer and research fellow in the Department of Military History at the Faculty of Military Science at SU. Katz is also an active member of the Andrew Mlangeni Regiment. He is the author of *South Africans vs Rommel* (2019) and *General Jan Smuts and his First World War in Africa: 1914-1917* (2022).

www.ingramcontent.com/pod-product-compliance
Lightning Source LLC
Chambersburg PA
CBHW070327090426
42733CB00012B/2392

* 9 7 8 1 9 2 8 2 4 8 2 2 4 *